# CALGARY
## HARNESSING THE FUTURE

By Peter Lougheed and Tom Walker

Profiles in Excellence by
Sari Shernofsky

Captions by Mike Lamb

Art Direction by
Sandy Carter and Jil Foutch

Sponsored by the
Calgary Economic Development Authority

▲ CRAIG DOLICK / TAKE STOCK INC.

LIBRARY OF CONGRESS CATALOGING-IN-PUBLICATION DATA

Lougheed, Peter, 1928-
    Calgary : harnessing the future / by Peter Lougheed and Tom Walker
; profiles in excellence by Sari Shernofsky ; captions by Mike Lamb
; art direction by Sandy Carter and Jil Foutch.
        p.    cm. — (Urban tapestry series)
    "Sponsored by the Calgary Economic Development Authority."
    Includes index.
    ISBN 1-881096-49-1 (alk. paper)
    1. Calgary (Alta.)—Civilization.    2. Calgary (Alta.)—Pictorial
works.    3. Business enterprises—Alberta—Calgary.    4. Calgary
(Alta.)—Economic conditions.    I. Walker, Tom, 1955-    .
II. Shernofsky, Sari, 1948-    . III. Title.    IV Series.
F1079.5.C35L68  1997
971.23'38—dc21                                                97-40315

URBAN
TAPESTRY
SERIES
TOWERY
PUBLISHING, INC.

Towery Publishing, Inc., 1835 Union Avenue, Memphis, TN 38104

PUBLISHER: J. Robert Towery
EXECUTIVE PUBLISHER: Jenny McDowell
NATIONAL SALES MANAGER: Stephen Hung
REGIONAL SALES MANAGER: Michele Sylvestro
MARKETING DIRECTOR: Carol Culpepper
PROJECT DIRECTORS: Andrea Glazier, Joseph Powell, Karen Riva

EXECUTIVE EDITOR: David B. Dawson
MANAGING EDITOR: Michael C. James
SENIOR EDITORS: Lynn Conlee, Carlisle Hacker
EDITORS/PROJECT MANAGERS: Lori Bond, Jana Files
STAFF EDITORS: Mary Jane Adams, Susan Hesson, Brian Johnston
ASSISTANT EDITORS: Pat McRaven, Jennifer C. Pyron, Allison Ring

CREATIVE DIRECTOR: Brian Groppe
PROFILE DESIGNERS: Jennifer Baugher, Laurie Beck, Kelley Pratt, Ann Ward
DIGITAL COLOR SUPERVISOR: Brenda Pattat
PRODUCTION ASSISTANTS: Geoffrey Ellis, Enrique Espinosa, Robin McGehee
PRINT COORDINATOR: Beverly Thompson

# CONTENTS

CALGARY: HARNESSING THE FUTURE ............... 8
*By Peter Lougheed and Tom Walker*
"Calgary's highly educated work force, cutting-edge growth companies, and entrepreneurial spirit should allow it to take full advantage of the opportunities of the next millennium."

PROFILES IN EXCELLENCE ............................. 180
*By Sari Shernofsky*
A look at the corporations, businesses, professional groups, and community service organizations that have made this book possible.

PHOTOGRAPHERS ............................................. 316

INDEX OF PROFILES ......................................... 319

ost North Americans take pride in believing that their home city is different, unique, or special. But nowhere is this conviction as strong as in the Canadian city of Calgary, Alberta. ❋ The challenging objective of my introduction to this terrific book is to help readers understand why Calgary really is unique—and why more than three-quarters of a million citizens are so convinced it is such a special place to live.

Foremost in understanding Calgary's uniqueness is that dreams and visions are what help a community build upon its strengths and overcome its difficulties. Calgary has always had its share of dreamers and visionaries.

Personally, my mind goes back to my grandfather's arrival in Calgary. He arrived in a railroad handcart in 1883, well over a century ago—before the Canadian Pacific Railway was built, the railway that linked and created the nation. At that time, Calgary consisted of a handful of adventurers, surrounded by Native Indian tribes. Sir James, as my grandfather became known, arrived fresh from the civilized East with the plan—can you

imagine?—to practice law in a frontier town. I sense that he came with a spirit of adventure and with a vision that Calgary would grow to be a prosperous and strong community in his lifetime. And he was right!

For my mother, it was a different story. She was convinced by a charming westerner (my father) to leave her safe roots and large family in the established, East Coast city of Halifax to journey as a young bride to Calgary. In 1919, Calgary was still very much a frontier city. My mother's family feared they would never see her again as she journeyed west past Upper Canada—as Ontario was then known—to the Territories.

I recall as a young boy my mother telling me of her thoughts as she came west. She loved her sports—golf and tennis—and wondered if there would be any opportunities to play them. She also wondered how she would adapt to the area's male-dominated "cowboy culture." It was not too many years later when she was invited—imagine—by a group of men—imagine—to play poker every second Thursday night.

EAST OF CALGARY ARE THOUSANDS OF MILES OF OLD WEST PRAIRIES AND BADLANDS, SO CALLED BECAUSE THEY ONCE WERE ALMOST TOO TOUGH TO NAVIGATE ON HORSEBACK. TODAY, THE TERRAIN BECKONS HIKERS BY THE THOUSANDS AS WELL AS SIGHTSEERS ANXIOUS FOR A LOOK AT THE CITY'S PICTURESQUE SKYLINE.

BY PETER LOUGHEED

For me, as I look out my living room window at the blazing lights of the modern office towers of Calgary, with my grandchildren playing in the living room, I try to envision my city when these young children become adults. Will they find opportunity here, as I have? Will they have the quality of life that I now enjoy?

As I ponder these questions, I start to think about those unique—and complex—characteristics that make Calgary and its people so special: the evolving mix of fascinating people from diverse corners of the world who have made Calgary their home; the unparalleled volunteerism and community spirit; the keen entrepreneurship that has arisen from the city's focus on energy and ranching; the highest education level of any Canadian city; an outward international perspective; the full participation by Calgarians in all aspects of Canadian life; and a quality of life rated at or near the top of all cities in North America.

This blend of characteristics has created an interesting city with a colourful past and an exciting future. What made it so? What caused Calgary to become what it is and what it promises to be?

MORNING'S FIRST LIGHT STRIKES DOWN-TOWN CALGARY, THE FINANCIAL CEN-TRE OF WESTERN CANADA AND THE SITE OF MORE CORPORATE HEADQUAR-TERS THAN ANY OTHER CANADIAN CITY, EXCEPT TORONTO. ONLY MINUTES FROM CALGARY'S FINANCIAL CORE—AND WITHIN VIEW OF ITS TALL OFFICE BUILDINGS—ARE SOME OF THE GAS-PROCESSING PLANTS THAT FEED A GROWING WORLD DEMAND THROUGH A MASSIVE NETWORK OF PIPELINES.

## HOW CALGARY GREW AND PROSPERED

The Canadian West was settled very differently from the American West. History traces its peaceful evolution, in part, to the North-West Mounted Police (NWMP). The NWMP, whose discipline, temperament, and patience allowed the peaceful co-existence of white settlers with Native Indians, is a story in itself. Their legacy still lives on today. As a nation, we have developed an enviable international reputation as peacekeepers.

Calgary began as an outpost of the NWMP in August 1875, when a troop surveyed the site where the Bow and Elbow rivers meet. Shortly after, Fort Calgary was established to help manage the fur trade and the relationship with the adjacent Indian territories. These stages of development then followed: the trade of buffalo hides for basic groceries; the first herds of longhorn cattle; the arrival of the Canadian Pacific Railway; the establishment of the first ranches; the migration of settlers from the East and from Europe to farm the surrounding area; and, in due course, the emergence of a town to service these frontier endeavours.

These early phases of growth were followed by the first discovery of oil at Turner Valley (1914) south of Calgary, by further waves of immigration to establish nearby grain farms, and by a new breed of adventurers—called remittance men by some—who came to seek their fortune.

Above all, the most significant influence on today's Calgary was the discovery by Imperial Oil Limited in 1947 of tremendous reserves of crude oil and natural gas at Leduc, just south of the capital city of Edmonton. Unlike the freehold areas of—let's say—the state of Texas, the provincial government owns most of these reserves. The substantial royalties that continue to this day have allowed our government to develop world-class health, education, recreation, and other public services. Calgary, as one of the two metropolitan areas in the province, has been a major beneficiary of these revenues.

THE NORTH-WEST MOUNTED POLICE, WHICH FIRST MAINTAINED LAW AND ORDER ACROSS THE CALGARY PRAIRIE IN THE MID-1800S, ALLOWED NATIVE CANADIANS AND WHITE SETTLERS TO CO-EXIST IN A HARMONY NEVER BEFORE SEEN IN NORTH AMERICA. NOW KNOWN AS THE ROYAL CANADIAN MOUNTED POLICE, THE RED-COATED HORSEMEN JOIN WITH LOCAL LAW ENFORCEMENT TO MONITOR CITY STREETS. AS A RESULT, CALGARY HAS ONE OF THE LOWEST CRIME RATES ON THE CONTINENT.

MARK REINSTEIN

Shortly after oil was discovered at Leduc, a key event occurred that would shape Calgary's destiny. The question on many people's minds at that time was whether Edmonton or Calgary would become Imperial Oil's headquarters. Many thought it would be Edmonton, because oil was discovered so close to that city. But it was Calgary that was chosen.

Why did this happen? Rumour has it that the manager of Imperial Oil favoured the golf course in Calgary over Edmonton's. As a result of this capricious decision, Calgary would eventually become the major centre for the Canadian oil and gas industry—and, in turn, all industries. In fact, more head offices of major corporations are located in Calgary than in any other city in the country, except Toronto.

While Calgary was nurturing this fledgling oil and gas industry, the cattle business was growing as well, with great ranches springing up around the city. The major cattle auctions and number of cattle brokers in Calgary also influenced the city's culture.

Most people are surprised to learn that it was before World War I—in 1912—that the world-famous Calgary Exhibition and Stampede was established. Today, the Stampede still deserves its boast as the "greatest outdoor show in the world." In its early days, as well as now, the Stampede's success depended on volunteers. As the city grew, a place on the Stampede Board became a coveted goal for many ambitious businessmen and ranchers. The Stampede Board has always been the closest thing Calgary has to an elite class.

The Stampede is a two-week summer rodeo where everybody wears jeans and western hats and boots, decorates their places of business, and parties. These parties start with free downtown pancake breakfasts in the morning and end with late-night backyard barbecues throughout the neighbourhoods. The informal dress and absence of serious business promote enthusiasm and camaraderie. Everybody gets involved, convinced it's their civic duty to become what is known in the vernacular as a "drugstore cowboy."

On the other hand, because Calgary is so closely associated with the Stampede, visitors are often surprised when they see how sophisticated and urbane the city is today.

A NATURAL LOCATION FOR RANCHING, ALBERTA HAS NEARLY TWICE AS MANY COWS AS HUMANS—4.7 MILLION HEAD OF CATTLE COMPARED WITH A PROVINCIAL POPULATION OF 2.5 MILLION. AND AT THE HEART OF THE PROVINCIAL CATTLE INDUSTRY IS COWTOWN CALGARY, WHERE CALVING SEASON CAN BEGIN AS EARLY AS MARCH AND EXTEND INTO JUNE.

TROY & MARY PARLEE / TAKE STOCK INC.

## HARNESSING THE FUTURE

 his book is titled *Calgary: Harnessing the Future*. To me, that denotes harnessing our energy—our human, technical, natural, and financial resources—to expand opportunities for the future, while maintaining our enviable quality of life. ❀ The various organizations profiled in this book pay tribute to a fascinating cross section of Calgarians. They are dreamers and visionaries who are directing their energy toward a future of growth and opportunity. I believe the characteristics I mentioned earlier are the source of the energy.

## AN EVOLVING MIX OF FASCINATING PEOPLE

ho are today's Calgarians, and where did they come from? The city was initially built by immigrants from England, Scotland, and Ireland. They were the first pioneers, who co-existed with the Native Indian tribes. Later, there were immigrants from other parts of Europe, as well as a small Chinese contingent who helped build the railway. ❀ The Leduc oil discovery after World War II brought a wave of ambitious American oilmen from Texas, Oklahoma, and other oil-producing states. For a time, this group was a dominant force in the city's society.

However, the biggest change in the make-up of Calgary came during the 1980s and 1990s, with the arrival of large numbers of New Canadians, particularly from India and Pakistan, as well as Chinese from Southeast Asia.

These newcomers have been welcomed warmly and are now part of the fabric of the city. I'm proud to say that Calgarians as individuals have little class consciousness. People are judged on the basis of what they can contribute—not on their background.

Immigration in the past two decades has created a city that is diverse in its ethnic make-up and quite different from the Calgary of the early 1970s. Calgarians of all backgrounds are now just as likely, when dining out, to frequent new ethnic restaurants as they are the city's superb steakhouses. And thousands participate in ethnic celebrations, such as the annual Dragon Boat Festival on the Glenmore Reservoir. New Canadians have also contributed to the growth in both traditional and ethnic cultural activities, including theatre, opera, ballet, and the like. It all helps to make a very modern, international city.

A TRUE MELTING POT, CALGARY BOASTS A LARGE NATIVE POPULATION AND THOUSANDS OF IMMIGRANTS FROM PAKISTAN, LEBANON, GREECE, CHINA, VIETNAM, AND AFRICA. THE CITY IS ALSO HOME TO THE LARGEST CONCENTRATION OF AMERICANS ANYWHERE IN CANADA.

▶ BRIAN STABLYK / SCHULHOF PHOTOGRAPHY

## UNPARALLELED VOLUNTEERISM AND COMMUNITY SPIRIT

**W**hy is the volunteer spirit so incredibly strong in Calgary? Essentially, in my view, it's because of the "Stampede spirit." That spirit is contagious and filters down to the neighbourhood level. ❊ Other North American cities may also have a strong community spirit, but it's nowhere near as pervasive as it is here. One source might be the pioneer heritage of helping one's neighbour. And perhaps because Calgary is a medium-sized city, it's easier for people to feel a strong personal commitment to city events and activities.

While they might be motivated by civic pride, Calgarians also bring a special enthusiasm that makes any volunteer activity fun. When the Winter Olympic Games were held in Calgary in 1988, Juan Antonio Samaranch, President of the International Olympic Committee, told me that the degree to which Calgarians from every walk of life were donating their time—embracing even the menial tasks of ushering, ticket taking, and patrolling fences—had never occurred before at any other Olympic Games.

AS SYMBOLIZED BY *The Olympic Arch*, DESIGNED BY TONY GRIFFIN AND FRANCES SCHMITT PRIOR TO THE 1988 WINTER GAMES (OPPOSITE), THE PEOPLE OF CALGARY ARE KNOWN FOR THEIR WILLINGNESS TO LEND A HAND. ON A SNOWY DAY, EVEN THE TINIEST OF SCHOOLCHILDREN FIND A WAY TO PITCH IN (LEFT).

hy is Calgary so entrepreneurial in nature? The city's two major industries—ranching, and oil

and gas—are both definitely high-risk businesses, with revenues dependent on volatile world

markets. The term "wildcat" to describe an exploratory oil well reflects the high stakes and

gambling nature of the oil patch. ✼ Breeding cattle in Alberta's unpredictable climate is very

gh risk as well. When you talk to people in the ranching business, you quickly notice their individualism

d self-determination, traits that have been absorbed by many other Calgarians.

So, these two industries of a high-risk nature have bred into Calgary business people a keen entrepreneurial

irit. And while our rugged pioneer background has also contributed to the do-it-yourself social and political

titude of our community, Calgary's New Canadians are pioneers in their own right. They are helping to for-

y and rejuvenate this philosophy of hard work and self-reliance.

Finally, it's interesting to note that the most respected citizens in our city today are those who have used

eir entrepreneurial skills to generate wealth, and then have taken some of the proceeds to develop wonder-

l public facilities, such as the world-class equestrian centre at Spruce Meadows, south of the city, and the

ntre of Sports Excellence facilities at the Father David Bauer Arena, where Team Canada trains.

SPRUCE MEADOWS, ONLY A FEW MIN-
UTES FROM DOWNTOWN, IS A WORLD-
RENOWNED EQUESTRIAN VENUE THAT
ANNUALLY HOSTS THREE MAJOR SHOWS:
THE NATIONAL, HELD THE FIRST WEEK
IN JUNE; THE NORTH AMERICAN CHAM-
PIONSHIP, HELD DURING THE STAMPEDE;
AND THE INTERNATIONAL MASTERS,
WHICH HAS DRAWN RECORD CROWDS
OF UP TO 53,000. OF COURSE, IF A SET
OF WHEELS IS YOUR PREFERRED MODE
OF TRANSPORTATION, A NUMBER OF
OPTIONS—FROM CLASSIC MODELS TO
THE LATEST STYLES—CAN BE FOUND
THROUGHOUT THE CITY.

hy are Calgarians so highly educated? The answer to this is a complex mix of factors. ❋ First, the original pioneers brought with them dedicated teachers who nurtured successive genera-tions of splendid educators. ❋ Second, in order to be profitable, the oil and gas industry has required continuing research to develop new technologies both to improve productivity and to ·cess existing reserves economically. The industry has also bred a generation of computer-literate teams in ·ismic, geological, engineering, and financial activities.

Many of these people have migrated to both small and large high-tech companies, a significant component ·f the city's diversifying economy. For example, one of the world's leading telecommunications manufactur-·s, Nortel, has expanded its Calgary plant, which produces products destined for customers in every part of ·e world.

At the same time, with its significant oil and gas revenues, the provincial government had the foresight and ·sources to create a first-class public education system with small class sizes, as well as world-renowned ·ostsecondary institutions, including technical schools, a community college, and a university. According to ·e Organization for Economic Cooperation and Development, Canada has a greater per capita commitment ·· education than the United States and many other countries. And within Canada, Calgary leads.

IN RECENT YEARS, CALGARY HAS JUMPED TO THE FOREFRONT OF THE COMMUNICATIONS INDUSTRY, THANKS TO ADVANCEMENTS MADE BY SUCH COR-PORATIONS AS NORTEL, FORMERLY KNOWN AS NORTHERN TELECOM, AND DOZENS OF SPINOFF COMPANIES.

ow has Calgary developed such an international perspective? Historically, Alberta's prosperity has depended on the export of commodities—grain, beef, lumber, coal, and oil and gas. Calgarians have always been focused on export and international markets. ❊ And in recent years, a growing number of high-tech companies have taken advantage of the Canada-U.S. Free Trade Agreement, as well as the North American Free Trade Agreement, to market their products and services in the United States, and then to spread their wings, so to speak, across the Pacific. On the other hand, foreign investors have been lured by the Calgary success story, and in many cases have invested in local firms.

Some statistics report Calgary as leading the world's major cities in business air travel on a per capita basis. Dinner parties in Calgary with business people usually have as a focus of discussion a guest who has just returned from a business trip to Kazakhstan or Thailand.

Finally, the increasing ethnic diversity of the city has certainly helped develop the confidence, skills, and sophistication needed to be a successful player in the international marketplace.

GRAIN ELEVATORS ARE A COMMON SIGHT IN NEARBY CARSTAIRS, WHILE BACK IN THE CITY, ELEVATORS OF A DIFFERENT SORT WHISK PASSENGERS TO THE TOP OF THE CALGARY TOWER IN ONLY 48 SECONDS. BOTH THE TOWER AND ITS NEIGHBOR, THE PANCANADIAN BUILDING, CELEBRATED THE 1988 WINTER OLYMPICS IN STYLE. THE TOWER WAS TURNED INTO A HUGE NATURAL GAS TORCH, AND THE PAN-CANADIAN BUILDING SPORTED A GREEN LASER OUTLINE OF A HOCKEY PLAYER.

ow does Calgary fit within the mainstream of Canadian life? In the past decade, a growing army of Calgarians have received awards and national recognition for their work and volunteer activities. Honoured citizens include academics, scientists, athletes, and performers. Our professional associations and organizations also receive accolades. For example, University of Calgary researchers, funded by the Alberta Heritage Foundation for Medical Research, have been recognized nationally and internationally for their important medical research.

The impact of Calgarians can be seen in the political arena as well. With its dreamers and visionaries, Calgary has often been the birthplace of new political movements and ideas. The Social Credit movement of the 1930s, which governed Alberta for almost 40 years, was born in Calgary. The current federal party—the Reform Party of Canada—is headquartered in and led from a Calgary base. And the Progressive Conservative Party of Alberta, which has been the governing party in Alberta for more than 25 years, was started by a group of Calgarians.

CLOSING EACH DAY OF THE CALGARY STAMPEDE IS A SPECTACULAR FIREWORKS DISPLAY. ADDING ITS OWN COLOUR TO THE SKY IS THE CANADIAN FLAG WITH ITS UBIQUITOUS MAPLE LEAF.

## A SUPERB QUALITY OF LIFE

**W**hat factors give Calgary the quality of life that attracts newcomers—whether from overseas or from other provinces? Our city's growing ethnic diversity and community spirit enhance our quality of life immensely. ❋ In addition, the Canadian Rockies are only 45 minutes away by car and provide numerous family recreation opportunities in both national and provincial parks—from camping and hiking to horseback riding, rock climbing, and skiing. Kananaskis Country, a recreation area in the nearby Rockies, is a wonder of natural beauty and provides a variety of outdoor experiences.

The city itself provides unmatched public recreation, including an extensive bicycle and jogging path system, golf courses, swimming pools, leisure centres, and even a local ski hill. Some of these facilities are the legacies from the 1988 Winter Olympic Games.

The Bow and Elbow rivers that meander through the heart of Calgary provide opportunities for fishing and rafting, while many areas have been kept in their natural state, to the delight of bird-watchers and other nature lovers. Fort Calgary, Heritage Park, the world-renowned Calgary Zoo, Calgary Science Centre, Calgary Tower, and Glenbow Museum attract tourists and locals alike. These recreational facilities are matched by

orld-class cultural facilities, including the Calgary Centre for Performing Arts.

Nearby is the world's leading paleontology museum, the Royal Tyrrell Museum, which received its "royal" signation during a 1990 visit by Queen Elizabeth II to Alberta.

Calgarians are also fortunate to enjoy a health support system that is as good or better than anywhere se—especially for senior citizens, I'm finding out. We also have low unemployment, high-quality jobs, and latively safe, crime-free neighbourhoods.

While the weather in Calgary can have its ups and downs, there are more days of sunshine here than in just bout any other Canadian city. And when it's really cold, we know we can look forward to a chinook—the sudden, arm winds that break over the mountains, allowing us to bask in our shirtsleeves in the middle of February.

Calgary, as a medium-sized city, can thus provide an affordable scope of activities in a manageable traffic nd urban environment.

Finally, Calgarians enjoy an above-average disposable income, so most of us can take advantage of our city's ctractions, delight in the mountains, partake of the diverse culture, and enjoy an authentic western party.

TRAIL RIDES ARE A COMMON SUM-
MER DIVERSION IN THE ROCKIES, ONLY
A LEISURELY DRIVE WEST OF THE CITY
LIMITS. ONCE THERE, YOU'LL FIND
BREATHTAKING SCENERY AND CAMP-
FIRE CHATS DURING TRIPS THAT RANGE
IN LENGTH FROM A DAY TO A MONTH.
OFFERING A GLIMPSE AT ANOTHER
SIDE OF THE EARLY WEST IS THE WORLD-
RENOWNED HERITAGE PARK, A HISTORI-
CAL VILLAGE THAT RE-CREATES LIFE IN
PRE-1914 CANADA.

udging by the companies and organizations profiled in this book, the future of my city appears

very bright. ❀ If tomorrow belongs to those engaged in worldwide knowledge-based activity,

then Calgary is superbly positioned. Its highly educated work force, cutting-edge growth com-

panies, and entrepreneurial spirit should allow it to take full advantage of the opportunities of

e next millennium.

I hope my grandchildren will be among those pioneering the next century—the next generation of dreamers

d visionaries. ∎

IF YOU'VE GOT A STRONG ARM, YOU COULD ALMOST HIT CALGARY'S SKYSCRAPERS FROM THIS VANTAGE POINT ON SCOTCHMAN'S HILL (OPPOSITE). UNLIKE MANY URBAN CENTRES, METROPOLITAN CALGARY ABRUPTLY MEETS FOOTHILLS, PINES, AND DAFFODILS, NOT TO MENTION A FEW CANOLA FIELDS (LEFT). ONE OF THE MAINSTAY PRODUCTS OF ALBERTA'S AGRICULTURAL ECONOMY, CANOLA SPREADS ACROSS 4 MILLION ACRES OF PROVINCIAL PRAIRIE LAND AND IS USED IN EVERYTHING FROM HIGHLY PRIZED COOKING OIL TO PRINTER'S INK, COSMETICS, AND MARINE LUBRICANTS.

THE SETTING SUN LEAVES ITS GOLD-en mark on Calgary, illuminating downtown office buildings, the Centre Street Bridge, the Calgary Tower, and an area park. The sun's rays also lend added drama to a chinook arch, which marks a mid-winter warming trend as mild Pacific air blows over the Rockies and drops on Calgary's doorstep (BOTTOM RIGHT). Winter temperatures can rise 40 degrees in only 24 hours.

COFFEE, TEA, OR JUST COME AND read! Calgary hosts dozens of java joints and specialty tea haunts, and there's no better way to spend a morning than drinking a cup of fresh Brazilian blend while reading one of the city's daily newspapers or weekly entertainment guides.

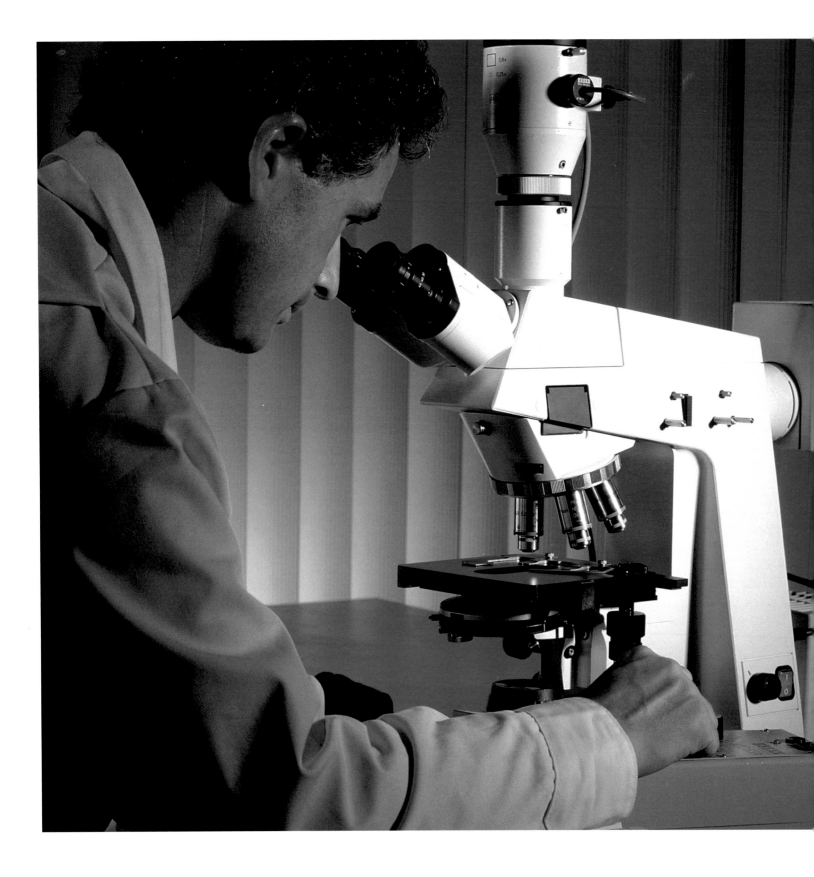

DESPITE ITS ONE-TIME COWTOWN image, Calgary has developed its share of industry. Locals are sure to get the job done, whether it's making scientific discoveries in the lab or manning the presses to get the finished product out on time.

ALGARIANS ARE PROUD TO BOAST
the highest level of education
among all Canadians. As a result,
the community can claim hundreds
of specialists, whose talents range
from programming and installing
computers (ABOVE) to removing
asbestos insulation (OPPOSITE).

ROM FINE-TUNING THE CENTURY-
old clock at City Hall to repairing all manner of machinery,
Calgary's wealth of skilled labour-
ers lend an experienced hand.

WHITE OR NOT, CHRISTMAS IN Calgary means plenty of bright displays. Here, patterns of light decorate Olympic Square (OPPOSITE) and issue a holiday greeting at the McDougall Centre (BOTTOM), while a familiar figure salutes passersby at the Festival of Lights in nearby Airdrie (TOP). More subtle decorations, like this wreath hung on the fence at an area ranch (CENTRE), are a reminder of the many ways to celebrate the season.

MARK VITARIS PRODUCTIONS

**C**ALGARY'S PETRO-DRIVEN skyline changed dramatically in the late 1970s and early 1980s when the Arab oil embargo drove the price of fuel through the stratosphere. City planners tried desperately to control the building boom, but skyscrapers managed to go up faster than the oil prices.

DOWNTOWN CALGARY'S NUMEROUS steel-and-glass towers, which house some of the world's most successful corporations, were considered ahead of their time when they were built, even serving as a futuristic backdrop for *Superman III*. Today, many of the structures are connected by a massive series of above-ground, windowed pathways, called Plus 15s, which allow workers to walk between buildings without subjecting themselves to snow and bitter winds.

CALGARY'S STEPHEN AVENUE WAS born in the late 1800s, but when record grain harvests brought a seemingly endless stream of settlers in 1908, entrepreneurs decided it was time to match the bustling business districts of the East. As a result, wooden storefronts were razed and replaced by elegant sandstone structures, which today include (CLOCKWISE FROM BOTTOM) the Bank of Nova Scotia, LH Doll Building, Bank of Toronto, Lancaster Building, and Canadian Imperial Bank of Commerce Building.

MODERN, GEOMETRIC ARCHITEC-
ture is one of the many delights
at Eau Claire Market, located on
the banks of the Bow River. After
strolling among the indoor stalls
filled with fresh produce and seafood, baked goods, and plenty of
beef, visitors can patronize any of
the market's specialty shops and
restaurants or take in a movie at
the IMAX Theatre.

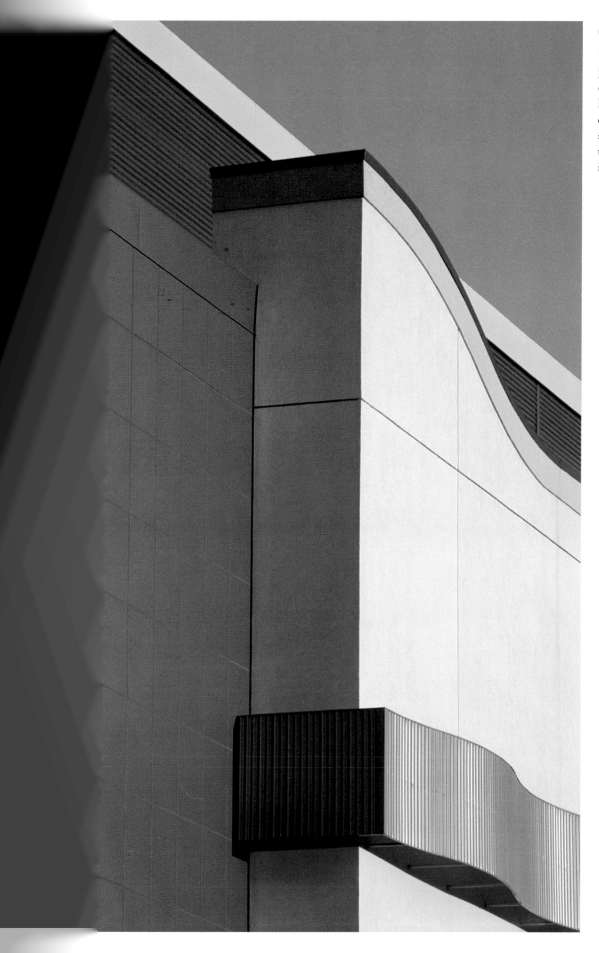

BUSINESS PEOPLE LUCKY ENOUGH to work in downtown's shiny 'scrapers can enjoy views of the majestic Rockies or the prairies that only a century ago brought settlers here via covered wagon. Two of the city's tallest structures are the 37-storey Nova Building (PAGE 54) and the 46-storey Canterra Tower, built in 1988 (PAGE 55).

ALAN MARSH / FIRST LIGHT

**W**ITH THE ARRAY OF ETHNIC groups living in Calgary, it's only natural that the city would also have a number of ethnic restaurants. Options range from Italian food at Teatro in Olympic Plaza to Indian fare cooked in a tandoor and from spirits reminiscent of the Yucatán at Coconut Joe's to the Asian offerings of the Silver Dragon Restaurant in Chinatown.

COUNTLESS ETHNIC TRADITIONS are celebrated in and around Calgary, especially during the Heritage Day Folk Festival, held at Centennial Park in nearby Canmore (LEFT).

Many of Calgary's Chinese citizens make their home near the Bow River in Chinatown, the third-largest neighborhood of its kind in Canada. In addition to a museum and gallery, 800-person auditorium, 40,000-volume library, and huge restaurant, the Calgary Chinese Cultural Centre boasts intricate tiling and a spectacular dragon mosaic that hangs 20 metres above the floor (OPPOSITE).

**T**HANKS TO THE NUMEROUS FES-
tivals held in the city on nearly
every summer weekend, Calgary
may very well have more clowns
and jugglers than the world's largest circuses.

WHILE SOME CALGARIANS PREFER to have their fire and eat it too, others recognize the danger in out-of-control blazes. Fortunately, local firefighters are up to the task, responding quickly to emergencies of every magnitude.

◄ DAVE OLECKO

► WES RAYMOND / TAKE STOCK INC.

THE ARRIVAL OF THE OLYMPIC torch from Athens in time for the 1988 Winter Games signified the start of one of Calgary's most historic events. Nearly a decade later, its legacy includes this bronze statue in Canada Olympic Park, located on the western outskirts of the city.

WHETHER IT'S A RACE TO GET clothes off the line before an afternoon shower or a contest featuring some speedy swine, the victor is the one who moves his feet (or hooves) the fastest. At the Rangeland Derby chuck-wagon races, one of the Calgary Stampede's most popular events, thousands of spectators delight in the risky business of galloping around a dirt oval at breakneck speeds (PAGES 66 AND 67).

WHILE THE BREED OF TRANSPORtation may vary, Calgarians love to go along for the ride. At the Stampede, you'll find an ostrich race and Mutton Busting, where aspiring cowboys and cowgirls jump aboard the wool and stay on as long as they can. During Calgary's mild winter days, some common— and not-so-common—sights include a horse-drawn toboggan and a llama-driven cart.

▼ RICK RUDNICKI / TAKE STOCK INC.

▼ BRIAN STABLYK / SCHULHOF PHOTOGRAPHY

CATTLE AND HORSES ARE SO MUCH a part of everyday life in Calgary that they're often immortalized in everything from hot-air balloons to colourful oil derricks.

**P**UBLIC ART ILLUSTRATES THE local importance of horse power, as Calgary's "statued" steeds graze, amble, and buck their way across the urban terrain.

More than 1,000 public statues, created by local and international artists, dot the cityscape. Some try to reflect the moment, but all make a statement, leaving the message up to the observer.

CALGA

THE FAMILIAR IMAGE OF A LONE cowboy finds a place, even in the heart of the city.

WHILE THE 1988 WINTER OLYM-
pics drew thousands of visitors
and millions of television viewers,
Calgarians themselves took a 10-
day holiday to participate in the
once-in-a-lifetime experience.

WITH PLENTY OF MOUNTAINS and snow, locals can revel in such exciting wintertime activities as skiing and snow boarding. Scattered over the Rockies and area foothills are dozens of ski resorts, the most famous of which are Sunshine Village and Lake Louise in nearby Banff National Park. The two internationally renowned resorts attract visitors from around the world.

WHETHER GLIDING OVER AN expanse of green near Cochrane, bouncing at the Stampede, or enjoying a bird's-eye view of the Calgary Tower and a free-falling dinosaur, Calgarians love to reach new heights. The city is unofficially known as the hot-air balloon capital of Canada, and it's not uncommon to see dozens of enthusiasts aloft on a clear morning.

C ALGARY'S PROXIMITY TO SOME
of the world's best fossil beds
and glacier-shaped badlands has
lured many archaeologists and pale-
ontologists to the area. Paying homage to the mammoth creatures that
lived here in prehistoric times are
Dinosaur Provincial Park, a UNESCO
World Heritage Site that features
the remains of more than 300 dinosaurs (PAGE 84), and the world-
renowned Royal Tyrrell Museum
of Paleontology, home to 50 full-
size, reconstructed skeletons that
were unearthed nearby (PAGE 85).

**E**STABLISHED IN 1929 ON ST. George's Island, the Calgary Zoo, Botanical Gardens, and Prehistoric Park annually attracts more than 850,000 visitors to its spectacular exhibits, featuring more than 1,000 familiar and exotic animals in natural environments. In addition to an extensive indoor butterfly garden, the zoo boasts the Prehistoric Park, which houses replicas of dinosaurs and mastodons, and hosts a survival breeding program for 22 endangered species, including the rare whooping crane.

LOCATED AN HOUR SOUTH OF Calgary on the outskirts of the Peigan Nation Reserve, Head-Smashed-In is one of North America's best-preserved buffalo jumps, so called because Plains Indians would drive thousands of bison over a cliff to their death. Under the guidance of archaeologists, the provincial government spent millions of dollars building a museum into the sandstone cliff. Known as the Interpretive Centre, the facility chronicles prairie life over nearly 10,000 years.

I T'S NEARLY IMPOSSIBLE TO AVOID wildlife in and around Calgary, where elk crossings are more common than you'd think. Unfortunately, drivers who don't stop in time might end up with a new hood ornament.

W HETHER YOUR GOAL IS A QUICK honeymoon getaway or a herd of well-fed cattle, four wheels and a full tank of gas couldn't hurt.

I N THE 1880S, ALBERTA'S PIONEER farmers used sod-bustin' horses to till and harvest the land. Steam-driven, wood-and-coal-fed, metal-wheeled tractors followed, but today, farmers use powerful diesel machinery to create the huge, round bales of hay that are a common sight along Calgary's fringe each July.

COWBOYS (OR "COWPERSONS," to be politically correct) are synonymous with Alberta landscapes, where many a long day is spent in the saddle rounding up strays and mending fences. Oftentimes, the reward for a hard day's work is a peaceful night under the stars.

OLITUDE HAS ALWAYS BEEN PART of a cowboy's life. After all, being the caretakers of Alberta's 4.7 million cattle takes a lot of work and dedication. The province is the sixth-largest producer of cattle in North America, and some of its ranches spread as far as the eye can see.

GREG FULMES

**N**O MATTER THEIR BACKGROUND, Alberta's children have at least two things in common: a rich past and a promising future. Here, an Indian girl, a Hutterite child, and an aspiring cowgirl seem prepared to face the future head on.

P LENTY OF BREATHTAKING LAND-scapes—both rural and urban—can be enjoyed from heights in and around Calgary. Seeing is believing, whether through the eyes of a curious child atop Sulphur Mountain (OPPOSITE), or a group of tourists at the Calgary Tower (ABOVE). Of course, nothing beats an aerial view of the entire city on a clear day (PAGES 104 AND 105).

IMPRESSIVE, CLEAN, AND SAFE ARE words often used to describe downtown Calgary, which has strived to harmonize its construction with the natural surroundings. From a business district that reaches over the serene Bow River Valley to a placid fountain outside the new City Hall, Calgary has worked to maintain and enhance its beautiful setting.

GIVEN THE ABUNDANCE OF AREA lakes and rivers, water sports abound in Calgary, from wind-surfing on Ghost Lake in Kananaskis Country to braving the rapids in a kayak, paddle boating through Bowness Park, and fly-fishing in the Bow River, considered by some to be the world's best waterway for trout fishing. During hot summer days, residents can also find solace at any of Calgary's 21 public swimming pools.

WHETHER YOUR GOAL IS SWIM-ming laps or merely getting your feet wet, Calgary can accommodate. In addition to the Lindsay Park Sports Centre, which offers extensive recreational facilities to area athletes (TOP), there are plenty of wading pools for local children and their parents to enjoy (BOTTOM). Each summer, Olympic Plaza is flooded with water, providing residents with another cool oasis on a warm day (OPPOSITE). The same surface is frozen during winter months, much to the delight of ice-skaters.

WHATEVER THE MEDIUM, THERE'S no better way to spend a day than building a castle. During the Calgary International Children's Festival, held in May, participants can construct a milk carton palace (OPPOSITE LEFT), while revellers at the Calgary Winter Festival flock to the famous frozen fortress at Winter Village (OPPOSITE RIGHT). To the delight of skaters and other onlookers, ice sculptors work their magic each year at Lake Louise (ABOVE).

THE CASTLELIKE BANFF SPRINGS Hotel, a major landmark in Banff National Park, was built out of beautiful Rundle rock (OPPOSITE). Opened in 1888, it features more than 800 guest rooms, as well as a nine-bedroom penthouse that includes its own lap pool. Across the Bow River from the hotel is the town of Banff, the world's largest urban centre located within a national park (ABOVE).

FOTOPIC / TAKE STOCK INC.

JERRY KOBALENKO / FIRST LIGHT

**B**ANFF NATIONAL PARK OFFERS plenty of exciting activities, exquisite views, and elegant hotels. Visitors can stroll around charming downtown Banff, enjoy a game of golf, or take in the beauty of Lake Louise. For those planning to stay overnight, the Post Hotel offers 17 different types of bungalow-style rooms (OPPOSITE RIGHT), and Chateau Lake Louise, opened in 1890, provides breathtaking views of its emerald green namesake and nearby Victoria Glacier (OPPOSITE, BOTTOM LEFT). Of course, the historic Banff Springs Hotel has an inviting elegance all its own (BOTTOM RIGHT).

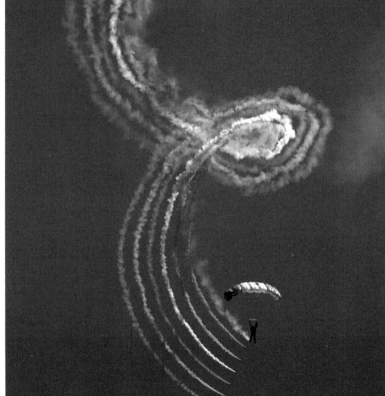

**H**IGH-FLYING SOULS CAN FEED their need in and around Calgary, from climbing 1,000 metres on the Jasper Tramway to sightseeing in a helicopter outside Canmore. Though stunt planes and crop dusters will get you from point A to point B, most people leave the flying to the commercial airlines. Served by 18 major carriers, the Calgary International Airport is ranked number one in North America and number three in the world for business passenger convenience. Of course, there are also those who throw caution to the wind and leave the plane behind altogether.

Two PROFESSIONAL SPORTS TEAMS make their home in Calgary. The Canadian Football League's Calgary Stampeders, who won the Grey Cup Championship for the third time in 1992, run and pass the pigskin at McMahon Stadium, a facility that was doubled in size to accommodate the opening and closing ceremonies of the 1988 Winter Olympics (TOP). The former Stanley Cup Champion Calgary Flames, a National Hockey League franchise that moved here from Atlanta during one of Calgary's many boom periods, compete in the Canadian Airlines Saddledome, a 20,000-plus-seat stadium that's known as one of the best sports venues in North America (BOTTOM).

OR SPORTS LOVERS WHO AREN'T content to sit in the stands, Calgary hosts dozens of footraces each year and boasts more than 20 public, semiprivate, and private golf courses. Among the city's popular marathons is Forzani's Road Race.

DANGER
QUICKSAND

▼ DARWIN A. MULLIGAN / TAKE STOCK INC.

I T'S NOT UNUSUAL ON SUMMER AND winter weekends to see a mass exodus from the city as recreation-loving Calgarians take to their favourite pursuits of camping and fishing. Although catch-and-release angling is encouraged for stream-run wild rainbow, brown, brook, and cutthroat trout, hundreds of lakes are stocked for those seeking a day of fun and a tasty meal afterwards.

A BRILLIANT SUN LIGHTS UP CASTLE Mountain along the upper Bow River in Banff National Park (PAGES 124 AND 125). The appropriately named landmark, which consists of 500 million-year-old rock perched atop 200 million-year-old rock, is a familiar sight for folks heading west to Lake Louise, home to one of the largest ski areas in the world.

THE CHANGING SEASONS BRING ALL manner of outdoor delights. Each autumn, Banff's high-elevation larch trees turn from dark green to bright yellow, luring photographers and hikers who hope to capture the moment (RIGHT). Nearby, melting snow creates the perfect reflecting pool just in time for sunset (OPPOSITE).

FOXTAIL BARLEY AND TOADFLAX— weeds despised by Alberta farmers—nonetheless provide an irresistible photo opportunity for hikers through Horse Creek Valley (PAGE 128).

Cat-tails and aspen dominate a pond in Water Valley, north of Calgary (PAGE 129). Ponds like this are why Alberta is one of North America's premier producers of mallard and pintail ducks. In fact, the skies are literally filled with migrating waterfowl each spring and fall.

▲ LYLE KORYTAR / TAKE STOCK INC.

M OUNTAIN CLIMBING IS A POPULAR activity in and around Calgary, thanks to the area's abundant rock formations. Climbers can scale the bluffs near Barrier Lake in Kananaskis Country (LEFT) or near Lake Louise in Banff National Park (RIGHT). Hoodoos, mushroom-shaped rocks formed by eons of water and wind erosion, can be found by the thousands in Alberta's badlands along the Milk and Red Deer river valleys, both within a leisurely drive of Calgary (OPPOSITE).

USIC WEAVES ITS WAY THROUGH-
out life in Calgary, whether
it's part of the three-mile-long
Stampede Parade or merely in
celebration of a sunny day.

I T'S NO SURPRISE THAT CALGARIANS usually have a lot to sing about. In 1996, Canadian Celine Dion (BOTTOM RIGHT) performed at the Saddledome, a modern, acoustically perfect venue that has attracted the likes of Frank Sinatra, ZZ Top, and Alan Jackson.

F OR MORE THAN 30 YEARS, THE Alberta Ballet (TOP LEFT) has wowed audiences with brilliantly choreographed contemporary and classical pieces, even performing before Queen Elizabeth II and at the opening ceremonies of the 1988 Winter Olympics. Still, ballet can sometimes play second fiddle to square dancing (RIGHT) or the always entertaining and challenging Indian hoop dance, performed here by the Red Thunder Native Dance Theatre of Alberta (BOTTOM LEFT).

CALGARY BOASTS A WORLD-CLASS performing arts community, including 10 professional theatre companies, an opera, an orchestra, and a ballet company. From a stage full of youthful ballerinas to con- certs at the Centre for Performing Arts to memorable productions at Theatre Calgary, the city aims to please. Most shows sell out almost as quickly as tickets are made available.

OCCUPYING A FIVE-BLOCK AREA in downtown Calgary is Stephen Avenue, a pedestrian mall featuring cafés, souvenir shops, and dozens of turn-of-the-century, sandstone buildings that were given historic designation in the 1980s. Although the avenue is alive with lunching business people during midday, the carpets roll up after 8 p.m. Planners are now trying to encourage additional residential development nearby to keep the area vibrant into the night.

SHOPPING OPTIONS IN DOWNTOWN
Calgary run the gamut. The
Bay, Alberta's largest department
store, offers top-end merchandise
in a historic 1913 landmark (OPPO-
SITE). Boasting 781,000 square feet
of retail and office space, Calgary
Eaton Centre has lured countless
shoppers since its opening in 1992
(LEFT).

PEOPLE OF ALL ETHNIC TRADITIONS find a welcome home in Calgary. At the North American Native Cultural Centre, Canadian Indians can be found making and selling intricate works of art (LEFT), while merchants in Chinatown offer everything from dried lizards to special-formula noodles (OPPOSITE TOP).

DESPITE ITS GROWING REPUTATION as an international commercial centre, Calgary has not forgotten its ranching roots. The city arguably has the best boot-making and saddlery artists in the world.

NOTHING GIVES AWAY A TRUE Alberta cowboy more than leather chaps, a lariat, and a pair of old, faded bluejeans—unless, of course, it's a huge silver belt buckle won during a rodeo. Forget the typical trophies awarded in other sports. An oversized buckle can be worn anytime, and it won't collect dust on the mantel.

L IFE ON THE PRAIRIE CAN BE down-and-dirty work sometimes, but half the fun is cleaning up after a hard day of wrangling.

I N CALGARY, IT SEEMS THAT EVERY-
one and his dog wears a cowboy
hat. One of the city's most popular
symbols, the ubiquitous western
headgear has many uses, from fend-
ing off charging bulls at the Calgary
Stampede to blocking the sun on a
bright day. A hot-air version even
serves as a floating advertisement
for a local car dealership.

A LTHOUGH CALGARY IS A TRUE city of contrasts, it often succeeds in bringing people together. Only a kilometre from the city limits, a group of small-town residents must travel to an outdoor "post office" to collect their mail. On a grander scale, people from virtually every nation came together in Canada Olympic Park, a focal point for the 1988 Winter Olympics. Today, flags commemorating the countries that participated in the competition still stand tall in the park.

FARMING METHODS HAVE COME A long way since the times when windmills were the main source of power, but Albertans haven't given up on the nonpolluting energy that comes from prolific Pacific wester-lies. As an old-fashioned mill charms visitors to Heritage Park near the Glenmore Reservoir (ABOVE), a modern-day version fills the land-scape at Cowley Ridge, a two-hour drive south of Calgary (OPPOSITE). Canada's largest and most energetic wind farm, featuring 52 modern turbines, the three-year-old facility annually churns out enough energy to light and heat 8,200 homes.

ATTRACTING 300,000 VISITORS each year, Heritage Park is a historical village that re-creates life in Alberta around the turn of the century. The 66-acre park features some 45,000 donated artifacts, ranging from covered wagons and butter churns to crank telephones and old-fashioned pianos. More than 100 buildings, which were either moved from their original locations or reconstructed from original drawings, round out the authentic experience.

PERHAPS INSPIRED BY THE CANA-
dian Pacific Railroad, which
transported many of the city's first
settlers and relocated its corporate
headquarters here in 1996 (LEFT),
Calgary has developed one of the
fastest, quietest, and cleanest transit
systems in the world. The LRT line
runs from all four corners of the
city to the downtown area, and rid-
ership has remained high throughout its two decades of existence
(OPPOSITE TOP). For those who are
less concerned with speed and more
interested in the view, the steam-
driven train through Heritage Park
is the way to go (OPPOSITE BOTTOM).

V INTAGE PUMPS AT A RURAL GAS
station hark back to 1914,
when oil was discovered in Turner
Valley, just southwest of Calgary.
Today, the oil and gas industry
remains the backbone of the provincial economy, providing 25
percent of Alberta's revenue and
463,000 jobs nation-wide.

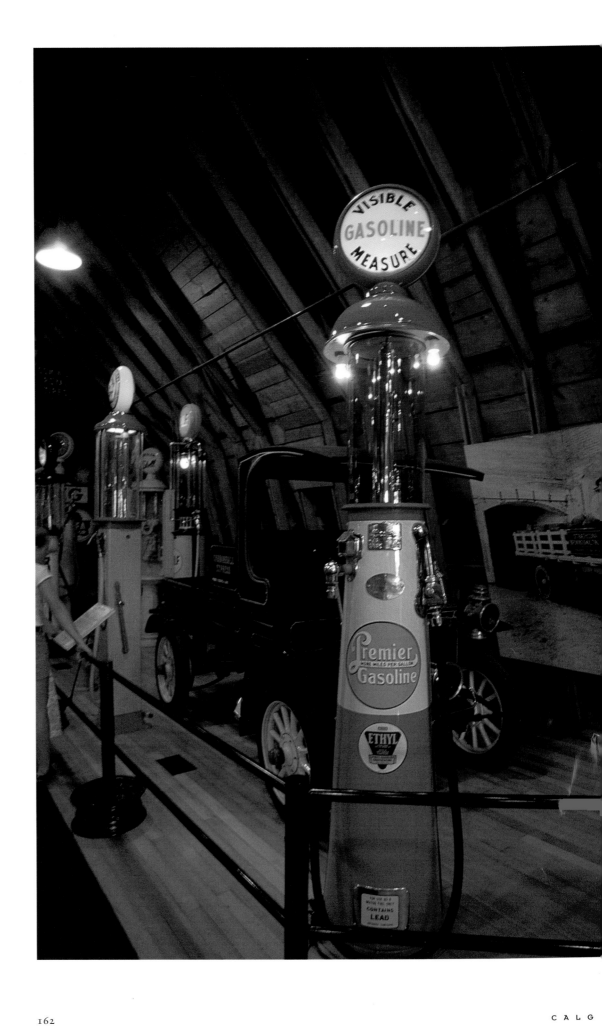

ERITAGE PARK PAYS HOMAGE
to Calgary's long-time role in
the oil and gas industry with exhibits that feature turn-of-the-century
gas pumps and other memorabilia.

A T TIMES, THE LINES BETWEEN ART
and industry are not so clearly
drawn: A contemporary sculpture
on the University of Calgary campus (OPPOSITE) seems to echo the
curves and contours of an old-
fashioned hay rake (ABOVE).

A N ANTIQUE WAGON WHEEL FINDS
new life as a rustic greeting at
one of the many cattle ranches that
dot Alberta's landscape (PAGES 166
AND 167).

WHAT WOULD THE GREATEST outdoor show in the world be without a midway? Each July, the Calgary Stampede lures its share of rodeo lovers, as well as more than a million people who like thrills of another sort, like spinning, twirling, and rocketing through the sky.

Some of North America's largest dogsled races are held each winter in and around Calgary. The exciting events bring plenty of participants, pooches, and patrons from across the continent.

THANKS TO THE EFFORTS OF AVID conservationists, Alberta's lakes, prairies, and foothills are home to a diverse range of wildlife, including (CLOCKWISE FROM OPPOSITE TOP) Canada geese, Richardson's ground squirrels, bighorn sheep, and elk.

174

CALGAR

**B**LACKFOOT PETROGLYPHS THAT were created thousands of years ago at the Head-Smashed-In Buffalo Jump (OPPOSITE) stand in contrast to the 100-year-old cattle brands stamped into a wooden wall at Heritage Park (ABOVE). Both have left their mark on local history.

**T**HANKS TO STEADY OIL AND AGRI-cultural prices, today's Calgary is seeing the greatest surge in economic activity since the boom of the late 1970s. The recent increase in home and office construction has brought on yet another influx of skilled workers, and local employment rates remain among the highest in Canada.

WHETHER ILLUMINATED BY A street lamp or the light of a full moon, downtown Calgary and its tall, glassy buildings are a metaphor for the city's growth over the years and its proven ability to harness the future.

# PROFILES IN EXCELLENCE

A LOOK AT THE CORPORATIONS, BUSINESSES, PROFESSIONAL GROUPS, AND COMMUNITY SERVICE ORGANIZATIONS THAT HAVE MADE THIS BOOK POSSIBLE. THEIR STORIES— OFFERING AN INFORMAL CHRONICLE OF THE LOCAL BUSINESS COMMUNITY—ARE ARRANGED ACCORDING TO THE DATE THEY WERE ESTABLISHED IN CALGARY.

ALBERTA ENERGY COMPANY LTD. ❋ A.R. WILLIAMS MATERIALS HANDLING LTD. ❋ ASM INDUSTRIES ❋ BPB WIRELINE SERVICES ❋ BURNCO ROCK PRODUCTS, LTD. ❋ CALGARY CHAMBER OF COMMERCE ❋ THE CITY OF CALGARY ❋ CITY OF CALGARY ELECTRIC SYSTEM ❋ CALGARY COOPERATIVE ASSOCIATION LIMITED ❋ CALGARY ECONOMIC DEVELOPMENT AUTHORITY ❋ CALGARY FLAMES ❋ CALGARY HERALD ❋ CALGARY OLYMPIC DEVELOPMENT ASSOCIATION (CODA) ❋ CALGARY PHILHARMONIC SOCIETY ❋ CALGARY STAMPEDERS ❋ CANADA SAFEWAY LIMITED ❋ CANADIAN AIRLINES INTERNATIONAL, LTD. ❋ CANADIAN FRACMASTER ❋ CANADIAN HUNTER EXPLORATION LTD. ❋ CANADIAN NATIONAL RAILWAY ❋ CANADIAN PACIFIC ❋ CANADIAN PACIFIC RAILWAY ❋ CANFER ROLLING MILLS LTD. ❋ CARMA DEVELOPERS LTD. ❋ CLAY-ROBINSON LTD. ❋ COCA-COLA BOTTLING LTD. ❋ COLT ENGINEERING ❋ ECL GROUP OF COMPANIES, LTD. ❋ GALVANIC COMPANIES ❋ GIMBEL EYE CENTRE ❋ HONGKONG BANK OF CANADA ❋ IMPERIAL OIL ❋ INTERNATIONAL HOTEL OF CALGARY ❋ MAXX PETROLEUM LTD. ❋ MOUNT ROYAL COLLEGE ❋ MULLEN TRANSPORTATION INC. ❋ NORTEL ❋ NOVA CORPORATION ❋ NOVATEL ❋ PANCANADIAN PETROLEUM LIMITED ❋ PETROLEUM INDUSTRY TRAINING SERVICE ❋ PROGAS LIMITED ❋ PRUDENTIAL STEEL LTD. ❋ QUANTEL VECO ENGINEERING LTD. ❋ THE RIDER TRAVEL GROUP ❋ RIGEL ENERGY CORPORATION ❋ ROBYN'S TRUCKING SERVICES LTD. ❋ ROYAL BANK OF CANADA ❋ RYAN ENERGY TECHNOLOGIES INC. ❋ SAP CANADA INC. ❋ SHAW ❋ SHAW NEE SLOPES GOLF COURSE ❋ SHELL CANADA LIMITED ❋ SILCORP ❋ SOUTHERN ALBERTA INSTITUTE OF TECHNOLOGY ❋ SPM/CALGARY INC. ❋ STONE & WEBSTER CANADA LIMITED ❋ TELUS ❋ TRANSALTA CORPORATION ❋ TRI-LINE FREIGHT SYSTEMS ❋ TRIMAC CORPORATION ❋ TRIZECHAHN CORPORATION ❋ UNITED WAY OF CALGARY AND AREA ❋ UNIVERSITY OF CALGARY ❋ VALMET AUTOMATION ❋ VICTORIAN ORDER OF NURSES ❋ WALLACE & CAREY LTD. ❋ WESTERN ATLAS INC. ❋ WESTFAIR FOODS, LTD.

| | |
|---|---|
| 1875 | THE CITY OF CALGARY<br>CITY OF CALGARY ELECTRIC SYSTEM (1905)<br>CALGARY ECONOMIC DEVELOPMENT AUTHORITY (1983) |
| 1881 | CANADIAN PACIFIC |
| 1883 | CALGARY HERALD |
| 1883 | CANADIAN PACIFIC RAILWAY |
| 1885 | TELUS |
| 1891 | CALGARY CHAMBER OF COMMERCE |
| 1897 | VICTORIAN ORDER OF NURSES |
| 1907 | ROYAL BANK OF CANADA |
| 1911 | MOUNT ROYAL COLLEGE<br>SOUTHERN ALBERTA INSTITUTE OF TECHNOLOGY (1916)<br>UNIVERSITY OF CALGARY (1945) |
| 1911 | TransAlta CORPORATION |
| 1912 | BURNCO ROCK PRODUCTS, LTD. |
| 1912 | IMPERIAL OIL |
| 1913 | CANADIAN NATIONAL RAILWAY |
| 1919 | COCA-COLA BOTTLING LTD. |
| 1921 | WALLACE & CAREY LTD. |
| 1929 | CANADA SAFEWAY LIMITED |
| 1933 | CLAY-ROBINSON LTD. |

**T**HE CORPORATION OF THE CITY OF CALGARY PROVIDES A COMPLETE RANGE of municipal services to the Calgary community. The City is one of Canada's leading municipal corporations, supporting a successful and internationally focused business sector, and an enviable quality of life for Calgary citizens.

Calgary was founded by the North-West Mounted Police in 1875, and named after Calgary Bay on the Isle of Mull, Scotland. By 1881, Calgary had a total population of 75 and saw the arrival of its first big herd of cattle, which initiated the area's world-famous ranching industry.

The coming of the Canadian Pacific Railway in 1883 opened up Calgary to settlers, and in 1884, with a population of 1,000, Calgary incorporated and became a town. In 1894, Calgary officially became a city, with a population of approximately 3,900.

In the next two decades, a number of well-known institutions were established, including the world-famous Calgary Stampede. But in 1947, the community took a major leap forward with the discovery of oil in nearby Leduc. It was only a matter of time before Calgary would become the Canadian headquarters for the oil and gas industry.

By the early 1980s, Calgary boasted four postsecondary educational institutions, including the University of Calgary; three important regional hospitals; a major international airport; and an internationally respected zoo.

During the 1980s, the city acquired a new NHL hockey team, built a unique performing arts centre, and won the honour of hosting the 1988 Olympic Winter Games. The Olympics made Calgary a truly international city, endowed the community with world-calibre sports facilities, and transformed Calgary into a major national sports training centre.

---
### CALGARY TODAY
---

Today, Calgary is the sixth-largest city in Canada, with a gross area of 721.36 square kilometres and a population of 800,000 and growing. In addition to a strong energy and agricultural industry base, Calgary has manufacturing, research and development, and advanced technology sectors, as well as a burgeoning film industry. Calgary has the second-largest number of corporate head offices of any city in Canada.

Calgary is also ranked first among Canada's largest cities for its quality of life, and second for giving taxpayers the most for their money. Calgary's quality of life ranked 12th in a survey of 118 cities worldwide.

---
### THE MUNICIPAL
### CORPORATION
---

Calgary's quality of life is partly due to how The City is managed. "Sound local government forms the basis of a fine city," says Mayor Al Duerr. "We've worked hard to ensure the good management of The Corporation that

CALGARY IS RANKED FIRST AMONG CANADA'S LARGEST CITIES FOR ITS QUALITY OF LIFE. THIS VIEW SHOWS DOWNTOWN CALGARY LOOKING WEST OVER THE BOW RIVER.

rves this municipality. We're oud of our contribution to aking Calgary one of the best ties in which to live."

One major advantage for algary is its ability to manage ban growth under a single risdiction. As a "unicity," e municipal government can an, finance, construct, and ovide city-wide utilities, trans-rtation infrastructure, recre-ion, and other services on comprehensive, integrated isis.

Another advantage of e City is its financial strength. espite a high level of municipal rvices, municipal taxes are nong the lowest in the country. e City of Calgary has success-lly met the challenges of main-ining a balanced budget, sorbing significant cuts in ovincial grants, and reduc-g its debt, while continuing to velop and deliver the quality rvices needed by the growing pulation.

One source of Calgary's ccess has been its ability develop innovative partner-ips with community organi-tions. With Calgary's strong dition of volunteer involve-ent, community partnerships ve proved very successful in advancing civic initiatives.

A strong customer service focus, another of The City's key principles, is built into every municipal operation. For ex-ample, when city crews are scheduled to work in a neigh-bourhood, local residents receive prenotification via brochures and door hangers. When the work is completed, residents are asked to comment on the conduct of the crew and the quality of the work.

The Calgary Police Service applies the same principles. It has a national reputation for its commitment to innovative, community-based policing.

The City's major operating departments are at the heart of its success in meeting the needs of Calgary citizens and businesses. The Engineering and Environ-mental Services Department handles public works services such as the collection and dis-posal of waste and materials for recycling; the design, con-struction, and maintenance of roads, lanes, and sidewalks; water and waste water treatment facilities; and animal services. The City's residential recycling program, established in 1990, is the largest in Canada.

Parks and Recreation ac-quires, develops, and maintains parkland and open spaces in the city, as well as developing and operating recreational facilities and programs. For example, the department operates nine municipal golf courses and numerous leisure centres, pools, and ice rinks. The City's well-used pathway system, much of it along the edge of the Bow and Elbow rivers, is one of the most extensive in the country.

The Transportation Depart-ment provides public transit services, including the state-of-the-art light rail transit system, called the C-train. Calgary is also among the few cities that have completed a formal, long-term transportation plan, with extensive public consultation. The 1995 GoPlan will serve as a blueprint for land use and bud-get decisions in the decades to come.

"The 1990s represent a decade of change," says Duerr. "We've used strategic planning and maintained fiscal responsi-bility to cope with challenges and uncertainties. We're confi-dent that we have prepared the foundation for a secure future, and we're excited about the potential and possibilities that await us as a city."

**T**HE CITY OF CALGARY HAS COME A LONG WAY SINCE 1875, WHEN IT WA founded as a fort and trading post by the North-West Mounted Polic By the early 1970s, Calgary had become an international oil and gas centr attracting top-ranking businesses that eventually would establish the city

the business and financial capital of Western Canada. With the growing need to further diversify the city's economy, the Calgary Economic Development Authority (C.E.D.A.) was founded as a collaborative effort in 1983 by The City of Calgary and the Calgary Chamber of Commerce. Since C.E.D.A.'s establishment, Calgary's economy has diversified into areas of advanced technology, manufacturing, retail trade, distribution and transportation, and tourism. Today, it is home to the second-largest concentration of corporate headquarters in Canada.

"Calgary is now poised to lead Canada's economy into the next century," says John G. Jung, President and CEO of C.E.D.A. "The chief economist of the Royal Bank of Canada has said that Canada will lead the G-7 nations in growth, Alberta will lead Canada, and Calgary will lead Alberta."

NEARLY 7 MILLION PASSENGERS TRAVEL THROUGH THE CALGARY INTERNATIONAL AIRPORT EACH YEAR, MAKING IT THE THIRD-BUSIEST AIRPORT IN CANADA.

AN IMPRESSIVE URBAN SKYLINE AND CLOSE PROXIMITY TO THE ROCKY MOUNTAINS MAKE CALGARY A PERFECT STAGE FOR A BURGEONING FILM INDUSTRY AND AN EXCELLENT LOCATION FOR SUCH TELEVISION SERIES AS *Viper*.

CHRIS LARGE

### ONE-STOP SHOP FOR INFORMATION

Calgary's reputation and business success is bolstered by C.E.D.A.'s

focus and commitment to positioning the city for the 21st century. A major milestone was the opening of the Calgary Business Information Centre in 1996. Unique in all of Canada is the co-location of C.E.D.A., the provincial government's Economic Development and Tourism department, and the federal government's Industry Canada department.

"The centre provides a one-stop shop with valuable market information for both companies and individuals. It has fostered the integration of products, services, and expertise across three levels of government," notes Jung, "and is a testament to the entrepreneurial spirit that prevails in Calgary. It's one example of the many advantages of doing business in this city."

Other economic development agencies, such as Western Economic Diversification and Aboriginal Business Canada, are now located in adjacent space. A Synergy Centre was established in November 1996 to provide affordable office space for the growing number of associations

and businesses with whom C.E.D.A. collaborates.

The Client Services depart ment also emerged to meet th needs of both internal and ex ternal clients for information, technology, research, commun cations, and marketing assistanc It provides new high-end tools to deliver better business infor mation to clients, including in formation obtainable on the World Wide Web (www.ceda calgary.ab.ca/calgary), the deve opment of a CD-ROM on the city, videos, and other tools a methodologies. In addition, C.E.D.A. also manages a Busi ness Development group, the Strategic Leaders Council, re lated strategic alliances, and the Calgary Film office, as well a administering the province's Alberta Film Commission.

C.E.D.A. acts as an initia tor, facilitator, and partner. F example, C.E.D.A. helps comp nies find joint venture opportu ties and form economic allianc actively promotes and marke Calgary as a destination for business and investment; and participates regularly in trade ows and in overseas trade ssions. C.E.D.A. also produces, ordinates, or participates in oducing industry directories. E.D.A. has partnered with the algary Airport Authority to eate an interactive multimedia osk at the Calgary airport— e first of its kind in Canada. E.D.A. also develops and ordinates business forums, nferences, and events.

By analyzing Calgary's instment development strengths d weaknesses, C.E.D.A. has entified five high-priority instries that should help the city's onomy grow: value-added od processing, manufacturing ecifically plastics), environental services and products, stribution, and the emerg-g industries of new economy vices and products. With put received from focus oups, C.E.D.A. has devel-ed action plans for each these sectors.

## "YOU OUGHTA BE IN PICTURES"

e film industry is an especially gh-growth sector. Calgary is w perceived as the entry point : all film and television produc-ns in the province. In 1996 one, 16 major motion pictures re filmed in the province. locations photo library has erged to provide quality loca-n photos and promotional ckages for international com-nies considering filming in lgary.

C.E.D.A. is also active in edu-ion and training. For example, artnership with the Employ-nt Leadership Council for uth has helped the Council est in industry-driven train-; programs to create employ-nt opportunities.

Recognizing that the eco-my of the region does not p at municipal borders, rural mmunities in the province

benefit from C.E.D.A.'s activi-ties through Prosperity South. This initiative explores potential linkages and collaboration opportunities in various sectors.

C.E.D.A. also fosters Calgary's Sister Cities relationships to cultivate export market development. "Initially established to promote international harmony and friendship, Sister Cities has grown into an effective tool for promoting trade, investment, and general business opportunities between strategically twinned communities," notes Jung. In addition to Sister Cities relationships with Daqing, China; Taejon, South Korea; Naucalpan, Mexico; Quebec City, Canada; Jaipur, India; and Phoenix, Arizona, C.E.D.A. initiates strategic alliances with other municipal economic development organizations in areas such as Colima, Mexico, and Szolnok, Hungary.

Finally, Calgary is Canada's leading beta-test centre. Telecommunications and related high-technology industries and applications are key to Calgary's diversification. C.E.D.A. works closely with the Calgary Research and Development Authority to promote and assist this sector. C.E.D.A. also nurtures the development of start-up associations, such as the International Smart Cities Institute, whose

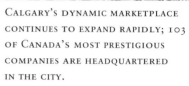

goal is to provide communities world-wide the ability to share information through the use of communications and telecommunications.

"According to a 1996 study, Calgary ranked first among 54 urban areas in Canada for overall market potential," notes Jung. "Any consumer product or service company seeking success in Canada must put Calgary at the top of the list for either new or expansion sites. Calgary is a dynamic and cosmopolitan business city renowned for its entrepreneurial spirit. Whether it's the Olympics or pioneering in emerging international markets, Calgary's business spirit shows a willingness to take on the world."

CALGARY'S DYNAMIC MARKETPLACE CONTINUES TO EXPAND RAPIDLY; 103 OF CANADA'S MOST PRESTIGIOUS COMPANIES ARE HEADQUARTERED IN THE CITY.

HOME TO THE ALBERTA STOCK EXCHANGE, CANADA'S FASTEST-GROWING EXCHANGE, CALGARY IS THE FINANCIAL CENTRE OF WESTERN CANADA.

THE MUNICIPALLY OWNED CITY OF CALGARY ELECTRIC SYSTEM DATES BACK to 1905, when it was formed to actively compete with Peter Prince's Calgary Water Power Company in supplying lighting to Calgary's residents and commercial enterprises. More than 90 years later, the Electric

System has now become a wholly owned subsidiary corporation of The City of Calgary. This move is part of the organization's preparation for competition in the electric utility industry, a result of provincial deregulation that began in the mid-1990s in Alberta.

"We will no longer be a department of The City of Calgary," notes General Manager Ken Bosma. "We will have a separate board of directors. Our vision is to be a customer-valued, competitive, profitable participant in the energy marketplace."

In achieving its vision, the Electric System expects to be- come a provider of total energy solutions to its customers. New products and services will be developed to strengthen its ability to retain existing customers and attract new ones.

### COMPETING FROM A POSITION OF STRENGTH

"We are fortunate to have a number of strengths which will help us in the move to deregulation," says Bosma. "We have an existing franchise area, with customers we know and who know us. Our pricing approval process is less cumbersome than that required by privately owned utilities, and we own the distribution facilities through which the power must flow to get to the customer."

While its headquarters is located near the Stampede grounds, and its engineering and construction divisions are in southeast Calgary, parts of the Electric System are visible all over the city—there are more than 35 substations, as well as distribution lines, transformers and wires crisscrossing the city and reaching into all homes and businesses.

Currently serving approximately 300,000 residential and commercial customers in a 940 square-kilometre area, the Electric System provides revenue to The City of Calgary and plays a key role in helping to keep property taxes as low as possible. At the same time, Calgarians are fortunate that their electricity rates are also low. In fact, Calgarians pay some of the lowest rates in the country and the Electric System is committed to keeping it that way.

The Electric System further demonstrates its commitment to Calgary not just by keeping the lights on, but also by acting in the community's best interests. For example, rebates are provided to local community associations for skating rink lighting in the winter. The electricity for the magnificent display of Christmas lights at Confederation Park is donated as well.

The City of Calgary Electric System is committed to maintaining its reputation for reliability and dependability. With a strong customer focus, the Electric System continues to be an asset for all Calgarians.

CLOCKWISE FROM TOP RIGHT: BIG ROCK BREWERY LTD. AND THE CITY OF CALGARY ELECTRIC SYSTEM WORK TOGETHER TO FIND SOLUTIONS TO POWER QUALITY, ENERGY MANAGEMENT, AND BILLING NEEDS.

ENERGY TRADING SPECIALISTS MANAGE THE PURCHASE OF ELECTRICITY FOR CALGARY THROUGH THE POWER POOL OF ALBERTA.

CLEANING INSULATORS REMOVES CONTAMINATION, WHICH HELPS TO MAINTAIN THE RELIABILITY OF THE ELECTRICITY SUPPLIED TO CUSTOMERS.

THE VICTORIAN ORDER OF NURSES (VON) WAS ESTABLISHED IN 1897 in Alberta, and in 1909 the Calgary Branch was founded. The first president was Mrs. James Lougheed, local president of the National Council of Women, and later Lady Lougheed. The Calgary Branch began with one

nurse with a bicycle—and she completed 2,175 visits, including 112 assisted births, in her first year.

The organization's mission, vision, and philosophy are as relevant today as they were when the Canadian charity was formed 100 years ago, and named to honor the 60th anniversary of Queen Victoria's ascent to the throne.

"We are a charity that operates as a three-legged stool," says Mary Perry, Executive Director of the Calgary Branch. "We have a non-profit leg, which carries out regional home care and government contracts at cost. We also have a charitable leg, which offers community nursing services and subsidized home care. And our third leg is for profit, since we have a number of contracts with businesses. We try to maintain equal emphasis among the three different legs, using revenues from the profitable contracts to subsidize our charitable programs."

VON has developed a wide range of wellness and community care programs that complement those offered through Family and Social Services and the Calgary Regional Health Authority. A surprising variety of services for seniors, children, new mothers, and surgery patients is available, including home and day support programs, palliative nursing, school programs for special needs children, respite care, parish clinics, and more.

### DEVELOPING GRASSROOTS INITIATIVES

In the mid-eighties, the introduction of regional home care

programs forced VON to change its focus," notes Perry. "Our programs became more community based and more grassroots oriented. But now, with the current cutbacks in health care, we have more opportunities than ever to fill the gaps in health and social services."

One of VON's newest services is its Homesharing Program, which matches single, older home owners with adults or young families who require accommodation and can carry out some household tasks. "The program is intended to promote well-being and independence," says Perry. "It allows older people to stay in their homes longer and decreases the need for formal support services."

The Calgary Branch also offers a wide range of services that benefit local companies and their employees. VON provides assistance in conducting insurance assessments, care for sick and special-needs children so parents can go to work, occupational health screening, sick time monitoring, and environmental hazards testing, to name only a few. Wellness services, such as flu shot clinics and individualized employee support programs, are also available.

The Calgary Branch's newest challenge is the expansion of its boundaries in late 1996. The organization is now responsible for all of south central Alberta and is developing programs and services for other communities, including Banff, Canmore, and Red Deer. With the dedication of its volunteers and staff, the next 100 years should provide many more opportunities for the Calgary Branch of the Victorian Order of Nurses.

THE CALGARY BRANCH OF THE VICTORIAN ORDER OF NURSES BEGAN WITH ONE NURSE WITH A BICYCLE—AND SHE COMPLETED 2,175 VISITS, INCLUDING 112 ASSISTED BIRTHS, IN HER FIRST YEAR (LEFT).

TODAY, VON OFFERS A VARIETY OF SERVICES FOR SENIORS, CHILDREN, NEW MOTHERS, AND SURGERY PATIENTS, INCLUDING HOME AND DAY SUPPORT PROGRAMS, PALLIATIVE NURSING, SCHOOL PROGRAMS FOR SPECIAL NEEDS CHILDREN, RESPITE CARE, PARISH CLINICS, AND MORE (RIGHT).

# C

ANADIAN PACIFIC IS A VITAL ENGINE OF GROWTH IN WESTERN CANADA. I transportation, energy, and hotel subsidiaries are major participants in the industries that keep the Western Canadian economy on the move. ❋ Can dian Pacific and the City of Calgary have had a close relationship since th

building of the railway more than 110 years ago, but it wasn't until 1996 that Canadian Pacific made Calgary its principal base of operations. From its new headquarters in Bankers Hall, Canadian Pacific can keep an eye on a number of its subsidiaries. In fact, with the railway across the street and the PanCanadian and Fording head offices, as well as the Palliser Hotel, close by, the Canadian Pacific group of companies has virtually taken over Ninth Avenue.

Canadian Pacific is the largest public company based in Western Canada, with an enterprise value of more than $15 billion. There are more than 5,000 Canadian Pacific employees in Calgary and more than 17,000 in Western Canada. The company's capital expenditure program in 1997 totals approximately $2 billion, the majority of which will be spent in Western Canada.

Along with the move to Calgary, Canadian Pacific completed an ambitious corporate restructuring program in 1996. A new Canadian Pacific Limited, with just one class of shares, was created to be the parent company of the Canadian Pacific group. The railway was reorganized to be a separate subsidiary, rather than a division of the parent company.

"The restructuring simplified our capital structure, narrowed our business focus, and positioned us for more profitable growth in the future," says

David O'Brien, Chairman, President, and Chief Executive Officer. "We have an usually strong collection of assets that we can expand internally and through selective acquisitions in the years ahead."

## SUBSIDIARIES PLAY AN IMPORTANT ROLE

Canadian Pacific Railway play an important role in linking Western Canada's agriculture and mining industries to expo markets. Canada is the second largest exporter of wheat in th world, and grain represents about 25 percent of the railway volume. Coal, sulphur, and fertilizers account for approxi mately 33 percent.

"We're also an important user of transportation," notes O'Brien. For example, Canadian Pacific subsidiary Fordin Inc. is a major customer of the

THIS SLANT DRILLING RIG OPERATING IN NORTHERN ALBERTA IS TYPICAL OF PANCANADIAN PETROLEUM'S USE OF ADVANCED TECHNOLOGY TO MAXIMIZE SUCCESS RATES AND MINIMIZE COSTS (LEFT).

CANADIAN PACIFIC RAILWAY PROVIDES EFFICIENT TRANSPORTATION THAT HELPS WESTERN CANADIAN INDUSTRY COMPETE SUCCESSFULLY IN INTERNATIONAL MARKETS (RIGHT).

DANIEL WIENER

DANIEL WIENER

DANIEL WIENER

ilway. Fording's export coal mines are located in southeast British Columbia, some 600 miles from the west coast port Roberts Bank. "Fording must compete with Australian mines that are much closer to tidewater," adds O'Brien. "So it imperative that Fording, and so the Canadian transportation and port systems, be more ficient."

Calgary-based Fording Canada's largest and most versified metallurgical coal rporter and also provides ermal coal for electric power neration in Alberta. Fording's ajor export market is blast rnace steel producers. The mpany's U.S.-based subsidry, NYCO Minerals, mines ad processes wollastonite ad tripoli for markets in North merica and abroad. NYCO the world's largest producer wollastonite, which is used plastics, abrasives, adhesives, ramics, and building materis. In 1997, Fording will start oduction at the world's largt wollastonite mine in Mexico.

Another Calgary-based bsidiary, PanCanadian Petrom, is the second-largest oducer of conventional oil ad gas in Western Canada, ne of the top two drillers, ad the largest publicly traded stream energy company.

PanCanadian exports about half of its natural gas production and two-thirds of its conventional crude output to the United States.

Canadian Pacific Hotels is Canada's largest hotel chain. It owns, leases, or manages hotels (many of which are heritage properties) in 26 locations across Canada, 13 of which are in Western Canada.

Canadian Pacific Hotels is a cornerstone of Alberta's tourism industry. The company's Alberta hotels have more than 1 million room nights available for occupancy annually. The prestigious, completely renovated Palliser Hotel was opened in 1914, and at nine storeys, was the tallest building in Calgary until the 1960s. A second Calgary property, the Calgary Airport Hotel, was opened in 1979. Other internationally recognized Canadian Pacific hotels in Alberta are Chateau Lake Louise, the Banff Springs Hotel, Jasper Park Lodge, The Lodge at Kananaskis, Hotel Kananaskis, and Hotel Macdonald in Edmonton.

"We have fully exploited the suggestion of William Van Horne, Canadian Pacific's second president," notes O'Brien. "He stated, 'If we can't export the scenery, we'll import the tourists.'"

Canadian Pacific's other subsidiary, CP Ships, is the largest carrier of containers on the North Atlantic and serves major markets across Canada and in the United States.

For both Canada and Canadian Pacific, prosperity depends on the ability to compete in international markets. In the West, this means developing the country's abundant natural resources and moving them efficiently to export markets.

"In the end," notes O'Brien, "Canadian Pacific is a trading company in a trading nation. Although we have operations in every province, our centre of operations is in Western Canada and our future lies in Western Canada. With the Alberta advantage, I believe that both Calgary's and Canadian Pacific's best years are yet to come."

THE *Calgary Herald*'s STORY BEGINS IN 1883, WHEN TWO ADVENTUROU men from Ontario set out looking for opportunity in the wester frontier. Thomas Braden, a teacher, arrived in Calgary just ahead the Canadian Pacific Railway, and waited for his friend Andrew N

Armour, a printer, who brought a hand press with him on the first train to arrive in the frontier town.

Braden and Armour's fledgling newspaper, then called the *Calgary Herald, Mining and Ranche Advocate and General Advertiser*, made history as one of the first three companies to set up business in Calgary. It hit the streets in 1883 with a four-page issue.

As Calgary grew, so did the *Herald*, helping businesses prosper and people stay informed by getting news and advertising to a growing number of loyal readers. Nearly 100 years later, in 1981, riding the coattails of

the energy boom, the *Herald* built a new $70 million publishing plant off Deerfoot Trail, on a bluff overlooking the city's burgeoning skyline. In 1987, the *Herald* made Canadian history by becoming one of the first companies in Canada to establish an on-site day-care centre for staff members.

---

### THE HERALD TODAY

Like many of the city's other corporate icons, the *Herald* weathered the ups and downs of Calgary's volatile economy during the 1980s, and during the early 1990s the company restructured various departments into leaner, more efficient work teams. Layoffs were not *de rigeur*, however, as the *Herald* has always regarded its people as one of its greatest strengths.

By embracing the latest technological advances, the *Herald* has become an industry leader at using computer technology throughout the full production process of the newspaper. It was the first newspaper in the world to use digital cameras, with its

first fully digital edition produc in April 1995.

With a new, more entrepr neurial owner, Hollinger Inc., taking over the *Herald*'s pare company, Southam Inc., in 199 the *Herald* began more aggre sively marketing and promotir its strengths under the slogan It's a New Day.

"Our editors are more attuned to community needs," says *Calgary Herald* Presiden and Publisher Ken King. "For example, when Canadian Pacif Railway decided to move its head office to Calgary, we sav an opportunity to go after ne readers."

The newsroom produced special colour supplement aime at welcoming Candian Pacific Railway employees to Calgary and providing them with ever thing they needed to know abou the city. The supplement was distributed to all employees mal ing the move from Montreal, and the railway responded by purchasing one-year subscriptions for all transferred staff.

Since then, the supplemen has been redeveloped for differ

THE *Herald* HAS POSITIONED ITSELF AS AN INFORMATION COMPANY, PREPARED TO GIVE READERS TIMELY, INFORMATIVE, AND ENTERTAINING NEWS—FROM LOCAL EVENTS LIKE THE CALGARY STAMPEDE TO INTERNATIONAL TRENDS THAT AFFECT LOCAL INDUSTRIES LIKE OIL AND GAS PRODUCTION. LEFT: 1995 NATIONAL NEWSPAPER AWARD WINNING PHOTO BY LARRY MACDOUGAL, *Calgary Herald*

t audiences. A special edition as produced to showcase Calry in Hong Kong, and another ition was produced for devel-ers to distribute to potential me buyers. Yet another edition as produced for the Calgary rport Authority and is avail-le to everyone arriving in or ving Calgary at the airport.

In addition to the daily news-per and news supplements, the *erald* produces a number of onthly publications, including tal guides for apartments and ndominiums. The Special ojects Department develops he market publications.

*Discover Calgary* is full of formation about the blossom-g number of activities in the y, replete with maps and "news u can use," including an arts d entertainment guide. Says ng, "A new version is pro-ced every three months. With sh content and good adver-ing sales, the supplement is w a commercially viable tity."

The *Herald* also operates o Internet sites—Herald On-e, and calgaryhomes.com. ntly sponsored with the Cal-ry Home Builders Association, latter site is unique in Canada. sed on the newspaper's weekly w homes section, the Web e provides a virtual parade new show homes, local build-

ers, developers, and designers that can be accessed by poten-tial home buyers throughout the world.

## CONNECTED TO THE COMMUNITY

Although the *Herald* has always been a profitable undertaking, part of management's goal has been to ensure that employees understand that producing a newspaper is a business and readers are their customers. While maintaining editorial integrity, the editorial staff has a thorough understanding of the costs involved in producing a daily newspaper and the neces-sity of producing a paper unique and relevant to the community.

"Quality local news written with accuracy, balance, passion, and excellence is our goal," says Managing Editor Joan Crockatt.

The *Herald* has received numerous journalism awards, including 10 Canadian National Newspaper Awards since 1990, in areas from spot news photog-raphy to a special project on the Charlottetown constitutional accord. Three Roland Michener Awards for meritorious Public Service Journalism have been bestowed on the newspaper, and in 1995, it received the pres-tigious Association of Opinion Page Editors (of North America)

Gold Award for a 10-day series on the changing health care industry.

The *Calgary Herald* was also recognized with an inter-national newspaper marketing award for its special education program. Under this program, the *Herald* provides newspa-pers and resource kits for local public school teachers to use as learning tools in the classroom.

In recognizing its com-munity's achievements, the *Herald* annually sponsors A Class Act, which profiles local high school students in the news-paper and then fetes those stu-dents and their parents at a special dinner.

"We can turn on a dime now," notes King. "We're inno-vative and we're listening to our customers. We have the best journalists and photographers to ensure we get the proper breadth of coverage. I believe we set the news agenda in Cal-gary—we're usually the ones to break the major stories.

"And Calgary is a wonder-ful place to be right now," King sums up. "We have a high level of education and affluence, which means more readers. We've posi-tioned ourselves as an information company, and we are prepared to give readers the timely, informa-tive, and entertaining information they want and need."

"ON SECTION 15 THERE IS A VERY GOOD LOCATION FOR A TOWN SIT and I have no doubt that when you see the place it will please you." Wi those words, wired on August 1, 1883, to General Manager W.C. Va Horne, the Canadian Pacific Railway began its long association with wh

Clockwise from top:
Truck trailers in Montreal are loaded on an Iron Highway train, CPR's radically new trailers-on-train technology. Trucks can drive on and off a continuous platform train and slots can be reserved on a next-departure basis by phone or the Internet.

Canadian Pacific Railway's new Network Management Centre in Calgary is the hub for freight operations.

A CPR double-stack container train crosses the St. Lawrence River bridge near Montreal.

today is the booming city of Calgary.

By the turn of the century, the town site along a narrow, winding river had grown into a bustling town and a thriving division point for the new railroad, with freight yards and roundhouse and turntable that were among the most modern of their era. Within a few years, Canadian Pacific Railway would become the largest employer in the town.

Since then, huge investments in the railway, hotels, oil, and gas, as well as a host of other economic activities, have made

Canadian Pacific Railway and its parent company, Canadian Pacific Limited, among the biggest investors in Alberta. So when the railway moved its head office from Montreal to Calgary in 1996, it was a return to roots deeply embedded in the West.

Today, Canadian Pacific Railway, or the CPR as it is commonly known, is one of the largest railway systems in North America, with about 17,000 miles of rail line in Canada and the United States, and close to 22,000 employees.

"Our move to Calgary recognized pragmatically that about 75 percent of our traffic and revenue is derived from bulk commodities, such as grain and coal, that move west of the Great Lakes. Calgary is a crossroads for that business," says Hugh MacDiarmid, the CPR's Executive Vice-President, Commercial. "At the same time, our senior management and support were spread across four time zones in two countries and five cities. Consolidating in

Calgary made a great deal of sense, with opportunities to reduce costs and speed decision making."

The relocation to Calgary ranks as one of the largest corporate moves in Canadian history A new telephone prefix had to be issued to accommodate the demand created by about 1,300 people moving into Gul Canada Square in Calgary's downtown core. From the new offices, employees supervise the CPR's core network, which runs across North America like a wishbone from Vancouver east to Toronto and southeast to the Twin Cities and Chicago From Toronto and Chicago to Montreal and the eastern seaboard, operations are handle by CPR's subsidiary, the St. Lawrence & Hudson Railway

## COMMITMENT TO CALGAR

The CPR is proud of how effi ciently the move to Calgary was accomplished. "The city and its people have given us a warm Western welcome,"

ys MacDiarmid. "We're all
eased with how easily we
ave fit in."

In return, the railroad
striving to make a positive
ontribution to its new home
d neighbours. It is partnering
ith the Canadian Football
ague's Calgary Stampeders
a special program, called
ear the Track, that reaches
it to youth with a stay-in-
hool message. Stampeders
allenge junior and senior
gh school basketball teams
exhibition matches during
e off-season, delivering their
essage in pregame talks with
e youngsters.

The CPR is sponsoring
e program, boosting its visi-
lity with posters, pamphlets,
shirts, and ball caps. At
e same time, the CPR uses
e program to reinforce an
iportant stay-off-the-tracks
fety message: "Anytime is
iin time."

In another community
irtnership program, the CPR
sponsoring the Alpine Skill
wards in Alberta and British
olumbia. The program helps
ildren improve their skiing
ills and rewards them for pro-
ess with skill achievement

badges, while reinforcing both
ski and railway safety messages.

## THE SPIRIT LIVES ON

After six years as CP Rail
System, the company returned
to its original name, the Canadian Pacific Railway, when
it moved its head office to
Calgary. "People have a deep
attachment to the Canadian
Pacific Railway name," notes
MacDiarmid. "While we've
gone through a complete reengineering of all railway functions
and restructured the company
for greater effectiveness and
profitability, we recognize that
our heritage is a very positive
ingredient in the mix."

In fact, the halls at the CPR's
head office are replete with strategically placed memorabilia from
the railroad's rich past—everything from large posters announc-
ing "Homeseekers Fares" to the
Prairies and round-the-world
steamer cruises to "Ports of a
Thousand Romances" to old
time-punch clocks.

"We're fortunate to have
such a rich tradition to draw
on," says MacDiarmid. "The
picture of the man in the railway
station tapping out a telegraph

is still a graphic railroad image
in the minds of many people
in North America."

However, advanced technology now pervades the railroad
as much as it does other facets
of modern business. For example,
the CPR has introduced a radically new trailer-on-trail technology called Iron Highway.
Trucks can drive on and off
a continuous-platform train
that has uniquely smooth handling characteristics. It operates
on a slot-reservation system
similar to seat reservations in
air travel, with space reserved
on a next-departure basis by
phone or the Internet.

The CPR is also introducing
a new generation of leading-
edge computer applications
and platforms for day-to-day
rail operations, and has a new
Customer Service group employing the latest voice and data
technology.

Yet, there are still times
on the railroad when grit, as
much as technology, is needed.
Whether it's blasting tunnels
through towering, snow-capped
mountains; cleaning weeds out
of ballast; or punching through
a blizzard, the old Canadian
Pacific Railway spirit lives on.

A CPR GRAIN TRAIN CROSSES LETH-
BRIDGE VIADUCT IN ALBERTA. THE
VIADUCT, WHICH WAS BUILT IN 1909,
IS THE HIGHEST RAIL BRIDGE IN CAN-
ADA, TOWERING 320 FEET ABOVE THE
OLDMAN RIVER AND EXTENDING
5,300 FEET. (LEFT)

GIANT GANTRY CRANES SWIFTLY
HANDLE INTERMODAL CONTAINERS
AT CPR'S BIG VAUGHAN TERMINAL
NEAR TORONTO. THE TERMINAL IS
ONE OF THE MOST ADVANCED CON-
TAINERIZED FREIGHT HANDLING
FACILITIES IN NORTH AMERICA.
(RIGHT)

**J**UST AS CALGARY HAS COME A LONG WAY IN THE PAST CENTURY— from a small fort beside the Bow River to a bustling city making its mark in the global marketplace—so has the province's own telecommunications company, TELUS. Since its inception in 1885, when the

A NUMBER OF TELUS SUBSIDIARIES HAVE THEIR HEAD OFFICE IN CALGARY: TELUS MOBILITY, TELUS ADVANCED COMMUNICATIONS, TELUS ADVERTISING SERVICES, CANADIAN MOBILITY PRODUCTS, AND TELUS MARKETING SERVICES. CALGARY IS HOME TO ABOUT 3,700 OF THE COMPANY'S 9,000 EMPLOYEES (LEFT).

THE COMPANY HAS LAUNCHED ONE OF CANADA'S MOST INNOVATIVE MULTI-MEDIA TRIALS, USING A FIBRE-OPTIC NETWORK FOR 3,400 CUSTOMERS IN CALGARY AND EDMONTON (RIGHT).

first phone was installed in Calgary, TELUS has undergone continual change and growth to keep up with the times.

By 1906, a provincially owned and managed telephone system was in operation in the province, growing each year as new communities were developed. But by 1958, the Alberta Government Telephones (AGT) Commission was established, ending direct government involvement. In 1990, AGT was reorganized into TELUS, a company with both regulated and non-regulated subsidiaries. At $896 million, TELUS' privatization resulted in Canada's largest-ever initial public offering. Thousands of Albertans jumped at the opportunity to become shareholders; today, about 65,000 Albertans own shares in the company.

In 1994, TELUS prepared for the beginning of long-distance telephone competition, bringing in a new President and CEO, George Petty. Petty brought with him 25 years of experience as a senior executive with AT&T in the United States.

TELUS purchased municipally owned Edmonton Telephones in 1995 and, the following year, launched a campaign to bring the corporation's companies and products under one unified identity. The AGT and ED TEL brands were honourably retired.

"We have a rich history that continues to serve us well," notes Petty. "We now are united under the TELUS name. The complex task of changing the look of more than 17,000 public telephones, 2,300 vehicles, 260 buildings, and countless other items was daunting. But the truth is, this is a new company, and the people of TELUS are writing a new book for their shareholders, their customers, and themselves."

Now Canada's third-largest telecommunications and information management services company, TELUS is a widely held public company, managing assets of more than $4 billion. The Calgary office is home to about 3,700 of the company's 9,000 employees, who work in 75 Alberta communities and strive toward the goal of "enriching lives, taking responsibility, working together, and creating value."

A number of TELUS subsidiaries have their head office in Calgary: TELUS Mobility, TELUS Advanced Communica-

ns, TELUS Advertising Services, d Canadian Mobility Products, well as TELUS Marketing rvices.

## EMPHASIS ON CUSTOMER SERVICE

a competitive environment, way for any business to suc-d is to satisfy its customers. d TELUS' customer service tiatives are felt throughout company's operations.

For example, TELUS Com-unications, the company's larg-subsidiary, has introduced *ur Way* Long Distance, a ple, price-competitive savings n geared toward residential stomers. In addition, the com-ny now provides 24-hour, en-day-a-week customer ser-e for its residential customers.

Business customers' data eds are addressed through LUS Advanced Communi-ions. This specialized busi-s unit offers complete data utions and provides a fully egrated portfolio of products d services, including the inte-tion of both core (lower-speed) d enhanced (high-speed) data vices, as well as videocon-encing. "This integration

sets us apart from our competi-tors," notes Petty.

Data solutions range from basic Internet service to fully managed applications, such as long-distance medical diagnos-tics and highly sophisticated seismic data transfers for the oil and gas industry. The com-pany is currently working on the Cybercity project to link all public buildings in the city of Grande Prairie with a high-speed data network. "This project will position Grande Prairie as an information gate-way to the North, while foster-ing further economic growth," explains Petty.

TELUS Mobility, Alberta's leading supplier of wireless mo-bile communications, including cellular, paging, and radio sys-tems, is focusing on improving the quality of its network and expanding cellular coverage. Satellite service provides unin-terrupted coverage, even in the most remote areas of the province, to almost 300,000 subscribers.

To meet the unique needs of cellular customers, the subsid-iary has introduced a number of innovative services, including Prepaid Cellular Cards, First

Incoming Minute Free (on a trial basis), and Multi-ring, which offers simultaneous ring-ing of up to three phones, one of which may be a home or busi-ness phone. Personal Commu-nications Systems (PCS), a new wireless service integrating voice, data, and video, will offer in-creased mobility to more Albertans than ever before.

"Our commitment to service continues to pay off," says Petty. "In 1996, 88 percent of our cellular customers rated our service as either good or excellent."

## TECHNOLOGY PROVIDES NEW OPPORTUNITIES

TELUS Advertising Services publishes the white and yellow pages directories in 20 Alberta communities, as well as audio/text services such as the Talk-ing Yellow Pages. In 1996, the subsidiary introduced Canada's first complete Internet-based yellow pages directory—www.alberta.com.

"With this service," says Petty, "advertisers get better value for their money and can tailor and update information that is accessed by potential

TELUS' DATA SOLUTIONS RANGE FROM BASIC INTERNET SERVICE TO FULLY MANAGED APPLICATIONS, SUCH AS HIGHLY SOPHISTICATED SEISMIC DATA TRANSFERS FOR THE OIL AND GAS INDUSTRY (LEFT).

VIDEOCONFERENCING IS ANOTHER OF THE SERVICES PROVIDED TO HANDLE CUSTOMERS' BUSINESS NEEDS (RIGHT).

"Our commitment to service continues to pay off," says George Petty, President and CEO of TELUS. "In 1996, 88 per cent of our cellular customers rated our service as either good or excellent (left)."

The company provides 24-hour, seven-day-a-week customer service for its residential customers (right).

customers both locally and around the world."

TELUS continues to invest significantly in R and D to develop advanced network technology and customer information systems. As a result, TELUS has launched one of Canada's most innovative multimedia trials, using a fibre-optic network for 3,400 customers in Calgary and Edmonton.

### PROVIDING ADVANTAGES FOR CALGARIANS

TELUS' presence in Calgary provides a number of unique advantages for the city as well as the province. As an Alberta-based company, TELUS' revenues stay in the province, funding future telecommunications projects and establishing a strong tax base.

TELUS also supports a number of local municipal initiatives. The company was the first major corporate sponsor for Calgary's bid to host EXPO 2005, committing assistance and funds totalling $250,000 to the bid phase alone.

Under a partnership called Team Alberta, TELUS and the Alberta government are market-

ing Alberta's expertise in telecommunications, information technology, and business infrastructure to North American businesses, encouraging them to relocate or set up call centres and related activities in Alberta.

The City of Calgary and the Province of Alberta have officially joined with TELUS in financially supporting the transformation and expansion of convention facilities in Calgary. The existing and expanded city convention facility will be named the TELUS Convention Centre. The existing centre has been renovated and will be connected to the new facility to be constructed across Stephen Avenue mall. The combined complex will feature added exhibit space, more meeting rooms, and the use of advanced communications technologies to link Calgary and the world electronically.

For Petty, the partnership with the Convention Centre is a natural one. "We see an opportunity in the Convention Centre to make an important contribution to the vitality of Calgary and to do a lot of good things for TELUS customers, employees, and shareholders."

TELUS is also one of the largest private sector employe in Calgary, and estimates tha the direct and indirect emplo ment effects of its activities i the city translate into about 6,000 jobs.

### PARTNERING IN THE EDUCATION AND HEALT SECTORS

Guided by its motto, Using Bright Technology, We Creat Bright Minds and Bright Futur TELUS invests people, dollar and technological support to enrich the lives of Calgarians As a participant in the Imagi program, the company donat 1 percent of its revenues to nc profit projects. The company sponsors a number of events and sports activities in the cit including the Spruce Meadov Masters and the Calgary TELU Open Golf tournaments, part of the Canadian professional golf circuit.

In addition, in 1996, the TELUS Bright Futures Found tion launched TELUS World Learning, a $7.2 million initi tive to provide all of Alberta' elementary and secondary scho with free Internet service and gh-speed network access ntil 1998.

Students are the beneficiaries another educational support ogram—the first of its kind Canada. Under a partnerip with the Calgary Board Education, FOCUS (Funding ur Children's Unlimited Sucss) provides financial support individual schools within the algary district. When TELUS stomers sign up for *Your Way* ng Distance, the company ontributes a portion of its ng-distance charges to the hool of its choice.

TELUS' technology also is creasing the efficiency of health re delivery in Alberta. The mpany's ultimate health care sion is a comprehensive Alberta tegrated Health Information etwork to link all members of e health care community, which uld eventually save $220 milon each year in health care sts.

As a first step, the TELUS emote Consultative Network as introduced in 1994 to link imary health care practitioners in rural areas with specialists in urban centres to help with diagnosis through interactive multimedia communication.

Other community commitments include the establishment of a videoconferencing/telemedicine room for the Calgary Regional Health Authority, and the establishment of a multimedia training and education development program for the Alberta Shock Trauma Air Rescue Society (STARS). And, as part of Stentor, a national alliance of 11 Canadian telecommunications companies, TELUS is working with Health Canada and Industry Canada to develop a national health care infrastructure.

Employees also make important community contributions. Each year, Calgary employees give generously to charitable organizations through a fundraising campaign that the company matches dollar for dollar. Employees also help the community by volunteering their own time on local projects. One recent successful volunteer effort was a Feed the Homeless Dinner, in which 500 people were fed at the TELUS Calgary office tower. TELUS also contributes $200 to a not-for-profit or charitable organization of each employee's choice for every 60 hours of volunteer time.

TELUS employees take special pride in working for a full-service, fully integrated telecommunications company. "Our goal is to be seamless, from beginning to end," says Petty. The company now provides a single point of contact for all residential and business communication needs—one-stop shopping for customer ease.

"TELUS is committed to serving Albertans with the communications solutions they need to live richer, more productive lives," Petty concludes. "Our commitment is to become more competitive, flexible, and customer-focused. In this age of communications, every home and enterprise depends on our services. We're in a great business."

IN 1996, TELUS INTRODUCED CANADA'S FIRST COMPLETE INTERNET-BASED YELLOW PAGES DIRECTORY (LEFT).

THE TELUS BRIGHT FUTURES FOUNDATION LAUNCHED TELUS WORLD OF LEARNING, A $7.2 MILLION INITIATIVE TO PROVIDE ALL OF ALBERTA'S ELEMENTARY AND SECONDARY SCHOOLS WITH FREE INTERNET SERVICE AND HIGH-SPEED NETWORK ACCESS (RIGHT).

THE CALGARY CHAMBER OF COMMERCE IS DEDICATED TO LEADING AND serving the Calgary business community, with the goal of creating a environment in which the city and its citizens can prosper. Nowhere Calgary's volunteer spirit demonstrated so strongly as in the activiti

THE CALGARY CHAMBER OF COM-MERCE OFFICES ARE LOCATED IN DOWNTOWN CALGARY IN THE HERI-TAGE BUILDING, WHICH WAS BUILT IN 1912. THE CHAMBER'S IMPACT, HOWEVER, EXTENDS FAR BEYOND THE BUILDING'S WALLS DUE TO THE ONGOING EFFORTS OF HUNDREDS OF VOLUNTEERS.

of this volunteer organization. Formed on May 2, 1891, as the Calgary Board of Trade, the Calgary Chamber of Commerce today represents the interests of approximately 4,000 individual members and 2,700 companies.

"With almost 7,000 corporate and individual members, our chamber is the second-largest and the most active chamber of commerce in Canada," says Glenn Tibbles, Managing Director and Chief Operating Officer.

Under the direction of its volunteer Board of Directors and its Managing Director and staff, the Chamber provides information and assistance to the public, produces targeted business publications, and organizes general meetings, seminars, and special events geared to improving the business climate in the city, province, and country.

### PROMOTING BUSINESS VIEWS

The Calgary Chamber's Policy Committees are the mainstay of the organization. Without its strong committee structure—and the invaluable contribution of more than 500 volunteer committee members—the Chamber could not continue to be an effective voice for Calgary businesses. Most of these committees monitor government policy at all three levels and make recommendations and submissions to promote the interests of Calgary's business people. In addition, the committees are active in creating public awareness about business issues and in promoting the city and its industries. For example, a Small Business Week is held annually to recognize Calgary's many entrepreneurs.

In addition to the opportunity to participate in the Chamber's activities, members receive regularly published newsletters and a membership directory—a publication that is well used for networking purposes by a large number of members.

In fact, the Chamber provides many networking and socializing opportunities, includ ing monthly Contact Breakfas and Business After Hours. Men bers can sponsor seminars and other marketing initiatives through the Chamber, which regularly sponsors a number of prominent, high-profile gues speakers from the political or corporate sectors.

The Chamber's facilities, conveniently located in the heart of downtown, include numerous meeting rooms that members can use for staff sem nars, presentations, shareholde meetings, corporate dinners, or office parties. The Commer Club provides an elegant dinin room on the fourth floor for members to entertain their bus ness guests, and has more casua dining in the second floor lounge; the Fireplace Dining Room is a private dining roon for intimate gourmet dinners.

The Commerce Club offe a variety of leisure time dining experiences for members and guests, and special buffets are held in honour of major holiday The club also offers special events such as wine tastings, and members are able to rent the club's facilities for events such as weddings and other receptions.

With its strong volunteer spirit and entrepreneurial focu the Calgary Chamber of Com merce truly reflects a city that embraces progress while creat ing a vision for the future.

The Chamber would like to thank NOVA Corporation for its generous gesture in con tributing this page to the Calgar Chamber of Commerce.

STABLISHED FOR THE BENEFIT OF ALL ALBERTANS IN 1954, NOVA Corporation (NOVA) has grown from a natural gas pipeline company serving local gas producers to an international company whose economic impact ripples across Canada and the United States, into South America,

ad around the world.

Incorporated by a special t of the Alberta legislature, lberta Gas Trunk Line Company Limited was granted the ghts to build, own, and oper- e a province-wide natural is transmission system. Since at time, the company, now nown as NOVA Gas Transmission Ltd. (a subsidiary of OVA Corporation), has ex- anded its gas transmission usiness and become a pioneer the development of Alberta's orld-scale, gas-based petro- emicals industry.

Today, NOVA is an inte- ated natural gas services d petrochemicals company, nploying more than 6,000 ople in more than 100 facil- es throughout the world. he company is structured to three businesses: NOVA hemicals Ltd., NOVA Gas ransmission Ltd., and NOVA as International Ltd.

The largest industrial buyer Alberta natural gas, NOVA hemicals Ltd. produces poly- yrene, ethylene, styrene, and olyethylene at nine plants in anada and the United States.

NOVA Gas Transmission d. is the largest-volume trans- orter of natural gas in North merica through one of the orld's most technologically lvanced and cost-efficient atural gas transmission systems, ith facilities in more than communities throughout lberta.

Focusing on Canada, the nited States, Mexico, Asia cific, and South America, OVA Gas International d. invests in natural gas pportunities and provides

consulting services to natural gas and petrochemicals indus- tries worldwide. The business has participated in more than 300 projects in 50 countries.

## COMMITMENT TO CALGARY

"NOVA has evolved into a large, international company alongside Calgary's emergence as a world- class city. We've grown up to- gether," says Ted Newall, Vice- Chairman and CEO. "Although we've broadened our focus sig- nificantly since our early years, we intend to remain a Calgary- based, Canadian-owned company."

The company has main- tained a substantial employee base in Calgary, with about 2,500 employees. "We're build- ing expertise and knowledge that we can export worldwide," notes Newall. "And while Calgary provides a top-quality work force, if we need to recruit employees from other areas, the city and its quality of life are a big attraction."

In addition to its role as a major employer in the city, NOVA continues to add value to the communities where it op- erates. More than 85 percent of its $10 billion in assets are located in Canada. The company is also one of Alberta's largest investors in technology and product devel- opment, employing a full-time research group of scientists, engi- neers, and technical support staff at its world-class research facili- ties in Calgary. A recent major innovation was the development of Advanced SCLAIRTECH™ technology to produce excep- tional-quality, high-performance polyethylene resins.

And, in an era when non- profit organizations are look- ing to the corporate sector for increasing support, NOVA is taking a leadership role in the community through its corpo- rate contributions program. "Our mission is to invest in the growth, diversity, and well- being of the communities we share in by lending a hand to organizations dedicated to im- proving the overall quality of life," says Newall. About 70 percent of the company's cor- porate contribution dollars are invested in Alberta.

As NOVA grows and evolves in the 21st century, the company will continue to play a signifi- cant role in strengthening and diversifying the Alberta economy, creating jobs and new opportu- nities for many more Calgarians.

BRIAN HARDER

NOVA CORPORATION, A CALGARY- HEADQUARTERED COMPANY, IS BUILD- ING EXPERTISE AND KNOWLEDGE IN THE NATURAL GAS SERVICES AND PETROCHEMICAL INDUSTRIES IN ALBERTA THAT IT WILL EXPORT WORLDWIDE.

PAUL CONNOR

BRIAN HARDER

ORLD-CLASS POSTSECONDARY EDUCATION INSTITUTIONS ARE AMONG TH many attributes that make Calgary an ideal place to live and work. Calga is fortunate to have three major institutions—The University of Calgar Southern Alberta Institute of Technology, and Mount Royal College-

each with its own focus, yet working collaboratively to provide Calgarians and their employers with the skills and knowledge to keep the city on the leading edge of the information age. These institutions, along with the Alberta College of Art and Design and the Alberta Vocational College, help Calgarians and Calgary's businesses compete and succeed in the global marketplace.

"Education and training hold the keys to our collective economic future and our individual well-being," says Mount Royal College President Thomas Wood. "Corporations and individuals who invest most effectively in them will thrive."

In response to changing needs, Mount Royal College (MRC), The University of Calgary (U of C), and Southern Alberta Institute of Technology (SAIT) are developing a multitude of new programs—in many cases joint ventures with businesses or other institutions—to ensure that postsecondary institutions not only meet emerging demands, but that they also help guide and lead community growth and development. Approximately 150,000 Calgarians take advantage of programming offered by the postsecondary institutions each year. Indeed, Calgarians are the most highly educated population in Canada.

"It's now almost as commc to see five-year-olds and 60-year-olds in our halls as it is t see traditional young, full-tim students," notes U of C Presider Terry White. "All of Calgary' postsecondary institutions are active in the community, offer ing a variety of programming such as summer camps, contin ing education programs, and open houses."

### ROOTS GO BACK TO 191

The oldest postsecondary insti tution in Calgary is Mount Roy College, which opened its doo in downtown Calgary in 191 By 1931, MRC was offering first-year university courses in affiliation with a number o Canadian and American unive sities, and the college has con tinued to expand its program base, now offering more than 50 career credit diploma and certificate programs. Mount Royal College offers two of

lberta's eight applied degree ograms—Bachelor of Applied ommunications and Bachelor Applied Small Business and ntrepreneurship—and has one- d two-year university programs ansferable to Canadian and .S. universities. A major focus on entrepreneurial training d preparing students and aduates for global challenges.

Southern Alberta Institute Technology was founded in 16 to fill the growing demand r skilled workers in the prov- ce. The institute now offers 7 diploma and certificate pro- ams, as well as 27 appren- ceship and pre-employment ograms in business, commu- cations, engineering technolo- s, health sciences, hospitality, ansportation mechanics, and cility operations. SAIT also fers two applied bachelor's grees and more than 1,900 urses and seminars, many of hich are customized to suit nployers' training needs.

"Our programs are driven industry's need for skilled nployees and learners' needs r employment or self-employ- ent," notes SAIT President Ken yhre. "Thirty of our diploma d certificate programs and further 19 apprenticeship pro- ams are now nationally accred- d. Employment rates for our aduates average more than percent."

The youngest member of e trio is The University of lgary, which originated in 45 when the Calgary Normal hool became a branch of the niversity of Alberta's education culty. After sharing a build- g with SAIT, it moved to its rrent northwest Calgary mpus in 1960 and gained ll autonomy as a degree-grant- g institution in 1966. Today, e U of C is a dynamic re- arch and teaching university growing national and inter-

national stature, with 16 facul- ties and more than 60 academic departments and major program areas. Programs lead to bache- lor's, master's, doctoral, and professional degrees in both tra- ditional and interdisciplinary fields.

## STRONG FOCUS ON RESEARCH

The U of C's strong research initiatives distinguish it from other postsecondary institu- tions and are helping to achieve worldwide recognition for Calgary. Virtually all faculty members engage in research, scholarship, and creative activ- ity—ranging from the structure of chromosomes to the origins of the universe, from ancient Greek poetry to modern art, and from critical care nursing to biomedical engineering.

Faculty at the U of C are members of nine of the 14 fed- eral Networks of Centres of Excellence (NCE). The U of C is headquarters for the Canadian Bacterial Diseases NCE, and the Canadian International Development Agency has rec- ognized the U of C as a Centre of Excellence in International Development. The World Tour- ism Organization approved the U of C's International Tourism Education and Re- search Centre—one of only two such centres outside of Europe.

SAIT also provides facilities and technical support to com- panies engaged in applied re- search. Recently, the institution has worked with Mobil Oil to design specialized training equip- ment for that company's overseas training, and is conducting re- search into the recycling of electrical transformer oil.

Mount Royal College has established the Suncor Centre for Applied and Environmental

Research in the Faculty of Science and Technology.

## COLLABORATION PAVES THE WAY FOR CHANGE

Meeting educational needs in the 1990s and beyond requires extensive collaboration among Calgary's three public institu- tions. Twenty years ago, stu- dents opted for either degree or diploma programs. Now, how- ever, employers are looking for a combination of theoretical and practical skills.

As a result, an increasing number of programs are being offered jointly. For example, in 1995, the first group of stu- dents graduated with a degree from the Calgary Conjoint Nursing Program offered by MRC and the U of C. The joint

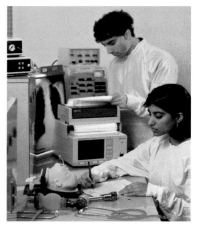

Bachelor of Hotel and Resort Management is offered by SAIT and the U of C, whereby students take a two-year diploma at SAIT and have the option to continue on to a degree at the U of C.

The institutions are also community partners and collaborate with business. In 1997, SAIT completed the second year of its innovative School to Work Transition Program, where high school students interested in pursuing careers in engineering technologies take relevant courses from SAIT and apply what they have learned in a business environment. SAIT works closely with employers to determine relevant courses and content, and also takes on the training requirements for some of these companies and their clients. Businesses such as Nortel, Engineered Air, Amoco, and CIBC are formal training partners with SAIT. The result is labs and facilities featuring the latest technology to benefit the students, employees, and employers alike.

MRC also has ongoing partnerships with companies. Royal Bank has sponsored the development of leading-edge educational materials for would-be small-business owners and entrepreneurs, and Petro-Canada has funded the Innovator Awards program to support innovative teaching and research.

The U of C has more than 30 endowed research chairs bringing together government and industry partners in a collaborative effort to increase society's knowledge base. These teams are examining topics from plant biotechnology to ethnic studies, and from intelligent manufacturing to natural resources law.

## CULTURAL AND LEISURE ACTIVITIES

In keeping with SAIT's mission to deliver skill-oriented training, much of the institute's contribution to Calgary's culture and leisure centres upon the application of technology. Students of several communication programs assist local television networks in sport and cultural coverage. For example, SAIT provided logistical and network support during the 1988 Olympics. Television students produce a weekly cable news show combining news and cultural coverage. Logistical and technical support is also provided to production companies shooting films and commercials in southern Alberta.

The U of C offers leading edge programs in art, drama, music, and dance. In addition, the 1988 Olympics left the university a legacy of sports facilities that are among the finest North America. And important lecture series, including the James Palmer lectures, bring in many world-renowned speakers such as John Kenneth Galbraith and Rajmohan Gandhi, the grandson of Mahatma Gandhi.

The Mount Royal College Conservatory has a national reputation for music excellence including the Academy of Music Program for gifted young musicians, and the new Calgary Organ Academy. MRC also offers free outdoor theatre performances each summer through its Shakespeare in the Park series.

The postsecondaries of the future will likely be very different from the ones of today. With international training and distance education gaining in importance, much of the learning may take place outside of traditional centralized campus environments. The explosive growth of the Internet as a learning medium has provided great opportunities for Calgary's postsecondary educational institutions to expand their horizons globally, and they have all been quick to rise to the challenge. In taking their education and training to learners in other countries, and in welcoming international learners onto the campuses at home, Calgary's postsecondaries are helping people in countries everywhere realize what Calgarians have known for nearly a century—Mount Royal College, Southern Alberta Institute of Technology, and The University of Calgary truly do represent a world of educational opportunity.

ITH ITS MISSION OF "SERVING CALGARIANS, ONE CUSTOMER AT A TIME," the Royal Bank of Canada has been a local institution since 1907. ❋ The bank has a strong presence in Calgary, with more than 2,000 employees working in sales and service, and in the company's district headquarters and processing centre located in the city.

Royal Bank has leading positions in Canada in most financial service markets, with profitable and growing global operations in 35 countries. Serving more than 10 million consumer and business customers throughout the world, the Royal is more than a bank.

In Canada, the company has leading market shares in residential mortgages, consumer loans, personal deposits, and Canadian-dollar business loans. Royal Bank is also the largest money manager, third largest in mutual funds, and owns the largest full-service investment dealer, RBC Dominion Securities Inc. Royal Bank Action Direct, its discount brokerage operation, is the second largest in Canada, while in insurance, Royal Bank ranks among the top providers of creditor insurance.

## THE COMMUNITY

We're committed to the community," says Gord Tallman, Senior Vice-President and General Manager for Alberta and the Northwest Territories. "There's not much that we're not involved in. We're one of the largest corporate donors in Canada," he notes. "We donate more than $16 million each year across the country, with $1.25 million in Alberta alone."

The funds are primarily targeted at a range of education and health care initiatives. For example, the bank has made a $700,000 donation to the University of Calgary's capital fund-rais-

ing campaign and a $200,000 donation to Mount Royal College to sponsor the Royal Bank Entrepreneurship Study Series.

More than $500,000 has been donated to the Calgary Regional Health Authority's Partners in Health campaign, with funds targeted at breast cancer research—since more than 75 percent of the bank's employees are women. And another $100,000 has been donated to the STARS air ambulance service to purchase helicopters.

The bank is also a key supporter of the United Way. In fact, it's the United Way's largest corporate donor in the country.

"A company's business success is tightly linked to the economic and social conditions in which it operates and grows," says Tallman. "Through the bank and its subsidiaries, and through the Royal Bank of Canada Charitable Foundation, we're committed to donate at least 1 percent of our annual net income before taxes."

Over the years, Royal Bank has grown from a traditional bank, delivering products and services through its many branches, to a broadly based financial services enterprise serving customers through a variety of channels, 24 hours a day, seven days a week. In the future, Royal Bank will continue to respond to changing customer needs and intense competition by focusing on quality and innovation, while maintaining its tight links to the community.

ROYAL BANK CONTINUES TO RESPOND TO CHANGING CUSTOMER NEEDS AND INTENSE COMPETITION BY FOCUSING ON QUALITY AND INNOVATION, AS WELL AS OFFERING CUSTOMERS SUCH CONVENIENCES AS PC BANKING (TOP).

WITH ITS MISSION OF "SERVING CALGARIANS, ONE CUSTOMER AT A TIME," THE ROYAL BANK OF CANADA HAS BEEN A LOCAL INSTITUTION SINCE 1907 (BOTTOM).

THE CONTINUING DEREGULATION AND RESTRUCTURING OF THE ENERGY industry is making it necessary for many North American utilities to reinvent themselves to operate in a more competitive global environment. In Canada, one of the leaders in this change process is TransAlta.

Providing electric energy in Alberta since 1911, the Calgary-based company's growth has paralleled the growth and development of the province, whose water resources were first tapped with a number of small hydro-electric plants. In later years, following the discovery of abundant, low-cost, low-sulphur coal reserves, larger coal-fired plants were built to supply the province's growing electric power requirements. Throughout the years, Albertans have been fortunate to have abundant supplies of electric power at rates that are among the lowest in North America as well as in the world.

TransAlta continues to be one of the few investor-owned electric utilities in Canada, and has always striven to be responsive to customers and shareholders. Well in advance of provincial industry restructuring in 1996, the company understood that it must prepare and change with the changing times.

TransAlta supports the movement toward a more competitive electric utility industry. The company holds the view that customer choice drives lower electricity prices and will strengthen Alberta's overall economy.

TransAlta owns and operates power generation, transmission, and distribution assets that supply more than two-thirds of the total electric energy needs of the province of Alberta. TransAlta is also in the business of electric and thermal energy production, gas and electricity distribution, energy services, and energy marketing in select regions of Canada, New Zealand, Australia, Argentina, and the United States.

### MOVING INTO THE GLOBAL MARKETPLACE

TransAlta is also seeking opportunities in other parts of the province, the country, and the world. As a result, a number of new ventures have been undertaken in recent years. One example is in New Zealand, where the company has ownership positions in two cogeneration plants and an electric distribution system that serves about 12 percent of the country's market. In 1996, TransAlta New Zealand Limited was created, with a goal of building an integrated energy company, increasing market share, and developing new, independent power projects.

"The New Zealand market provides a very good match for us," notes TransAlta Corporation's President and Chief Executive Officer, Stephen Snyder, who was appointed in 1996. "We're learning a lot from our experiences there and gaining competitive market insights."

TransAlta has 100 percent ownership in four other cogeneration plants—three in Ontario and one in Fort McMurray, Alberta. The company also has an interest in a cogeneration project in Australia and a hydro-electric project in South America.

In 1996, a TransAlta subsidiary was the first and only Canadian electric utility affili-

TRANSALTA IS IN THE BUSINESS OF ELECTRIC AND THERMAL ENERGY PRODUCTION, GAS AND ELECTRICITY DISTRIBUTION, ENERGY SERVICES, AND ENERGY MARKETING.

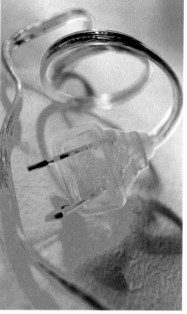

te to receive U.S. Federal Energy egulatory Commission approval o buy and sell electricity in ne United States. Once this approval was granted, the company commenced wholesale nergy marketing in the U.S. acific Northwest.

TransAlta has not been resting on its laurels in Alberta. In ddition to meeting the electric energy needs of Albertans ith 4,476 megawatts of genering capacity over 100,000 ilometres of transmission and istribution lines, the utility ontinues to record significant chievements.

For example, TransAlta nks best in its class in operaonal productivity and cost omparisons, according to the anadian Electricity Association. hile most other Canadian elecic utilities have experienced

cost increases, TransAlta's unit costs decreased by 4.7 percent during the last decade.

TransAlta is also the first company in the country to receive Industry Canada accreditation to test electric meters for other utilities and manufacturers. "Our in-house quality assurance expertise benefits customers by reducing costs and improving speed of service," says Snyder.

During 1996, TransAlta introduced a number of new products and services aimed primarily at helping oil and gas industry customers achieve optimum levels of production and energy usage, as well as reducing operating costs. For residential customers, the company operates a toll-free Energy Matters Hotline to provide energy efficiency information and advice.

TransAlta also received a national award in 1996 for its leadership in voluntarily promoting, developing, and implementing initiatives to mitigate climate change. Over the years, the company has received international recognition for its efforts to promote sustainable development. Those efforts have been partly responsible for TransAlta's success in New Zealand.

TransAlta intends to pursue new business opportunities that arise as a result of changing customer needs and market demand.

"As an investor-owned utility, we've always had a competitive tradition," says Snyder. "In addition to being an efficient, low-cost plant operator, we've maintained a strong focus on our customers' needs, exhibited financial strength and stability, and taken a proactive approach to environmental issues."

These strengths will be needed in the future as customers are given increasing choices regarding their electricity supplier and as electricity becomes a commodity, rather than a monopoly service. TransAlta is well prepared for the transition to an innovative, responsive, entrepreneurial culture.

FROM MODEST FAMILY BEGINNINGS, BURNCO ROCK PRODUCTS LTD HA grown to be a major supplier of high-quality aggregate, concrete, asphal packaged products, and precast concrete throughout the province o Alberta. BURNCO has supplied materials for such landmarks as th

Calgary Tower, the Edmonton Rapid Transit Tunnels, and the Banff Springs Hotel addition, all of which stand as testimonials to the company's strength, its progress, and the permanency of its products.

"Whether providing concrete for a bridge or packaged sand for a child's sandbox, our customers receive the same care and attention," says President Scott Burns. "We are committed to doing it well and doing it right."

J.F. BURNS II AND A PARTNER STARTED TRUE-MIX CONCRETE IN 1950. PICTURED AT RIGHT IS THE COMPANY'S FLEET OF READY MIX CONCRETE TRUCKS AND THEIR DRIVERS.

IN 1912, JAMES F. BURNS FOUNDED A CONCRETE AND EXCAVATING BUSINESS IN CALGARY. MATERIALS WERE HAULED IN HORSE-DRAWN DUMP WAGONS UNTIL THE 1920S.

## THE GROWTH OF
## A FAMILY BUSINESS

In 1912, James F. Burns started a concrete and excavating business in Calgary. Materials were hauled in horse-drawn dump wagons until the 1920s, when Burns and his son, James F. Burns II, purchased their first motorized gravel dump truck. J.F. Burns II eventually branched out with his own concrete, sand, and gravel business with a stationary crushing, screening, and washing plant along the Bow River. J.F. Burns sold his business to his son in 1946.

J.F. Burns II and a partner started True-Mix Concrete, and introduced one of the first central mix plants to Alberta in 1950. Concrete delivery by truck permanently replaced job-site mixing, and the first of many portable crushing plants was purchased. In 1954, the asphalt paving operations began, and the third generation of the family, James F. Burns III, joined the company.

Five family companies were consolidated in 1969, forming BURNCO Industries Ltd. J.F.

Burns III purchased his father's interest and became president. Rapid expansion saw branches open in Canmore, Red Deer, Medicine Hat, and Airdrie. In 1977, a new operating subsidiary was formed, BURNCO Rock Products Ltd.

BURNCO grew to include a number of portable crushing and washing plants. In 1984, the asphalt paving business wound down, but asphalt batch plants were kept to supply contractors. A packaging plant was introduced to provide do-it-yourself, premixed products. Scott Burns, a member of the fourth generation of the Burns family, joined the company in 1986. Expansion continued throughout Alberta, and landscape materials became available through the company's Consumer Centre.

In the 1990s, Scott Burns became president, and the parent company, BURNCO Industries Ltd, became a sister company. To avoid confusion, BURNCO Industries changed its name to BURNSWEST Corporation. New operations began at Shepard Road, and today, expansion continues into Edmonton and

Fort McMurray. The compan has also purchased a concrete precast company, which has now become BURNCO's Precast Division.

## FOUR OPERATING
## DIVISIONS

The company is structured int four main operating divisions, each with its own group of spe cialists to serve customers' indi vidual needs. The Aggregate Division produces aggregate, a mixture of sand and gravel, from more than 25 company-owned or leased pits. Four portable crushing plants and two wash plants, along with one large, stationary wash plan

rocess the aggregate from raw material into a vast array of products.

BURNCO's Consumer Centres provide retail customers and ontractors with one-stop shopping for a wide assortment of ndscaping supplies, including aving stones, decorative rocks, d precast products. The Property Department plans the various pit operations, and oversees ermit approvals and the final clamation of the land.

The Ready Mix Division tilizes 12 stationary concrete ants that are strategically cated in Alberta's major centes, and two portable plants at supply various large industrial sites. All of these plants ombine aggregate, cement, ater, and special additives r delivery to job sites by the ompany's fleet of more than oo mixer trucks. BURNCO rovides complete concrete rvices, including pumping, acing, and finishing.

The Asphalt and Packaging ivision has three stationary phalt plants, located in Calgary d Canmore, which produce full range of hot and cold ixes. The division's packaging ant produces a wide variety

of products, including premixed concrete and mortar, play sand, concrete and asphalt repair products, and landscape products. These are packaged in sizes ranging from one-kilogram pails to special 1,100-kilogram bags for mining, tunnelling, and SiloMix applications.

The Precast Division's product base includes architectural and structural precast concrete panels for commercial and industrial building systems, as well as such standard products as concrete steps, barriers, brackets, parking curbs, septic and water cisterns, sidewalk blocks, and planters.

"When my great-grandfather, Jim Burns, started the

business in 1912, he recognized that supplying quality products was not enough," Scott Burns comments. "Friendly, dependable customer service was also important. We've been developing strong customer relationships ever since. At BURNCO, attention to the customer's needs continues to be the engine that drives our company."

In an industry dominated by corporate giants, BURNCO has retained the freedom to direct and control its destiny by remaining independent. BURNCO has long been a part of Alberta's history and is looking forward to continuing its steady, dependable growth into the next century.

CLOCKWISE FROM TOP LEFT: BURNCO OPERATES SEVERAL ENVIRONMENTALLY FRIENDLY ASPHALT PLANTS, INCLUDING ONE ON SHEPARD ROAD.

BURNCO OPERATES SEVERAL PORTABLE PLANTS FOR PROCESSING AGGREGATE. PICTURED IS THE INDUS WASH-PLANT NEAR THE BOW RIVER.

THE BURNCO FLEET INCLUDES MORE THAN 100 READY MIX CONCRETE TRUCKS.

HE COUNTRY OF CANADA WAS ONLY 13 YEARS OLD WHEN IMPERIA Oil Limited was founded in 1880. Since that time, the company' history has been, in many ways, a reflection of the development o Canada itself. In 1947, Imperial Oil, in what is probably the single mo

significant economic and historic event in the province of Alberta, discovered major oil reserves at Leduc. This discovery marked the true beginning of Canada's role as an important, world-class oil producer.

With corporate headquarters in Toronto, Imperial Oil's Calgary operations, established in 1912, are home to about 1,000 employees. Another 1,500 employees work in Edmonton and at field locations in western and northern Canada. The company is currently the largest producer of crude oil in Canada, and a major producer of natural gas. Imperial Oil is also the largest refiner and marketer of petroleum products—with a coast-to-coast supply network having the largest number of retail sites

in the country—and a major producer of petrochemicals.

### STRATEGIC PRIORITIES

"Our business plans and programs will continue to be guided by four strategic priorities," says Calgary-based Doug Baldwin, Senior Vice-President, Resources Division. "They are to achieve execution excellence by the most capable people; to grow profitable sales volumes; to achieve and maintain an industry first-quartile cost structure; and to improve the productivity of our asset mix through selective investment and timely divestment."

As the company positions itself for future growth, a major focus is its Northern Alberta oil sands operations, which have the potential to play as large a role in the company's history as the Leduc discovery. Imperial's wholly owned Cold Lake production project sits atop one of three massive deposits of heavy oil, called bitumen. These deposits contain approxi-

mately 1.7 trillion barrels of oil, equivalent to more than one and-a-half times the world's proved oil reserves. Of that amount, only a small percentage is judged to be economically recoverable with today's technology.

"Our Cold Lake project is the world's largest in situ oil sands operation," notes Baldwin With annual production averaging 35 million barrels, the projec accounts for one in every 20 barrels of crude oil produced in the country. It is Imperial's largest single asset, comprising about half of the company's total production of hydrocarbon liquids. By the turn of the century, the company expects to increase production at Cold Lake by about 30 percent.

The oil-bearing sands at Cold Lake are buried more tha 400 metres below the surface, so they're not amenable to the surface mining techniques used by other oil sands operators. The bitumen is also so heavy and viscous that it won't flow naturally to the surface using

DIRECTIONAL DRILLING FROM SURFACE PADS MINIMIZES LAND DISTURBANCE AT IMPERIAL'S COLD LAKE PROJECT, THE WORLD'S LARGEST IN SITU OIL SANDS OPERATION (LEFT).

RESEARCH SPECIALISTS USE A LABORATORY MODEL TO FURTHER DEVELOP THE CYCLIC STEAM STIMULATION PROCESS. TECHNOLOGY ADVANCES WILL ENABLE IMPERIAL TO CAPTURE PROGRESSIVELY MORE OF THE ENORMOUS HYDROCARBON PRIZE AT COLD LAKE (RIGHT).

CHRIS THOMAS

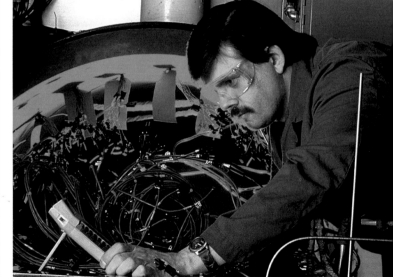

onventional production tech-
iques. Cold Lake production
 achieved using a thermal
rocess that Imperial pioneered
lled cyclic steam stimulation.

With a 25 percent interest,
mperial is also the largest share
wner in Syncrude Canada's
il sands operations near Fort
1cMurray, Alberta. Syncrude
roduces about 75 million bar-
ls a year of synthetic crude oil.

### RESEARCH AND DEVELOPMENT

"From the outset, develop-
ent at Cold Lake has been
riven by technology," says
aldwin. "Since start-up of
ommercial production in 1985,
e've increased our research
fforts devoted to Cold Lake
ear after year. To date, we've
ent more than a quarter of
 billion dollars on research
nd technology development
lated to Cold Lake."

That investment has helped
 reduce unit costs and increase
itumen recovery. Since 1985,
mperial has been able to reduce
nit costs by more than one-
iird, and recovery rates have
creased from about 17 percent
 25 percent. A number of
lternative processes are being
udied to further improve
covery.

"The focused investment
 scientific and technological

development over the past several
decades has created a profitable,
well-developed oil sands industry in Alberta and a strong foundation for the future," Baldwin
notes.

Along with research and
development, Imperial Oil also
exhibits a strong commitment
to environmental protection.
The company's operations
integrity management framework
provides a structured and disci-
plined approach to operating
facilities safely and reliably.
The company continues to demonstrate results, with increasingly
lower rates of safety-related
incidents and emissions. Significant progress is also being made
in the cost-effective clean-up
of depleted oil and gas wells,
decommissioned service stations,
and refineries.

### A PIONEERING COMMUNITY SPIRIT

Imperial Oil also demonstrates
its pioneering spirit in the development of innovative community
involvement projects. Through
the Imperial Oil Charitable
Foundation, the company supports hundreds of charitable
organizations each year, and
has donated approximately
$110 million in the last 10
years.

About 65 percent of its
current annual commitment

is directed to charities that benefit
children through the Esso Kids
Program, introduced in 1994.
Funds are provided for breakfast clubs, literacy and other
education programs, community
involvement for youth at risk,
children's theatre, and many
other cultural and recreational
neighbourhood activities.

"We believe the most meaningful, effective way we can
make a difference is by supporting programs that create and
foster healthy lifestyle choices
for children," says Baldwin.

"Companies that operate
in Canada have a responsibility
to help make Canada a better
place," Baldwin sums up.
"Businesses like Imperial Oil
operate because Canadians
give us the franchise to operate.
In return, Canadians expect
companies to invest in the future
by making a positive contribution to the quality of life in
their communities."

CONDUCTING ITS BUSINESS IN A SAFE
AND ENVIRONMENTALLY RESPONSIBLE
MANNER IS AN INTEGRAL COMPONENT
OF IMPERIAL'S OPERATIONS. THE
COMPANY'S SAFETY PERFORMANCE
IS AMONG THE BEST IN CANADIAN
INDUSTRY (LEFT).

IMPERIAL'S PROGRAM OF PHILAN-
THROPY IS ONE OF THE LARGEST
AND MOST EXTENSIVE IN CANADA.
SPECIAL CONSIDERATION IS GIVEN
TO PROGRAMS THAT ENRICH THE
LIVES OF CANADIAN CHILDREN;
ABOUT TWO-THIRDS OF IMPERIAL'S
DONATIONS GO TO THESE PROGRAMS
(RIGHT).

ANADIAN NATIONAL RAILWAY (CN) HAS PLAYED A VITAL ROLE I
Calgary's economy since the early part of the 20th century. The company
roots in the community date back to 1913, when the pioneer Canadia
Northern Railway built a rail line to connect the thriving new centre wi

rich coal fields in the Drumheller area. Six years later, Canadian Northern merged with several other rail systems to form the Canadian National Railway Company—a federal crown corporation that became, and remains today, Canada's largest rail system.

Now entirely investor-owned, CN operates Alberta's most extensive rail system, transporting almost two-thirds of all the products moved by rail into, within, and out of the province. Its coast-to-coast network—sixth largest in North America—reaches all of Canada's

major ports and serves all of the nation's resource-producing and industrial centres.

CN is a key element of the province's export-oriented economy, geared to distribute Alberta products quickly and efficiently in the markets of North America and around the world. The rail network connects Alberta importers and exporters with the West Coast getaways of Vancouver and Prince Rupert, facilitating trade with nations along the Pacific Rim. As for the North American marketplace, CN's own lines penetrate the United States, while strategic alliances with major U.S. railways enable the company to offer customers direct access to Chicago and beyond.

### CN'S PRESENCE
### IN CALGARY

Calgary is a key location for Canadian National. The city's economic strengths make it an ideal home base for CN's bulk commodities marketing group,

headed by Vice-President Pete Marshall, as well as account managers in the intermodal and merchandise business unit Marshall's bulk commodities group includes two marketing units that draw the majority of their business from the West: grain and grain products, and coal, sulphur, and fertilizers. "We want to be as close to ou customers as possible," says Marshall. "By being in Calgary we're right in the middle of where our primary businesses operate."

CN's major installations in Calgary include the Sarcee yard, with capacity for 800 ra cars, and an intermodal termi nal that serves as a hub for good moving in containers and trail ers throughout southern Alber and the Okanagan region. Alto gether, some 100 people work for Canadian National in Calgary.

### A BOON FOR CUSTOMER

The privatization of Canadian National in November 1995

INVESTOR-OWNED SINCE 1995, THE NEW CANADIAN NATIONAL RAILWAY LOOKS FORWARD TO SHARING A BRIGHT FUTURE WITH ITS CALGARY CUSTOMERS (LEFT).

CN UNIT TRAINS HELP WESTERN CANADIAN POTASH PRODUCERS MEET WORLDWIDE DEMAND FOR FERTILIZERS (RIGHT).

marked the culmination of a three-year process that essentially transformed the company into a highly competitive and focused force in the transportation marketplace. During that period, CN pursued an aggressive business plan involving three ambitious strategies: to sharply reduce operating costs; to significantly improve customer service; and to invest in initiatives that would both increase productivity and enhance service quality.

Under the leadership of President and Chief Executive Officer Paul M. Tellier, CN met its goals and was ready for privatization by the fall of 1995. The company's initial public offering proved to be Canada's largest and most successful ever, involving the sale of 83.8 million shares worth $2.26 billion within a day of their listing on the Toronto, Montreal, and New York stock exchanges.

CN's first full year as an investor-owned company—1996—was the best in the company's history. Now CN is aiming for new levels in profitability, shareholder value, and customer service. "We want to be the best railway in North

America," Tellier says. "We have new, more aggressive goals to grow our business, improve customer service, and operate more efficiently and safely."

## LOOKING TO THE FUTURE

To reach its ambitious goals, CN continues to keep a vigilant eye on costs while working to increase revenues by seeking out new business opportunities in partnership with customers.

Advanced technology is one of the key components in CN's drive to become North America's foremost railway. Over the past few years, CN adopted the industry's most advanced information technology for shipment management, making it possible to offer fully reliable service based on customer goals. Then, in 1996, CN became the first railway in North America to offer customers the option of tracking the progress of their shipments on the Internet.

At the same time, CN is renewing and strengthening its equipment fleet in response to growing customer demand. Powerful new locomotives, equipped with the very latest computer-based operating systems, are entering CN service to handle the needs of western producers. New, lightweight aluminum trainsets help to speed the movement of Western Canadian coal to distant markets.

"This is truly a new CN," says Tellier. "Across the system, there is a strong sense of excitement, shared commitment, and singleness of purpose. In today's competitive market, shippers have choices, and they expect value for their transportation dollar. To make shippers think of CN first, we will become Canada's most efficient railway and offer the industry's best customer service."

The new CN looks forward to sharing a bright and prosperous future with its Calgary and Western-based customers.

CN DELIVERS ALBERTA COAL TO THE ROBERTS BANK FACILITY AT THE PORT OF VANCOUVER FOR EXPORT TO PACIFIC RIM COUNTRIES (LEFT).

A SULPHUR-LADEN TRAIN MOVES TO THE WEST COAST FOR EXPORT (RIGHT).

THE BEST-KNOWN TRADEMARK IN THE WORLD, COCA-COLA WAS INVENTED in 1886 by Dr. John Pemberton, an Atlanta pharmacist. The syrup was initially promoted as a medicine, but once a fountain operator mixed it with carbonated water, the world's first soft drink was born.

By the turn of the century, Coca-Cola was being sold in some parts of Canada. In 1906, the company opened a manufacturing plant in Toronto, and Canada became the first country in which Coca-Cola could be bottled and sold outside the United States.

### A COKE AND A SMILE FOR CANADA

Coca-Cola opened its first plant in Calgary in 1919. In 1923, the Coca-Cola Company of Canada, Limited was incorporated, with its headquarters in Toronto, and the company continued to grow as plants sprang up across the country.

In 1997, the Canadian bottling operations were acquired by Coca-Cola Enterprises Inc., which is the world's largest marketer, producer, and distributor of Coca-Cola products, the most popular beverage brands in the world. Coca-Cola Enterprises is listed on the New York Stock Exchange under the symbol CCE.

Active in all of Canada's 10 provinces and employing more than 3,500 Canadians, Coca-Cola Bottling Canada is the largest bottler of soft drink products in Canada. The company bottles, cans, packages, distributes, and markets—under licence—Coca-Cola soft drink products. In addition, the company sells and distributes a wide variety of other beverages, including soft drinks, iced teas, juices, and bottled waters, to Canadian retail customers, as well as to wholesalers and other bottlers.

### ALWAYS COCA-COLA, ALWAYS CALGARY

As a head office centre for major companies such as Canada Safeway, Westfair Foods, and Calgary Co-op, the city of Calgary provides significant growth potential. The Calgary location also provides a number of other benefits. For example, the city is

COCA-COLA WAS BEING SOLD IN SOME PARTS OF CANADA BY THE TURN OF THE 20TH CENTURY. PICTURED IS THE DAVID BUILDING CIRCA 1912, WHICH WAS LOCATED ON 8TH AVENUE IN CALGARY.

ome to a number of can and ottle manufacturers who pro-ide Coca-Cola with containers or its products. Also, Calgary as quick access to other Alberta-roduced raw materials, such s sugar.

Calgary is now the regional ffice for the Alberta market nd part of the Western Canada ivision of Coca-Cola Bottling d. Located in northeast Calgary, e company operates from a 50,000-square-foot facility, hich provides the latest equip-ent and technology for its utomated packaging process. ere, the special syrup is com-ined with treated water to en-ire the uniform product that nsumers have come to expect. bout 250 local employees are volved in all phases of the pro-ss, from production to pack-ging, warehousing, marketing, nd distribution.

The company's results since structuring in early 1994 have een excellent. Case sales vol-mes and cash operating profits ave increased, while operating osts have decreased. As a result f the changes, Coca-Cola is enerating more revenue from smaller asset base.

Coca-Cola has two key com-etitive advantages: A product ne of premium brands that are nong the best-known brands the world, and a consolidated ottling system that delivers supe-or service to customers. These dvantages translate into a win-in relationship with customers. he company continues to focus n building a stronger sales ructure to support high rates f sustainable and profitable rowth in the future.

## STRONG COMMUNITY INVOLVEMENT

oca-Cola has established an xcellent reputation as a good orporate citizen wherever it perates. The company and its

associates support many com-munity programs and charitable organizations, both at the cor-porate level and through local fund-raising initiatives.

Coca-Cola has been a spon-sor of the Canadian Special Olympics since 1987. Through this sponsorship, the company is involved in chapter functions across the country and is a ma-jor contributor to the Sports Celebrities Festival fund-raising events.

The company actively supported Calgary's Winter Olympics in 1988 and is still involved with the Canadian

Olympic Development Associa-tion. There are also partnership agreements with such major sports teams as the Calgary Flames, Calgary Stampeders, and Calgary Cannons.

To continue its long tradi-tion of success, Coca-Cola strives to be a market-driven company supported by effective operations. As a company with the longevity to celebrate its 110th anniversary in 1996, Coca-Cola is clear on its pri-mary operating objective: to increase long-term operating cash flows through profitable increases in sales volume.

CALGARY IS THE REGIONAL OFFICE FOR THE ALBERTA MARKET AND PART OF THE WESTERN CANADA DIVISION OF COCA-COLA BOTTLING LTD. THE COMPANY OPERATES FROM A 250,000-SQUARE-FOOT FACILITY THAT USES THE LATEST IN EQUIPMENT AND TECHNOLOGY.

STAN BEHAL

TO ELIMINATE PRODUCT HANDLING AND REDUCE INVENTORY AT SALES CENTRES, TRAILER-TRAINS LIKE THIS ARE BECOMING COCA-COLA BOTTLING'S WAREHOUSES ON WHEELS.

# WALLACE &
# CAREY LTD.

Wallace & Carey Ltd. is a family-owned, Alberta-based national distribution company. The business has grown steadily from modest beginnings to become the largest independent wholesale distributor in Canada, with product listings of more than 7,000 items, including health and beauty, grocery, frozen, cooler, tobacco, sundry, food service, and confectionery products.

TODAY, WALLACE & CAREY LTD. IS A FAMILY-OWNED, ALBERTA-BASED, AND PROUDLY CANADIAN NATIONAL DISTRIBUTION COMPANY. PICTURED AT RIGHT ARE THE CALGARY BRANCH AND THE CENTRAL OFFICE.

WALLACE & CAREY BEGAN AS A MODEST CIGAR COUNTER, AND LATER OPERATED AS A WAREHOUSE IN THE BASEMENT OF A LOCAL HOTEL (BOTTOM LEFT AND RIGHT).

## THE EARLY YEARS

Wallace & Carey can trace its roots back to the cigar counter operated by Robert Wallace at a Lethbridge hotel in 1919. The business originally operated as a retail enterprise and expanded into wholesale as Wallace began providing cigars and tobacco products to other retailers. The business slowly grew over the years, and had become an attractive operation when Larry Carey first contemplated purchasing it while working there as a salesman in the early 1950s.

Wallace was now removed from the day-to-day operation of the business, which had grown into a regional wholesale company. He had not met Carey, but was aware of his innovative ideas and the honest approach he had toward business transactions. An arrangement was made so that Wallace would finance a large portion of the purchase price, but was not involved in the running of the company. He soon became both a mentor and a friend to Carey. For his part, Carey honoured his mentor and friend by retaining the Wallace name in the new company and providing an office that Wallace could use for the rest of his life.

Wallace & Carey was then operating out of the basement of the Colonial Hotel, and business often overflowed the confines of the cramped basement space. The budding wholesale business now drew the attention of the larger national chain wholesale companies that did not appreciate losing business to a company that was working from the basement of a hotel. Pressure was applied to the suppliers of tobacco products, and one of the largest advised Carey that it would no longer sell product to resellers such as Wallace & Carey. The loss of this essential product line was crippling, but Carey, with Irish stubbornness, would not concede defeat. Wallace & Carey persevered in the tobacco

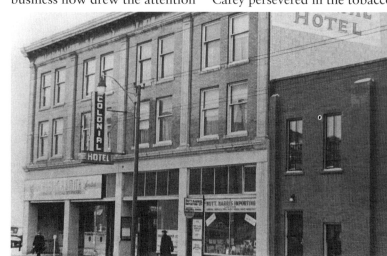

nd confectionery trade without
ne of the largest-selling lines.

rank Carey, the current presi-
ent and owner, joined Wallace
Carey in 1971 and purchased
e company from his father in
974. One of his first tasks was
travel east to convince the
bove-mentioned tobacco sup-
lier that it should sell product
Wallace & Carey. At that
me, Wallace & Carey's cusmer list consisted of a num-
er of local retailers in Alberta,
askatchewan, and British
olumbia.

It was by coincidence that
arey met the person in charge
f buying for the 7-Eleven chain
f convenience stores during a
les convention in Mexico. A
eal was struck shortly after
provide product to 7-Eleven
ores in Calgary; this soon ex-
anded to Edmonton in 1981,
ancouver in 1984, Saskatoon
1987, Regina in 1988, and
/innipeg in 1989.

A major challenge was pre-
nted in 1988, when 7-Eleven
ked Wallace & Carey to ser-
ce its stores in Ontario after
s supplier ceased to service
e convenience store trade.
arey, anxious to pursue the
pportunity, was on a plane
Toronto that day to prepare
r the new business, and the
anch in Toronto made its first
Eleven delivery six weeks later.

## THE PRESENT

he opportunity to supply a
tional convenience store chain
as permitted expansion in many
fferent markets. Wallace &
arey now supplies goods on a
tional basis to Shell Canada
oducts Limited, Cineplex
deon Theatres, Zellers, and
anadian Tire Corporation,
ong with its strategic alliance
rtners in Québec and Atlantic

Canada. It also serves Shoppers
Drug Mart, United Cigar Stores,
and Winks on a regional basis,
as well as a large number of independent chains and individual
accounts. The distribution network includes a work force of
400 employees working from
seven distribution centres from
British Columbia to Ontario.

Wallace & Carey provides
its customers with much more
than wholesale goods. Value-
added services include product
sales information provided to
assist customers to be more competitive in their markets. The
high fill-rate and picking accuracy ensure customers that they
receive the product that has
been ordered.

The company utilizes technology to improve fill-rate and
picking accuracy, both through
a sophisticated computerized
inventory control system and
through a computerized radio
frequency warehouse operations system.

## THE FUTURE

The wholesale distribution business has changed and evolved
dramatically, with Wallace &
Carey often leading the way.
The company was the first distributor to offer convenience
retailers the option of ordering
split cases of grocery products

and later introduced the Eaches
Program, where as few as three
units can be ordered. This allows
retailers to preserve valuable
shelf space and to carry a wider
variety of products. Wallace &
Carey led the convenience industry by supplying its customers TELXON units, which are
now the standard method for
product ordering, enabling retailers to place product orders
from their telephone at any
time of the day or night.

The explosion of fast food
and alternative beverages has
had a dramatic effect on convenience retailing, and the demographics of the consumer will
contiinue to demand more
diverse quality convenience
products.

In addition to anticipat-
ing the needs of its customers,
Wallace & Carey will continue
to lead the industry in technology. The company has pioneered
electronic data interchange technology in the convenience trade
and is continually expanding
the exchange of data with its
family of customers.

Wallace & Carey Ltd. has
a culture that has valued integrity and honest work for more
than 75 years. This business
philosophy is extended to its
customers, to the hundreds of
suppliers that provide product
to them, and to its employees.

FROM LEFT:

WALLACE & CAREY OPERATES SEVEN
MODERN DISTRIBUTION CENTRES,
SERVING 2,500 RETAIL SITES, FROM
OTTAWA TO VANCOUVER ISLAND.
ITS WAREHOUSES OCCUPY 275,000
SQUARE FEET, WITH MORE THAN 400
EMPLOYEES AND A DELIVERY FLEET
OF 60 VEHICLES.

ONE OF WALLACE & CAREY'S VALUE-
ADDED SERVICES IS THE EACHES
PROGRAM, IN WHICH CUSTOMERS
CAN ORDER AS FEW AS THREE ITEMS
FROM MORE THAN 1,500 SELECTED
PRODUCTS.

THE COMPANY CARRIES MORE THAN
7,000 ITEMS, INCLUDING HEALTH AND
BEAUTY, GROCERY, FROZEN, COOLER,
TOBACCO, CONFECTIONERY, AND
AUTOMOTIVE PRODUCTS.

EVERAL GENERATIONS OF WESTERN CANADIANS HAVE GROWN UP WIT Safeway. Canada Safeway Limited dates back to 1929, when the compan was chartered as Safeway Stores Limited in the province of Manitob. Walter J. Kraft, who came up from the United States in 1930 to establis

Alberta's first five Safeway stores, is widely regarded as the company's founding father.

By 1936, Safeway had acquired 69 Piggly Wiggly food stores and A. Macdonald & Company Ltd., a food wholesaler operating some 40 Canadian warehouses and cash depots. Three years later, Safeway purchased Vancouver-based Empress Manufacturing, the largest packager of jams and jellies in Western Canada.

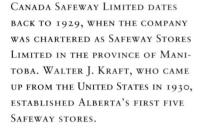

CANADA SAFEWAY LIMITED DATES BACK TO 1929, WHEN THE COMPANY WAS CHARTERED AS SAFEWAY STORES LIMITED IN THE PROVINCE OF MANITOBA. WALTER J. KRAFT, WHO CAME UP FROM THE UNITED STATES IN 1930, ESTABLISHED ALBERTA'S FIRST FIVE SAFEWAY STORES.

### PIONEERING IDEAS

Even in its earliest years, Safeway was known for its innovation. Free grocery delivery was available in the early 1930s, and once the automobile became popular, Safeway began to provide parking spaces and shopping carts for self-service. Other innovations in those years included pricing fruits and vegetables by the pound, special merchandising events, more sanitary milk transportation, and a guaranteed meat-trim program, which is still in effect today. Later, the company pioneered frozen food, when it introduced its private label Bel Air frozen peas.

WITH THREE OPERATING AREAS— SMO (SASKATCHEWAN, MANITOBA, AND NORTHERN ONTARIO), ALBERTA, AND BRITISH COLUMBIA—CANADA SAFEWAY NOW OPERATES MORE THAN 200 STORES FROM THUNDER BAY TO THE PACIFIC COAST, AND EMPLOYS MORE THAN 33,000 PEOPLE.

With three operating areas— SMO (Saskatchewan, Manitoba, and Northern Ontario), Alberta, and British Columbia—Canada Safeway now operates more than 200 stores from Thunder Bay to the Pacific Coast, and employs more than 33,000 people.

Safeway's company headquarters has been located in Calgary since 1984, and in 1994, the majority of the company's administrative functions were consolidated in a new corporate headquarters off Deerfoot Trail in the northeast part of the city. The company also operates 28 stores in Calgary.

"Calgary is a central location in Western Canada," says President and Chief Operating Officer Grant M. Hansen. "Fro here we have ease of distribution, whatever the mode of transportation."

In addition to its retail store Canada Safeway also operates four major distribution centre in Canada through its division Macdonalds Consolidated. An the company's manufacturing operations purchase, manufac ture, and process private label merchandise sold in Safeway stores under brand names suc as Safeway, Lucerne, and Safe way Select. These plants proce ice cream, bread, frozen food, eggs, fruit, and meat. In additior the company operates laborator facilities for quality assurance and research and developmen at some of its plants.

### ATTENTION TO QUALITY

"The Safeway story is a work in progress," notes Hansen. "Ot strategy is to provide maximur value to our customers by mai taining high store standards an offering high-quality products at competitive prices. We've intensified our efforts to elevate store standards, and provide friendly, helpful customer service."

The company places a strong emphasis on training for its employees. All retail staff receive training and orientation outside the store, as well as on-the-job training. Employees also are given additional training from time to time in communications skills and in new procedures. "We have the best employees in the industry," says Hansen.

The work in progress continues as Safeway's ongoing capital program is invested in remodeling and enhancing its stores and developing new merchandise. Specialty departments and special services are now available in many stores, including videotape sales, photo processing counters, and in-store automatic teller machines. "We try to provide one-stop shopping for today's busy shopper," adds Hansen.

In 1996, the company introduced a Parcel Pick-Up service for its stores. "This is especially convenient when the store is located in a mall," says Hansen. "Customers can go shopping in the mall before picking up their groceries. We keep the perishables refrigerated."

Safeway also continues to innovate with its products. In the late 1970s, the company introduced the Environmental Options program, which identifies hundreds of environmen-

tally friendly products to help consumers make informed purchasing decisions.

In 1995, the company introduced a line of more than 400 premium, private-label products under the banner Safeway Select. These products include soft drinks, pastas and pasta sauces, salsa, whole-bean coffee, cookies, ice cream, yogurt, pet foods, and laundry detergent. The line also includes Enlighten items, such as no-fat salad dressings and low-sodium, quick lunches. In 1995, Safeway introduced its Select Gourmet Club line of frozen entrees, such as lasagna, gourmet macaroni and cheese, pre-seasoned ground beef patties, and barbecued spareribs. More Select items will continue to be introduced in the coming years.

As a good corporate citizen, Safeway also "feeds" the community spirit. Each year Safeway works with more than 2,000 community groups and organizations, lending equipment, providing employee volunteers, and helping in promotional activities, as well as donating cash and in-kind merchandise. Hundreds of nonprofit groups take advantage of in-store programs, which include coin cans, Lucerne milk cartons, community bulletin boards, and brochure distribution.

The company's Commu-

nity Spirit program welcomes donation requests from local community organizations. In addition, Canada Safeway is a major sponsor of provincial summer games, national curling programs, local food banks, Special Olympics, Kids Help Phone Line, United Way, Variety Club, and Children's Festivals. In Calgary, the company sponsored the 1997 World Police and Fire Games, the 1997 Labatt Brier Curling Championships (which moves to Winnipeg for 1998), and the Calgary Exhibition and Stampede.

"We're one of the major grocery retailers in Western Canada," says Hansen, "and I believe we've been instrumental in helping set directions and policies in the grocery industry." It is apparent that Canada Safeway lives up to its company motto: Today's Better Way.

"OUR STRATEGY IS TO PROVIDE MAXIMUM VALUE TO OUR CUSTOMERS BY MAINTAINING HIGH STORE STANDARDS AND OFFERING HIGH-QUALITY PRODUCTS AT COMPETITIVE PRICES," SAYS PRESIDENT AND CHIEF OPERATING OFFICER GRANT M. HANSEN.

ITH MORE THAN 25,000 POLICIES FOR INDIVIDUAL AND CORPORATE clients, Clay-Robinson Ltd. is one of the largest privately held insurance brokers in Alberta. The company offers a full range of insurance products and services, from individual home and car insurance to commercial and corporate insurance plans for companies and groups.

With a legacy of 64 years of dependable, reliable service to Albertans, Clay-Robinson Ltd. services client needs throughout the province and territories from offices in Calgary. Principals also share joint ownership of a number of companies with offices on the west coast of British Columbia.

During its long history, Clay-Robinson has been able to establish long-term, positive working relationships with many major insurers. The company has successfully weathered the constant restructuring and changes that have taken place in the general insurance industry over the last decade.

"Many of our employees have been with us for 20 or 25 years," President and COO Scott Clay explains. "They're dedicated, they have lots of experience, and they've made a career of the insurance busi-ness—it's not just a job to them. Our client may be a large corporation, a small business, or an individual seeking car or home insurance," he adds. "In each case, they have put their financial future in our hands. Each client, regardless of size, is entitled to the best advice and service we can provide."

### PIONEERING TECHNOLOGY

In addition to a strong customer service focus, innovation is a key aspect of Clay-Robinson's operations. The firm is on the leading edge of computerization, and, together with its British Columbia partners, has pioneered and developed its own point-of-sale software that allows all transactions to be computerized, with full EDI capability. The system is networked through all the company's locations. "The software we developed ensures the prompt, efficient, and accurate delivery of insurance products," Clay notes. The company also provides a sophisticated call-forwarding system that allows clients to receive 24-hour emergency claims assistance.

Included in the Clay-Robinson portfolio is Grey Power Insurance Brokers (SA) Ltd., part of a national network of seven agencies providing insurance services exclusively to mature clientele (age 50 or older) in response to society's changing demographics.

In keeping with its long association with the city of Calgary, Clay-Robinson is actively involved in the community and regularly supports a number of local charities.

"The insurance business is always changing," says Clay. "Successful brokers must adapt quickly, and constantly add to their knowledge and experience. Our staff is constantly being educated, trained, and retrained to meet the challenge and remain current.

"Ultimately this is a people business," he adds. "Regardless of how large we grow, we will always be proud that our head office is in Calgary. Although many people conduct their insurance business over the phone or electronically, if people want to come to see us, we're here. And I believe we've positioned ourselves to compete successfully for at least another 64 years."

Clay-Robinson's corporate philosophy can best be summed up by the company's brief but meaningful mission statement: "Let's strive to prove our value to those we serve."

THE OFFICERS AND MANAGEMENT TEAM OF CLAY-ROBINSON INCLUDE (FRONT) PRESIDENT AND COO SCOTT CLAY, DIRECTOR DON CLAY, CHAIRMAN AND CEO BOB CLAY, (BACK) RON WOWK, CAMERON CLAY, LINDA WONG, MARY ANN STOREY, RICK SMITH, AND RON McLINTOCK.

# 1940-1973

| | |
|---|---|
| 1940 | UNITED WAY OF CALGARY AND AREA |
| 1942 | A.R. WILLIAMS MATERIALS HANDLING LTD. |
| 1942 | SHELL CANADA LIMITED |
| 1945 | CALGARY STAMPEDERS |
| 1947 | ECL GROUP OF COMPANIES, LTD. |
| 1948 | WESTERN ATLAS INC. |
| 1949 | MULLEN TRANSPORTATION INC. |
| 1954 | CALGARY OLYMPIC DEVELOPMENT ASSOCIATION (CODA) |
| 1954 | RIGEL ENERGY CORPORATION |
| 1955 | CALGARY PHILHARMONIC SOCIETY |
| 1956 | CALGARY COOPERATIVE ASSOCIATION LIMITED |
| 1956 | CANADIAN AIRLINES INTERNATIONAL, LTD. |
| 1958 | CARMA DEVELOPERS LTD. |
| 1961 | PETROLEUM INDUSTRY TRAINING SERVICE |
| 1961 | SILCORP |
| 1961 | TRIMAC CORPORATION |
| 1964 | GIMBEL EYE CENTRE |
| 1964 | TRI-LINE FREIGHT SYSTEMS |
| 1965 | SHAW NEE SLOPES GOLF COURSE |
| 1966 | PRUDENTIAL STEEL LTD. |
| 1969 | VALMET AUTOMATION |
| 1970 | INTERNATIONAL HOTEL OF CALGARY |
| 1971 | BPB WIRELINE SERVICES |
| 1971 | PANCANADIAN PETROLEUM LIMITED |
| 1973 | ALBERTA ENERGY COMPANY LTD. |
| 1973 | CANADIAN HUNTER EXPLORATION LTD. |
| 1973 | TRIZECHAHN CORPORATION |

**B**RINGING PEOPLE TOGETHER TO BUILD A STRONGER, HEALTHIER COMMUNIT is the goal of United Way of Calgary and area. With its high rate of volur teerism, nowhere is civic pride more evident than in the annual United W: campaign. Each fall, thousands of volunteers mobilize to raise millions

dollars to help their fellow citizens. And each year the people of Calgary set an ambitious target, and then prove themselves by exceeding it.

About 60 percent of United Way's revenues come from employees and individual donations, with 36 percent coming from companies and foundations. Approximately 84 percent of the funds raised goes toward helping more than 160 community programs and services. These programs strengthen and support families in need, improve the lives of children living in poverty or at risk, enhance community health and well-being, and support emergency shelter and help—in fact, about one in three Calgarians benefits from United Way-funded programs.

In addition to the many volunteers who participate in the United Way campaign, the Calgary media provide commitment and support. Local businesses and individuals donate their services to create the campaign, video, and informational materials. Other companies provide loaned representatives.

And throughout the city, United Way is helping more and more employee groups find ways to give more than money. Whether it's painting, repairing, providing computer training for agency staff, or preparing personal care packages for street people, employees connect with the causes they care about—and provide a valuable service to the community as well.

### NEW STRATEGIC DIRECTION

In 1994, United Way began a strategic planning process in-

volving public consultation th: resulted in the development of a new strategic direction.

"What was clear from the consultation was that United Way should focus its activitie in three distinct areas: commu nity leadership, impact on con munity issues, and providing linkages," says Ruth Ramsder Wood, President of United W: of Calgary and area.

Explains Ramsden-Wood "This direction represents a fundamental shift in emphasi for our organization—from or that was primarily based on i strength as a fund-raiser and funder, to an organization tha through active leadership, focuse on impact and the forging of links in the community to pro vide the best possible solution to its customers and the community at large."

That shift in direction ha: been exemplified in a number of new initiatives. For examp when domestic violence reach a crisis point with the murder of three women in Calgary, United Way responded immed ately to the call for leadership It provided funding to impro access to restraining orders. I

fluenced the provincial govern-
ent to waive its court filing
es for women in need. It pro-
ded the funding needed to
al with the backlog of men
aiting counselling for violent
haviour. And it worked with
e community to improve post-
elter services for women and
ildren. Today, United Way
ntinues to provide leadership
community initiatives that
ll one day make safety from
olence a reality for all
algarians.

United Way also mobilized
mmunity response to a crisis
homelessness during the two
ldest winters in recent mem-
y, inspiring an outpouring of
mmunity caring and funding
rvices to help the many "tem-
orarily homeless" get back on
eir feet again.

United Way also established
children's endowment fund
dicated to funding children's
ograms with an early inter-
ntion focus. And the organi-
tion is developing programs
conjunction with local schools
involve students, teachers,
mmunity services, and local
sinesses in helping to solve
oblems with youth at risk.

Over the next three to five
ars, United Way will increase
emphasis on the issues of safety
om domestic violence, learning
portunities for children and
ens, and economic self-suffi-
ncy for people who are poor.

The vision of a healthier,
fer community continues
guide the United Way's instment of public donations.
We are increasing emphasis on
ilding the community's ca-
city to care for itself," notes
msden-Wood. "We're work-
g with all funded agencies to
velop ways and means of
uging the impact of services
ovided. And we're working
th other funders to identify
ps and rationalize support
r services."

United Way funds stay in
the community, and are targeted
for results—with a range of
services that together focus on
the issues faced by the community as a whole. United Way
also offers a range of giving
options. Through the organization's donor choice program,
donors can decide when and
how they will give and where
their donations will be directed.
Finally, nearly 84 cents of every
dollar collected gets to where
it's needed most in the
community.

"We're proud of the low
cost of our fund-raising," says
Ramsden-Wood. "Thanks to
the work of thousands of volunteers and the generosity of
many sponsors, United Way
of Calgary and area is able to
keep fund-raising costs to less
than 10 percent of campaign
proceeds. Another 4 percent is
spent on community services
such as assessing community
needs, and selecting and review-
ing the programs funded. And
administration costs are largely
offset by other sources of
income."

With the United Way's
efforts, social conditions are
improved, the resources of the
community are focused, and
donors have the personal power
to do something significant.
As the organization states:
"Together we can make a
difference."

United Way gratefully
acknowledges Unocal Canada
Limited for its sponsorship of
this profile.

UNITED WAY DONATIONS SUPPORT A
NETWORK OF MORE THAN 160 LOCAL
SERVICES THAT WORK TOGETHER TO
STRENGTHEN AND SUPPORT FAMILIES
AT RISK, IMPROVE THE LIVES OF CHIL-
DREN, AND ENHANCE COMMUNITY
HEALTH AND WELL-BEING. AN ESTI-
MATED ONE IN THREE CALGARIANS
BENEFITS DIRECTLY FROM THE SER-
VICES FUNDED BY UNITED WAY.

ITH A HISTORY ALMOST AS LONG AS CANADA'S, THE A.R. WILLIAM companies sell and service forklift trucks, light construction equipmen and truck-mounted equipment. A.R. Williams Materials Handling Ltd. the exclusive distributor for Clark forklifts, Daewoo forklifts, and Selli

rough terrain forklifts in Alberta and Saskatchewan. A.R. Williams Western Ltd., operating as Bobcat of Calgary and Bobcat of Edmonton, represents Melroe loaders, Melroe excavators, JCB backhoe/loaders, and JCB telescopic boom handlers. A.R. Williams Truck Equipment Ltd. represents Hiab and USTC truck-mounted cranes.

All three are specialized successor companies to the A.R. Williams Machinery Company Limited, which incorporated in Ontario on March 19, 1895, to distribute machine tools and related supplies. Western expansion brought Alberta registration on July 6, 1942.

"Local market focus and industry specialization has been our guide to successful growth," says Arnie Charbonneau, who acquired the company in 1984. From a staff of 38 people and

two locations, A.R. Williams has grown to be a major player in the equipment industry, and today has 160 employees at 11 locations in the two provinces.

For the past four years, the firm has been a steadily ascending member of the top 100 private companies in Calgary.

## DIVERSIFIED CUSTOMER BASE

Headquartered in Calgary, the owner-operated companies serve broad segments of the economy. The materials handling group serves the manufacturing, distribution, building materials, transportation, mining, and food-processing sectors. The light construction group serves general construction, industrial, agricultural, and resource

industries. The truck-mounte equipment group serves the transportation, petrochemical resource development, waste management, utilities, and municipal sectors.

All of the companies offer a variety of options for ownership, including outright purchase, short-term rental, rental purchase, or leasing. A large selection of both new and used models is available for demonstration.

To properly serve its diver customer base, A.R. William has devised the solution of industry specialization, where individual dealerships are create to meet the demands of the different customer needs in those locations where volume and equipment warrant. Indu try specialization is best exemp fied through the three branch in Edmonton. Each location

A.R. WILLIAMS' REPUTATION AS AN INDUSTRY LEADER AND ITS GROWING MARKET SHARE HAVE BEEN BUILT ON LONG-TERM CUSTOMER RELATION- SHIPS AND A TEAM EFFORT.

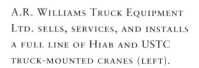

A.R. WILLIAMS TRUCK EQUIPMENT LTD. SELLS, SERVICES, AND INSTALLS A FULL LINE OF HIAB AND USTC TRUCK-MOUNTED CRANES (LEFT).

A.R. WILLIAMS IS PROUD TO HAVE MORE THAN 177 YEARS OF EXPERIENCE IN ITS CALGARY LIFT-TRUCK SERVICE DEPARTMENT ALONE (RIGHT).

ncentrates on the demands its individual customer base—aterials handling, light construction, or truck equipment—and ch dealership is staffed and quipped to respond to the ecific requirements of the quipment type it carries.

## FOCUS ON CUSTOMER SERVICE

he primary strength of A.R. illiams is its focus on customer rvice. The quality and design its products allow service es exceeding 40 years, and stomer service excellence is e basis for long-term partnerips with equipment users.

"The people are the key service success in any industry. eir motivation and training ll determine the response our customers' needs," notes harbonneau. "We are proud have more than 177 years experience in our Calgary t-truck service department one, and several technicians th more than 20 years expeence in the field." A.R. Wilms has received numerous alership distribution awards cognizing excellence in cusmer service.

The A.R. Williams compaes' strong commitment to ter-sales support provides competitive edge in lowering uipment operating costs for

their customers. Long experience in the industries served has enabled them to develop a broad supplier and vendor base to ensure a wide choice of replacement parts at competitive prices. All seven parts warehouses are on-line with each other, allowing each location to search other inventories and, if necessary, order parts for overnight delivery.

## LOCAL MARKET FOCUS

Another customer advantage of A.R. Williams is its neighbourhood market identity. Locally managed branches in Calgary, Edmonton, Regina, Saskatoon, Grande Prairie, Medicine Hat, Red Deer, and Lethbridge recognize the unique character of these western commercial centers. Service depot

staff share factory training for all products, and parts inventories reflect the demands of local applications and operation conditions. As responsible neighbours, all environmental standards are followed, and oils, antifreeze, paper, and cardboard are recycled. "We believe we have found the best combination of small dealer personal service and large dealer systems and support," says Charbonneau.

"The A.R. Williams reputation as an industry leader and its growing market share have been built on long-term customer relationships and a team effort, reinforced with our commitment to quality after-sales support," concludes Charbonneau. "I have a very strong belief in the people and economy of Alberta and look forward to a long and profitable relationship with both."

BOBCAT OF CALGARY AND BOBCAT OF EDMONTON REPRESENT BOBCAT LOADERS AND EXCAVATORS, JCB BACKHOE/LOADERS, AND JCB TELESCOPIC BOOM HANDLERS.

I N 1984, SHELL CANADA LIMITED WAS ONE OF THE FIRST MAJOR Canadian companies to make the westward trek to relocate its head office in Calgary. In fact, the company has a number of major firsts under its belt. For example, Shell was the first Canadian company

to produce chemicals from petroleum in 1953, launching a national industry now valued at more than $5 billion. It was the first to add an ignition-control ingredient to gasolines, the first to offer unleaded gas, and the first to eliminate lead completely. And Shell was the first major oil company to open self-serve gas stations, introduce convenience stores, and add tunnel car washes to the gas station format.

Shell's roots in Alberta go back 40 years before its head office relocation. A major worldwide shortage of oil products during World War II prompted

the company to embark on its first exploration program in the Western Canadian sedimentary basin in 1942. Unfortunately, the initial drilling found no oil. But a large natural gas field was identified two years later at Jumping Pound, not far from Calgary, and development began in the late 1940s. Shell then approached Canadian Western Natural Gas to hook up their existing grid system to Jumping Pound in order to provide Calgary, Banff, and adjacent areas with natural gas.

Shell Canada is now an integrated oil and gas company with exploration, development,

refining, and marketing businesses. Currently, the company is Canada's third-largest petroleum company, fourth-largest natural gas producer, largest sulphur producer, and third-largest refiner.

## COMMUNITY COMMITMENT

For Shell Canada, being part of the local community includes supporting that community through volunteerism and financial contributions. "Shell's support is especially focused on issues related to the environment, educational initiatives,

SHELL CANADA'S SERVICE STATIONS FEATURE A BRIGHT NEW DESIGN AND SELECT CONVENIENCE STORES (LEFT).

FROM THE 1940S TO THE PRESENT, SHELL CANADA GEOLOGISTS HAVE DISCOVERED ECONOMIC OIL AND GAS RESERVES (RIGHT).

id the United Way," says
on Blakely, Vice-President,
uman Resources and Public
ffairs.

For example, through its
ommunity Service Fund, Shell
lds financial support to the
olunteer commitment of its
nployees, retirees, and retailers.
he company awards grants of
o to $1,000 to any non-profit
rganization with whom a Shell
erson regularly volunteers. "In
996, this fund contributed to
early 80 organizations in Cal-
iry," notes Blakely.

Shell is also proud to be
e single biggest supporter
the Calgary United Way Cam-
iign, matching employee dona-
ons of more than $325,000
reach a total contribution
more than $650,000 in 1996.
nployees reinforced this con-
ibution with their commitment
time and effort to more than
Days of Caring projects.

Shell Canada has support-
I educational initiatives like
nior Achievement for a num-
r of years. The company is
significant supporter of the
algary Educational Partnerip Foundation, through which
maintains a community part-
rship with schools in six
algary-area school districts.
ie company also supports
ay-in-school programs and
ovides significant funding
postsecondary institutions
:e the University of Calgary.

## ENVIRONMENTAL PROTECTION LEADER

iell Canada is a leader in
ivironmental protection and
as one of the first recipients
a Voluntary Challenge and
egistry Climate Change Chal-
nge Award in 1996. The reg-
:ry is a federal government
itiative designed to encourage
anadian companies to stabilize
eenhouse gas emissions at
)90 levels by the year 2000.

SHELL PROVIDES FUNDING FOR
COMMUNITY ENVIRONMENTAL
PROJECTS LIKE THIS SCHOOL
VERMICOMPOSTING PROJECT.

"We hit that target in 1995,"
says Blakely, "and based on
the current level of operations,
we are projecting that Shell will
actually be at 94 percent of
1990 levels by the year 2000."

In addition, the Shell Environmental Fund, created in
1990, has granted more than
$5 million to more than 2,000
innovative, action-oriented environmental projects. In Calgary,
the fund has contributed to the
restoration of natural areas,
school recycling and environmental education programs,
education programs for wildlife conservation, and Clean
Calgary's teachers' environmental action guidebook.

In order to maintain its
industry leadership, Shell is
pursuing profitable growth
opportunities, as well as maximizing the leverage of its exist-

ing infrastructure. One major
opportunity involves a potential
commercial oil sands mining
operation on the company's
Athabasca lease holdings in
northern Alberta. These holdings are estimated to contain
about 9 billion barrels of recoverable bitumen.

Shell Canada continues
to strive for excellence. Its current
operational strategy involves
measuring performance in eight
key areas: health, safety and
environment, customer service,
reliability, growth, costs, employee relationships, and profitability. "To remain a top
company, we have to excel in
all these areas," says Blakely.
That commitment to excellence
has made Shell's corporate emblem—the pecten—one of the
most widely recognized around
the world.

OOTBALL HISTORY IN CANADA DATES BACK TO 1909, WITH TH emergence of the Calgary Tigers in the newly formed Alberta Rugh Union," says Ron Rooke, Vice-President of Marketing and Commun cations for the Calgary Stampeders Football Club. The Tigers were

dominant force in provincial football for four years, and captured the Western Canadian Crown in 1911.

But circumstances in Calgary precluded another Western championship for many years to come. Football teams playing under a variety of names and circumstances kept the sport alive, including the 1928 Tigers team that made history with the first forward pass in Canadian football. By World War II, organized professional football was halted to await the war's end, and the beginning of a new league that brought with it the Calgary Stampeders.

"The birth of the Canadian Football League Calgary Stampeders as we know them today took place in 1945," says Rooke.

"Their first game was played against the Regina Roughriders, with the Stamps winning 12-0 in front of 4,000 fans at Mewata Stadium."

In 1948, Calgary received its second Western championship and a Grey Cup, as the Stamps chalked up a 12-7 victory over the Ottawa Rough Riders in Toronto. That year the Stamps boasted a perfect 12-0 record and Calgarians christened a week-long celebration, which has now evolved into the annual Grey Cup Week festivities.

By 1960, the McMahon Stadium was built, transforming Calgary's football facilities from the worst in the country to the best. "McMahon is still one of the best parks to play

in the league," says Rooke. In 1971, the Stamps emerged victorious with their second Grey Cup win over the Toronto Argonauts.

---

### A SPORTS MIRACLE

By 1986, however, the footba club was in severe financial de and on the verge of folding. Bu a miracle in the history of Calgar sports occurred: An SOS—Sav Our Stamps—drive by the city and fans resulted in more than 22,000 season tickets being sold to save the club.

In January 1990, current head coach Wally Buono took over the reins. In his first year at the helm, the former Montrea Alouettes linebacker/punter guided the club to a first-place

THE CALGARY STAMPEDERS PLAY TO GREAT HOME CROWDS, AVERAGING MORE THAN 28,000 FANS PER GAME. IN 1997, 37,617 TICKETS WERE SOLD FOR THE LABOUR DAY CLASSIC—A COMPLETE SELLOUT.

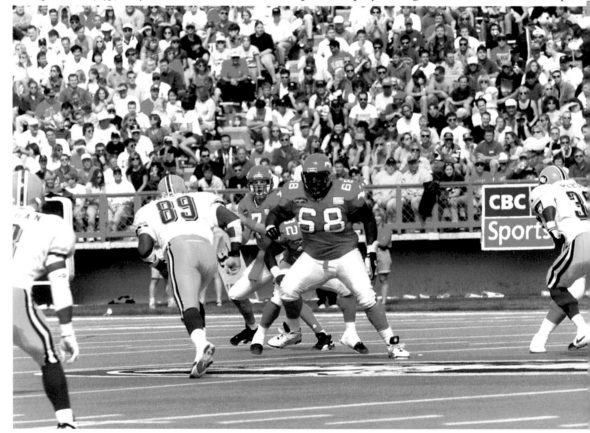

nish. In 1991, the commu-
ty-owned team was sold
 local businessman Larry
yckman. And in 1996, the
ub was sold again—to entre-
reneur and Hard Rock Cafe
wner Sig Gutsche.

"The '90s have been good
 the Stampeders," says Rooke,
oting that Buono has amassed
ore wins in the 1990s than any
her head coach in the Cana-
an Football League, and has
d the Stamps to a first-place
nish during regular season
ay in five out of the last six
ears. The Stamps have made
ree trips to battle for the Grey
up, and won the coveted trophy
ain in 1992. Buono himself
as named Canadian Football
ague Coach of the Year in
)92 and 1993, only the third
ach in history to receive this
vard two years in a row.

## MEMBERS OF THE COMMUNITY

he Stampeders now play to
eat home crowds, averaging
ore than 26,000 fans per game.
The annual Labour Day Classic
 always very popular with
algarians," notes Rooke, "with
ore than 37,000 tickets sold
st year."

But Stampeders team mem-
rs understand the important
le they can play in the local
mmunity, in addition to pro-
ding entertainment for thou-
nds of fans. One example is
e big Food Bank drive during
e Labour Day Classic, where
algarians are encouraged to
 a Fan, Bring a Can. Approxi-
ately $30,000 to $40,000 in
od and cash is donated at
is one event.

In addition to numerous
rsonal appearances at chari-
ble causes, the Stamps also
rticipate in a number of spe-
al programs targeted at young-
ers. Headed by team member
lark McLoughlin, the Stay in

School program was launched
in 1992. This program involves
players visiting local schools to
pass on the message that stay-
ing in school is the smart choice.
So far, more than 200 schools
have been visited in this program.

Another innovative program
called Clear the Track is jointly
sponsored with Canadian Pacific
Railway. Under this program,
headed by team member Greg
Knox, players visit junior and
senior high schools to play bas-

ketball against the schools' teams.
The players convey stay-in-school
messages, and emphasize railway
safety, since youngsters often
trespass on railway tracks and
sometimes enter freight yards,
both of which can be highly dangerous areas. To date, more than
20,000 students have participated
in the Clear the Track program.
There is also a Clear the Track
football camp, which is intended
to help develop high school
football programs in the Calgary area.

The Stampeders are currently
developing a joint project with
the *Calgary Herald* to promote
literacy by encouraging family
time in a shared reading program. In this project, youngsters
will receive football tickets for
reading a certain number of
books.

With a history of winning
seasons, community support,
and community involvement,
it is clear that the Stampeders
will continue to play an important role in Calgary for many
years to come.

IN AN INNOVATIVE PROGRAM CALLED
CLEAR THE TRACK, PLAYERS VISIT
JUNIOR AND SENIOR HIGH SCHOOLS
TO PLAY BASKETBALL AGAINST THE
SCHOOLS' TEAMS, AND CONVEY STAY-
IN-SCHOOL AND RAILWAY SAFETY
MESSAGES TO THE STUDENTS. SO FAR,
MORE THAN 20,000 STUDENTS HAVE
PARTICIPATED IN THE CLEAR THE
TRACK PROGRAM.

LTHOUGH ECONOMY CARRIERS LIMITED—THE PRECURSOR TO THE EC[
Group of Companies—began operations in Calgary in 1947, its roots stretc[
back a further 10 years to Jefferson, Alberta. At that time, Economy Feed ar[
Transfer was a small feed and fuel operation owned and operated by Em[

Fredericks, supplying bulk fuel from Maple Leaf Petroleum to the United Farmers of Alberta.

Following World War II, Fredericks and his three brothers-in-law, Harvey Bietz, Alvin Bietz, and Harry Bietz, decided that trucking offered them a promising future. Economy Carriers operated fuel and freight trucks from two downtown Calgary locations until 1952, when the United Farmers of Alberta awarded the company an exclusive contract hauling petroleum south of Calgary. New facilities were required, so the company located to Ogden Road on the outskirts of Calgary.

In the meantime, the company's home office moved from Cardston to Lethbridge, and, in 1963, Fredericks' son, Tom, joined the business. The remainder of the '60s saw the company grow progressively in the movement of refined petroleum products, while freight runs were gradually divested.

As Alberta's energy industry boomed, Economy seized opportunities to transport new products, such as liquefied petroleum gases and anhydrous ammonia. By the early '70s, Don Bietz, Harvey's son, had joined Economy. Its home office was established in Calgary and operations expanded into northern Alberta. With the retirement of the older generation in 1983, company ownership was assumed by President Tom Fredericks and Vice-President Don Bietz.

More dramatic changes were in store. The ECL Group of Companies was created, then grew to include seven divisions from 1988 to 1994, operating throughout Western Canada and the northwestern United States. During that period, the number of company employees grew from 100 to 600 Albertans. "We grew through the recessionary years," says Fredericks. "We went through a lot of rough water, but we made it. We're very proud of that."

### DIVERSIFICATION INTO SPECIALIZED SERVICES

The ECL Group of Companies now offers a range of transportation-related products and ser-

vices, including liquid bulk petroleum and liquid chemica[ transportation provided by Economy Carriers Limited, and oil field fluids sales and crude oil transportation throug[ the Wells Cargo Oilfield Servic[ and Freeman Trucking opera-tions. Liquid storage and rail siding services are provided by Starfield Terminals.

The company has also achieved expertise in environmental waste management through its hazardous waste transportation division, Hazm[ Transportation Services, whic[ boasts a fleet of vacuum truck[ and emergency response trail-ers to deal with chemical and product spills. The Environme[ tal Waste Management divisic[ provides project management services, including on-site secu[ rity, and transportation logistic[ tracking, and reporting for indu[ trial hazardous waste. Comple[ land reclamation and remedia[ tion services are provided by the Alberta Reclamation Man[ agement division.

"We've changed dramati-cally in the last decade," note[ Fredericks, "and we're now poised to change again. We will keep our focus on our core trucking business; how-ever, growth opportunities wi[ be measured by the extent to which they fit our long-term plans. In the future, we will emphasize those opportunitie[ that utilize the talents and ex-pertise of our people to help solve transportation, logistica[ and environmental problems for our clients.

"We're into the productiv[ ity and information age, wher[ ultimately employees will hav[

ECL HAS A FLEET OF 300 TRANSPORT RIGS, ONE OF WHICH IS PICTURED HERE AGAINST THE CALGARY SKYLINE (TOP).

AN ECONOMY CARRIERS DOUBLE TANKER UNIT PARKED IN FRONT OF CALGARY'S ORIGINAL CITY HALL (BOTTOM).

control over their own destinies," Fredericks adds. "We want to be on the leading edge in managing our employees to ensure their talents are developed to the fullest extent, for the benefit of the individual and the corporation. This means committing time and funding for education and training."

## GOING THE EXTRA MILE

One thing that Fredericks and Metz do not want to change is ECL's corporate culture, which emphasizes family values—respect, integrity, and trust. For example, since 1980, the company has been honouring employees' wives at a special annual ladies' awards banquet. "Truckers' wives are unique," according to Fredericks. "They play such an important role, often managing the household and raising children alone. Their success at home gives our professional drivers one less thing to worry about when the rubber hits the road."

Another commitment to employees is the ECL Deferred Profit Sharing Plan, where all individuals employed for one or more years share in the profits they help to achieve.

Participating in the community is also part of ECL's culture. For example, the company is a major supporter of the Alberta Literacy Foundation. In addition to providing direct financial support, the company encourages employees' families to help raise money for this worthwhile cause.

## EDUCATING THE PUBLIC

The company's award-winning King of the Highway program also helps raise money for charities, as well as educating the public about the trucking industry. The program offers a donation package for chari-

table silent and live auctions, which provides an all-expenses-paid trip to Banff in an 18-wheeler with a professional driver, a tour of ECL facilities, and assorted gift items.

"In addition to raising money for organizations such as Ducks Unlimited, the Alberta Youth Outreach Foundation, and Calgary Learning Centre," Fredericks notes, "thousands of people at the auctions become a little bit more aware of the trucking industry. The successful bidders experience and better understand the challenges professional drivers face on a daily basis."

Another innovative promotion was prompted by two employee suggestions—one was to use the company's trailers as travelling billboards to foster environmental awareness. The other suggestion was to educate the public about the need for professional truck drivers to maintain a speed limit of 90 kilometres per hour. A sign on the back of ECL trucks now notes that driving 90 kilometres per hour saves lives and conserves energy, and, at the same time, earns dollars for the Literacy Foundation.

Effective and innovative promotions such as these have provided ECL with recognition

by a variety of organizations. The company won international awards in 1995 and 1996 from the American Trucking Association for its promotional programs, competing against trucking companies from across North America. ECL has also been recognized by Arthur Andersen & Co. as one of the 50 best-managed private companies in Canada. Arthur Andersen recently ranked ECL 18th among the top 100 private companies in Calgary.

Through continuing strong and innovative leadership, ECL is ready to reinvent itself to meet the new challenges facing businesses as the 20th century draws to an end.

EMIL FREDERICKS FOUNDED ECONOMY FEED AND TRANSFER IN JEFFERSON, ALBERTA, IN 1937. HIS COMPANY WAS THE PRECURSOR TO ECL (TOP).

ECONOMY CARRIERS' TERMINAL IN DOWNTOWN CALGARY CIRCA 1950 (BOTTOM)

ISTED SINCE 1994 ON THE NEW YORK STOCK EXCHANGE, WESTERN Atlas Inc. is a major international oil field services and industrial automation systems company. With a presence in more than 70 countries around the world, Western Atlas has a number of long-established offices

in Calgary to provide oil field information services to the Canadian oil and gas industry. Two divisions are active in the Canadian market: Western Geophysical and Western Atlas Logging Services.

Established in 1933, Western Geophysical has been a leading international provider of seismic exploration services for imaging subsurface formations underneath land, deepwater, and shallow-water regions. The seismic data recorded in the field are typically transferred electronically to one of Western's data processing centres.

Western Atlas Logging Services, established in 1932, provides well-logging and data analysis services using state-of-the-art sensor and computing technologies to measure and characterize rock and fluid properties of oil and gas reserves. These services cover every phase of oil and gas drilling and production, including open hole logging, bore hole imaging, formation pressure testing and sampling, cased hole and pro-

duction logging, perforating and mechanical services, bore hole seismic surveys, and pipe recovery services.

"The services offered by Western Atlas Logging Services complement Western Geophysical's seismic surveys," says Canadian Area Manager Jeff West. While seismic surveys provide a 3-D microview of the reservoir, well logging provides the high-resolution bore hole information for each of the wells in the field. Geoscientists from both divisions work together to integrate surface seismic and bore hole data, providing clients with a more accurate understanding of a reservoir and its properties. Clients served from Calgary include all the major Canadian energy companies, as well as the smaller independent ones.

Western Geophysical's Canadian roots reach back to 1948, when the company's first field crew was sent to Calgary. Within a few years, the Calgary office became headquarters for the company's sec-

ond foreign subsidiary, Western Geophysical of Canada, Ltd. The Calgary office continued to grow over the years, along with the Canadian oil and gas industry.

Western Atlas Logging established its presence in Calgary in 1950, through Lane-Wells Canadian Company, a perforating company, and later, for many decades, through Dresser Atlas, which offered both perforating and logging services.

### THE LATEST TECHNOLOGY

"Western Atlas invests heavily in research and development, and uses the most advanced data acquisition technologies and equipment," says West. "Our ultimate goal is to help our clients improve exploration efficiency and productivity."

Western Geophysical has long been active in the latest seismic technologies—today, it is 4-D seismic, the fourth dimension being time—and recently shot a 4-D program

WESTERN GEOPHYSICAL IS A LEADING INTERNATIONAL PROVIDER OF SEISMIC EXPLORATION SERVICES FOR IMAGING SUBSURFACE FORMATIONS UNDERNEATH LAND, DEEP-WATER, AND SHALLOW-WATER REGIONS (LEFT).

WESTERN ATLAS LOGGING SERVICES, ESTABLISHED IN 1932, PROVIDES WELL-LOGGING AND DATA ANALYSIS SERVICES USING STATE-OF-THE-ART SENSOR AND COMPUTING TECHNOLOGIES TO MEASURE AND CHARACTERIZE ROCK AND FLUID PROPERTIES OF OIL AND GAS RESERVES (RIGHT).

SHARP PHOTOGRAPHIC PRODUCTIONS

the Rainbow Lake area of Alberta. Western runs about four field crews during the winter months—three in southern Alberta and one in the Northwest Territories—with a complement of about 450 employees or contractors.

About 65 percent of Western Geophysical's work involves proprietary surveys commissioned and owned by specific clients. The remainder of the division's work involves speculative multiclient surveys, owned by Western Geophysical and marketed at a lower cost than a proprietary survey to companies interested in the survey area.

Western Atlas Logging Services stays in the forefront of research by developing new generations of logging and data analysis technology. In fact, five new technologies were introduced over the past year.

One of the division's most recent innovations is the use of magnetic resonance imaging logging to produce a highly accurate measurement of the formation fluids in the rocks around the bore hole. Another premier service is the multipole array acoustilog, an instrument that provides acoustic data to determine porosity, lithology, and rock mechanical and formation fluid properties. The division also provides services to detect corrosion in down hole and surface pipe, using, for example, the microvertilog and the digital vertilog service.

The logging division, with 150 employees and Calgary as the area office, has established five field location offices in Alberta—in Bonneville, Calgary, Nisku, Grande Prairie, and Slave Lake. The division also has an office in Sarnia, Ontario, and has recently opened a base in St. John's to work under the Grand Banks Alliance on the Terra Nova project offshore from Newfoundland.

### QUALITY, SAFETY, AND PRODUCTIVITY

"Service is a key word for us," says West. "When we say we're going to do something, we do it. Our company's name has strong fiscal backing. And our investment in technology helps us continue to make our clients' operations more cost effective.

"A further, value-added advantage we bring to the table," he notes, "is our vertical integration, giving us the ability, through our two divisions, to verify and calibrate the big picture. We're a full-service company."

Both divisions strive for quality, safety, and productivity, and are currently working toward certification for ISO 9001 and 9002 international quality standards. The divisions also take pride in hiring their employees locally—from the Southern Alberta Institute of Technology for technicians and technologists, and from the University of Calgary for engineers. "The best thing we can do for Calgary is to help produce oil and gas and provide jobs," notes West.

And with Western Atlas' history of innovation, growth, and success, the company will be doing just that for many years to come.

THE SERVICES OFFERED BY WESTERN ATLAS LOGGING SERVICES COMPLEMENT WESTERN GEOPHYSICAL'S SEISMIC SURVEYS. WHILE SEISMIC SURVEYS PROVIDE A 3-D MICROVIEW OF THE RESERVOIR, WELL LOGGING PROVIDES THE HIGH-RESOLUTION BORE HOLE INFORMATION FOR EACH OF THE WELLS IN THE FIELD.

THERE HAVE BEEN A LOT OF CHANGES SINCE 1949, WHEN PATRIARCH ROLAN

Mullen founded Mullen Trucking Ltd. with just one truck. From tho:

modest beginnings, the company grew as a family business until Decemb

1993, when it became publicly owned. During the past decade, the compar

has expanded to more than 1,250 employees and 750 trucks.

In early 1997, Mullen completed an internal reorganization and changed its name from Mullen Trucking Ltd. to Mullen Transportation Inc. in recognition of its growing business. Four divisions—Truckload, Oilfield Services, Specialized Services, and Regional LTL—reflect the current scope of the company's operations across North America.

"We're not an overnight success," notes President and CEO Murray Mullen, now charged—along with two other brothers—with carrying out his father's vision. "We've had our tough times and we've learned a lot." One of Mullen's first priorities when he assumed the position of president in 1991 was to put in place a plan that would maintain the value system that had been instilled by his father, as well as position the company for future growth and prosperity.

## FOUR CORNERSTONES OF SUCCESS

"Safety is one of the four cornerstones of our success," comments Mullen. "We believe in using our highways responsibly, and we maintain a strong focus on education and training for our employees. Although we believe that safety and making money go hand in hand, we don't consider our safety program a proprietary competitive advantage, so we share safety information freely with the industry."

In 1995, Mullen was recognized by industry peers through the Grand Prize Safety Award from the Interstate Truckload Carriers Conference, a U.S.-based conference representing more than 650 trucking companies in North America. And in 1996, Mullen was the first recipient of the Premier's Business Award of Distinction in the province of Alberta.

A second cornerstone to success has been the company's

commitment to technology. In the early 1980s, Mullen was or of the first to computerize its operations. Satellite communi cation has been available sinc 1991. "Satellite communication gives us real-time inform: tion," notes Mullen, "because in these days of just-in-time ir ventory, it's important to kno exactly where each shipment is."

Diversification—by commodity and type of equipment as well as geographically—is the third cornerstone, and financial stability is the fourth. The company has achieved these goals through its acquisitions of competing and com plementary trucking firms, which have strengthened its financial base and helped the company broaden its scope.

## VALUED EMPLOYEES

"Trucks don't make companies, people make companies, could be the Mullen credo. When Mullen went public, al employees became shareholde and now participate in profit sharing; the company also fos ters an environment of mutua trust and respect. As a result, very low employee turnover is being experienced.

"We've created a really goc organization with really good people—people who understai their future and are aligned wi the company goals and objectives," Mullen continues. "Th company creates the jobs, but employees create value. I belie we've broken a number of ste eotypes of what the trucking business should be like. The best years are ahead of us."

IN 1949, ROLAND MULLEN FOUNDED MULLEN TRUCKING WITH JUST ONE TRUCK (TOP).

TODAY, MULLEN TRANSPORTATION, INC. BOASTS MORE THAN 1,250 EMPLOYEES AND 750 TRUCKS (BOTTOM).

**R**IGEL ENERGY IS SHOOTING FOR THE STARS. AND THE METAPHOR IS APT, since the medium-sized oil and gas company is named after the brightest star in the Orion constellation. ❀ Rigel originated in 1954 as French Petroleum Company of Canada Ltd., a wholly owned subsidiary of a French parent company. In the seventies, 50 percent of the company was sold to the public, and the company was renamed Total Petroleum (North America) Ltd. Following the parent company's complete divestiture of its Canadian interests in 1993, the company was reborn as Rigel Energy Corporation. The company is now widely held, primarily by Canadians, through pension funds and other investment holdings.

### INDEPENDENCE BRINGS CHANGES

This independence has presented many new challenges since 1993," says President and CEO Don West, who has been with the company for 17 years. "Our corporate culture has changed. We're our own masters now, and there's a greater range of things we can do."

Rigel has experienced significant growth since the 1993 milestone, with daily production doubling to more than 28,000 barrels of oil equivalent—split equally between light oil and natural gas. The company considers itself primarily an exploration and production company. "We drill for our daily bread," says West.

A significant exception to using the drill bit was the acquisition of Inverness Petroleum Ltd. in early 1996. The acquisition provided a unique opportunity for Rigel to improve cash flow; maintain a balance between oil and gas production; and gain significant undeveloped lands, supporting the company's commitment to grow through full-cycle exploration.

Operating primarily in the Western Canadian Sedimentary Basin, the company has also initiated some activity in the United Kingdom, which holds promise for significant light oil production. "We're seeing a decline in light oil production in Western Canada," says West, "and a stronger focus on heavy oil and synthetics. Since Rigel only produces light oil, we've had to look at international opportunities to maintain our oil/gas balance."

While a number of Calgary-based oil and gas companies have grown through acquisitions in the past decade, West believes that paying attention to costs has been a factor in Rigel's growth. This cost control has helped the company avoid the downsizing faced by the energy industry in the past years.

West also expresses pride in the company's commitment to the local community, as well as to the environment. For example, Rigel has co-sponsored a number of environmental initiatives in the Foothills area and has supported the Nature Conservancy.

Additionally, Rigel's Calgary-based employees have volunteered their time in the Partnership in Education Program, which pairs Calgary companies with local schools. "We deliberately chose a high-needs school," says West, "and we think we've had a positive impact." This initiative resulted in Rigel being presented with the 1996 Mayor's Excellence Award.

In summing up the competitive environment in the Canadian energy industry, West comments: "We must be constantly alert in order to react to the growing number of available opportunities." If the company's history is any indication, Rigel will continue to succeed.

CLOCKWISE FROM TOP: A RIGEL EMPLOYEE SURVEYS A GAS METER AT THE CORPORATION'S LEEDALE GAS PLANT LOCATED NORTHWEST OF CALGARY.

A SERVICE RIG COMPLETES AN OIL WELL FOR RIGEL AT THE ACME PLANT NORTHEAST OF CALGARY.

RIGEL'S CALGARY-BASED EMPLOYEES HAVE VOLUNTEERED THEIR TIME IN THE PARTNERSHIP IN EDUCATION PROGRAM, WHICH PAIRS CALGARY COMPANIES WITH LOCAL SCHOOLS.

THE 1988 WINTER OLYMPICS IN CALGARY MAY BE A PART OF THE PAST, BU the success of the Games lives on through the Calgary Olympic Developmen Association (CODA). World-class athletes, tourists, and local Calgarians ca benefit from the legacy of the Games, largely because of the organization'

vision, planning, and operation of Calgary's Olympic Winter Games facilities.

First established in 1954, CODA participated in three bids for Calgary to host the Olympic Winter Games before being successful in its fourth attempt in 1981. When OCO '88 was created in 1982 to organize the Games, CODA was restructured to ensure that there would be continuing use of the Olympic facilities for years to come.

CODA was quick out of the gate. Between 1982 and 1988, the organization negotiated long-term amateur sport benefits from the Canadian Airlines Saddledome, and ensured that the University of Calgary's Olympic Oval, Canada Olympic Park, and Canmore Nordic Centre would also be available to future athletes. After the Games, a Legacy Fund was established with part of the surplus revenues to allow CODA to subsidize the operation of facilities so that athletes could use them at nominal cost.

This foresight has paid off. Calgary is the only Winter Olympics city that has continued to operate all its venues for the training and competition of Canadian and international athletes.

With an annual operating budget of about $15 million, half of which is provided by the Legacy Fund and half by operating revenues at Canada Olympic Park (COP), CODA hosts numerous World Championships and World Cups at each Olympic venue. In addition, the association provides between $1 million and $2 million in annual grants to various Olympic winter sports organizations.

### STRENGTHENING THE VENUES

Nearly a decade after Calgary hosted what many consider to be the most successful Olympic Winter Games, the world-class facilities of the '88 Games continue to be among the most utilized in the world. No other Olympic Winter site can make such a claim.

Located 10 minutes from the downtown core, Canada Olympic Park represents the most visible example of the Olympic legacy where freestyle skiing, bobsleigh, luge, and ski jumping events took place. The venue consistently stages national and international competitions each year, and athletes from all over the world train year-round.

COP has evolved into Calgary's year-round sport an tourist facility, attracting more than 500,000 visitors each year. The park boasts one of the largest ski schools in West ern Canada, as well as the larg est Olympic Hall of Fame & Museum in North America. With such unique programs as Summer Sport Camps, the pub lic Bobsleigh Bullet ride, and Summer Luge rides, it's easy t see why COP continues to be

FROM LEFT:
CANADIAN TEAM MEMBERS PIERRE LUEDERS AND DAVE MACEACHERN ENJOY THE THRILL OF VICTORY AT CANADA OLYMPIC PARK.

ROB BOYD, A MEMBER OF CANADA'S ALPINE SKI TEAM, RACES FOR THE FINISH.

AMANDA FORTIER, MEMBER OF CANADA'S JUNIOR CROSS COUNTRY SKI TEAM

JOHN GIBSON PHOTOGRAPHICS

JOHN GIBSON PHOTOGRAPHICS

o well attended. The park continues to grow with the establishment of the city's first mountain bike park and dual slalom course, as well as a high-end miniature golf course and $1.4 million arts theatre expansion.

The Olympic Oval at the University of Calgary is another well-used venue. Comprising 26,000 square metres, it was the first indoor speed skating oval in North America to offer ice in both summer and winter. "Skaters and coaches claim the oval is the fastest in the world," notes CODA President Dennis Kadatz. The oval currently holds 24 of 30 official world records in long track speed skating. Some 15 of these records were set in 1996.

A national training centre for cross-country and biathlon teams, the Canmore Nordic Centre is also considered the best in its class. Canadian, American, Australian, and Japanese athletes all train on the best-developed trails in the world. In addition, since 1989, CODA has been operating a complementary summer training facility on the Haig Glacier from July through October each year. And in 1994, the $1.8 million Bill Warren Training Centre was opened at Canmore to encourage high-performance athletic development.

## SUPPORTING OLYMPIC WINTER SPORTS

CODA's focus is continuing to shift from being a facility operator to one of supporting Olympic winter sport," says Kadatz. "As CODA continues to operate COP more efficiently and economically, it's able to provide more support to the governing bodies of our 12 Olympic winter sports."

For example, CODA has partnered in establishing the National Sport Centre-Calgary, which works with athletes and coaches to ensure a positive and balanced approach to sport. The centre has assisted more than 150 nationally carded athletes in achieving their performance goals, and has helped many provincial-level athletes and coaches. Through the National Coaching Institute, provincial-level coaches learn new training techniques from high-performance coaches, while the Sport Science Support Group provides information on training methods.

In another partnership with the Calgary Board of Education, CODA has established the National Sport School at William Aberhart High School. This program helps student athletes achieve both their educational and their sport goals. The school operates year-round to accommodate training and competition schedules in conjunction with curriculum requirements.

"CODA continues to encourage national sport organizations to locate to the Calgary area," notes Kadatz, citing that Nordic Combined Canada has joined Alpine Canada in choosing Calgary as its head office. In the years to come, it's clear that these efforts will continue to pay off—for Calgarians as well as for the rest of Canada—as CODA achieves its vision to support the complete development of Canadian Olympic winter athletes through facilities, training, funding, event organization, and education.

CATRIONA LeMAY DOAN COMPETES AT THE CODA SPEED SKATING WORLD CUP AT THE OLYMPIC OVAL (TOP).

CANADA OLYMPIC PARK ATTRACTS MORE THAN 500,000 VISITORS YEAR-ROUND (BOTTOM).

ALGARY'S QUALITY OF LIFE IS A MAJOR ATTRACTION FOR A GROWING number of companies and individuals, and the Calgary Philharmonic Orchestra (CPO) is an important contributor to that quality of life. ✻ While many Calgarians love to two-step and line dance—especially during Stampede

week—city residents also have a passion for the orchestra. In fact, Calgary has the largest per capita subscription rate of all Canadian cities with populations of more than 500,000.

"We have the finest orchestra west of Toronto," notes Executive Director Leonard Stone. "Guest artists and conductors cannot speak highly enough of our musicians' capability and commitment. Clearly, Maestro Hans Graf has taken the orchestra to new heights."

The CPO has gained international recognition through its extensive recordings, national CBC broadcasts, and touring. In 1992, the CPO embarked on its first international tour, performing to critical acclaim in Toronto, Ottawa, Montreal, New York, Boston, and Washington, D.C.

At home in Calgary, the orchestra, with 64 full-time musicians, presents more than 100 performances to more than 100,000 people each season. The Jack Singer Concert Hall, where the orchestra plays, has been named one of North America's 10 finest pure music chambers, with superior yet flexible acoustics for a variety of performance styles.

WITH ITS CONTINUING SUCCESS, IT IS CLEAR THAT THE CALGARY PHILHARMONIC SOCIETY HAS FULFILLED ITS MISSION TO PROVIDE AUDIENCES WITH "A RICH, DIVERSE, AND UNEQUALLED SYMPHONIC MUSIC EXPERIENCE, WHICH EARNS BROAD COMMUNITY SUPPORT."

NOTES EXECUTIVE DIRECTOR LEONARD STONE, "GUEST ARTISTS AND CONDUCTORS CANNOT SPEAK HIGHLY ENOUGH OF OUR MUSICIANS' CAPABILITY AND COMMITMENT. CLEARLY, MAESTRO HANS GRAF (BOTTOM RIGHT) HAS TAKEN THE ORCHESTRA TO NEW HEIGHTS."

ALEXANDER W. THOMAS

ALEXANDER W. THOMAS

ALEXANDER W. THOMAS

Five series are offered each year, providing a range of music for everyone's taste. The two most popular series are the Pops Concerts and the Light Classics, while the CPO musicians find the Classics series the most challenging and inspirational. Attendance at the Baroque series has quadrupled over the last few years, and the Young People's Concerts are always sold out. In addition, the CPO plays for the Calgary Opera and the Alberta Ballet Company performances in the city.

## COMMITMENT TO THE COMMUNITY

The CPO takes its community involvement seriously. Special concerts for schoolchildren include lots of interaction to promote understanding and appreciation. More than 25,000 children attend these concerts annually. The orchestra also takes its concerts out into the community, playing at local community centres and throughout southern Alberta.

"Our orchestra reaches out to all levels—from elementary school children to senior citizens," notes Stone. "Music is a medium everyone relates to."

Calgarians regularly demonstrate their appreciation and commitment to the CPO by getting involved in fund-raising—the orchestra's Benny the Bookworm second-hand book sale has been a popular event in the city for more than 40 years. The orchestra is also grateful for increasing corporate sponsorships. Its annual Maestro Ambassador Ball is a source of funding but it also provides an opportunity for the business community to meet a number of ambassadors, opening doors for potential international trade.

With its continuing success, it is clear that the CPO has fulfilled its mission to provide audiences with "a rich, diverse, and unequalled symphonic music experience, which earns broad community support." And it is a mission that the Calgary Philharmonic Orchestra will continue to fulfill for many years to come.

ERSONS WHO ARE TRAINED BY THE CALGARY-BASED PETROLEUM Industry Training Service (PITS) receive petroleum industry training that will allow them to work anywhere in the world. Although approximately 80 percent of the 40,000 blue-collar workers who

enefit from PITS training ach year are Canadian, a walk rough the organization's train- g facilities will usually find assortment of visitors from ch countries as Russia, Libya, d Bangladesh.

## MEETING THE NEED

o meet the training needs f the growing Western Cana- ian energy industry, PITS was corporated in 1961 as a non- rofit society. For its first 12 ars, PITS received funding om supporting organizations, ch as petroleum industry trade sociations and the provincial overnment. In 1973, the orga- zation became self-supporting, enerating all of its operating nds through course fees. In 989, PITS' expanding role sulted in a new funding for- ula, whereby base funding provided by the oil industry rough the Workers' Com- nsation Board.

Currently, PITS offers out 75 courses in such areas petroleum engineering, field roduction operations, drilling d well servicing, safety, envi- nment, and supervisory and e-employment training. Thirty- ve instructors work on contract, hile a number of private sector nsultants also provide PITS aining programs. "We train e trainers, too," notes Presi- nt Paul Schoenhals, "as well offer customized programs meet a company's unique aining needs."

Schoenhals is especially oud of PITS' flagship train- g centre at Nisku, just south

of Edmonton. The 38-acre Nisku facility is a world-class training centre offering a complete petroleum training experience at one location. Approximately 7,000 workers receive training each year at Nisku, which boasts a fully operational drilling rig, a well control training faci- lity, a 1,000-metre well for production and work over training, state-of-the-art oil and gas production facilities, rescue training facilities, and a classroom building. "Nisku is the best hands-on oil and gas training facility in the world— bar none," says Schoenhals. PITS also has a presence on the East Coast, with a simula- tor and classroom located in Halifax.

While PITS strives to maintain its focus on meeting the Canadian energy industry's training needs, the Service has been doing a fair bit of inter- national work. When Canadian companies such as Canadian Fracmaster, Gulf, and Pan- Canadian began to work in the former Soviet Union, PITS

was part of the team, training their Russian nationals. While continuing to do significant training in Russia, PITS also does international work in many other countries.

"The nineties have been a time of significant growth for us," notes Schoenhals. "And that growth has been based on word of mouth alone. We've set the standards for training internationally." For example, PITS is the only Canadian registered assessment centre allowed to teach and certify workers in international well control. Students can receive simultaneous certification for Canadian and overseas work.

"We've been the train- ing arm of the Canadian up- stream oil and gas industry for a long time," Schoenhals concludes. "We believe that student numbers and inter- national contracts will increase, as the demand for high-quality training grows." And PITS will be around to meet that demand.

PITS' WORLD-CLASS TRAINING FACILITY IS LOCATED IN NISKU, ALBERTA.

"IRST IN FOOD—BEST IN SERVICE." THAT'S THE MOTTO OF CALGARY CO operative Association Limited, the largest retail co-operative in Canada. unique part of the city's culture, the Calgary Co-op is composed of 15 grocer stores (14 in Calgary and one in nearby Strathmore), most with gas bar

and some with added extras such as travel agencies and liquor stores.

Modelled after the British Rochdale Co-op, which was established in 1844 when a group of weavers pooled their resources to open their own store, Calgary Co-op was founded in 1956 with one store and 1,000 members. Today, the Calgary Co-op has grown to more than 330,000 members, with annual sales of more than $500 million. In addition, more

than 3,500 employees work at Co-op, making it among the top 10 employers in the city.

As an autonomous, self-help organization, the Co-op's basic principles are voluntary and open membership; democratic member participation in setting policy and making decisions; equal control of capital by members; education, training, and information for members so they can contribute effectively; co-operation with other co-operatives; and concern for the community. Each Co-op member has one share and one vote as a shareholder in the business.

### FOCUS ON CUSTOMER SERVICE

"As a co-operative, we're uniquely focused," says Glenna Cross, Division Manager, Communications. "Our community involvement and commitment comes from our roots and our values, and our competitive advantage is our customer service."

This means that all Calgar Co-op customers get their groce ies packed and carried out to their car; nearly all centres have a supervised Kiddies Korral, so that parents can shop without distractions; and recycling bins for newspaper, milk jugs, and check-stand bags are available with the revenue from some of these products distributed to non-profit organizations. An area in each centre is set aside for members to exchange books they no longer want, and members and non-profit groups have access to free pub licity through bulletin boards.

Members receive patronage refunds each year, based on a percentage of their yearly Co-op purchases. In recent years, an added-value program Value Plus, rewards members for different levels of spending And a special program offers a 5 percent discount on purchases for all registered charitable organizations. "Our goa is the collective good of all members," says Cross.

Listening to customers is another important aspect of Calgary Co-op's operations Before the Dalhousie store in northwest Calgary was renovated, Co-op did extensiv research in the local communit and with the store's staff. As a result, the renovated store, which opened its doors in October 1996, has wider aisle fresh fish, and bulk food depart ments. "Not only did we not los market share during the renovations," notes Cross, "but the store is doing much better than we projected. I believe customers feel good when they know they've been heard.

A MAJOR FOCUS FOR CALGARY CO-OP IS ENSURING THAT THE FRESH PRODUCE DEPARTMENTS ARE THE BEST IN THE MARKET (LEFT).

CUSTOMER INPUT MEANS THAT CALGARY CO-OP'S MODERN SHOPPING CENTRES ARE EXTREMELY USER FRIENDLY (RIGHT).

ANGUS OF CALGARY

ANGUS OF CALGARY

To reinforce the message that Calgary Co-op is listening, a customer satisfaction adviser is now available at its head office to respond to customers' concerns, to track issues, and to address problems early on.

## COMMUNITY INVOLVEMENT

Calgary Co-op has a lot invested in the city and surrounding area. Members are Calgarians who live and work in the community and shop at their local Co-op store. Profits are returned to the city through the patronage funds. "It starts and ends in the Calgary area for us," says Cross.

In addition, Calgary Co-op contributes a significant portion of its profits to local charitable organizations. Cash donations are given for a variety of causes, including women's issues, children's safety, breast cancer research, and children's nutrition. A further $1 million retail in groceries is donated to the Interfaith and Salvation Army food banks each year. And a major charity golf tournament is also held annually, which raises more than $100,000 for selected charities. Additional industry-supported sponsorships are undertaken, and each store has a small donations budget for the local Girl Guides group or hockey team. "It's very clear," says Cross. "You nurture the place that nurtures you."

## PLANNING FOR THE FUTURE

For the future, Calgary Co-op plans both renovation and expansion. A new store is planned for the Country Hills/Hamptons neighbourhood. And a gas bar/convenience store is planned for the Taradale area, which will expand to a full-service store when warranted by population growth. The company is also paying increasing attention to staff education, to ensure that employees know all the product lines now available.

"Of course, we're big business," says Cross, "but I believe we're big business with a conscience. Part of the fundamentals of being a co-operative are a strong sense of business ethics and corporate values. Those values have been continually articulated throughout the years. For example, in every management discussion when a decision is being made, someone always asks how the decision fits into our core values."

Those core values, and the total of $286 million Calgary Co-op has returned in patronage refunds to members over the last 40 years, are indicators that the organization will continue to meet the needs of Calgarians for many years to come.

CALGARY CO-OP'S STRENGTH LIES IN THE SUPPORT OF ITS MEMBERS. THIS LOYALTY IS REWARDED WITH A SHARE IN THE COMPANY'S SUCCESS THROUGH PATRONAGE FUNDS, SAVINGS PROGRAMS, AND A STRONG SENSE OF BELONGING TO AN ORGANIZATION THAT IS DEDICATED TO THE COMMUNITY (LEFT).

CUSTOMERS APPRECIATE CALGARY CO-OP EMPLOYEES FOR GOING ABOVE AND BEYOND THE CALL OF DUTY TO PROVIDE EXCEPTIONAL CUSTOMER SERVICE (RIGHT).

anadian Airlines International is the high-spirited descendant of a rugged past. The airline's roots are firmly set in the bush pilot era when skimming mountain peaks and surfing pristine lakes were common occurrences for biplanes and adventure-seeking pilots.

This entrepreneurial beginning has produced an airline determined to succeed in one of the world's most competitive business environments, reflecting the grit and adaptability of its international work force, the drive of its management team, and the experience of its board of directors.

Today, Canadian Airlines is a full-service international airline that offers passenger and cargo air transportation service to more than 160 destinations in 17 countries on five continents. In 1996, Canadian carried 11.6 million passengers. Including its regional affiliates, Canadian's fleet consists of 122 aircraft.

### TYING THE COUNTRY TOGETHER

The airline helps tie Canada together with a comprehensive schedule of local, regional, and national service. In partnership with several of the world's leading airlines, it also opens the doors of a beckoning world to all Canadian travellers.

It seems appropriate that an airline with such a colourful past, complemented by the prospect of an exciting future, would be headquartered in Calgary, a city known for innovation and vitality.

Such was the make-up of the pioneers who founded the airlines that ultimately merged to become Canadian Airlines. The corporation was founded on February 22, 1956, in Alberta, but it wasn't until March 27, 1987, that the West would welcome a new international carrier under the now familiar banner of Canadian Airlines International. It is the descendant of five predecessor airlines: Canadian Pacific Air Lines, Eastern Provincial Airways, Nordair, Pacific Western Air Lines (PWA), and Wardair Canada.

Each of these airlines contributed a unique personality. Canadian Pacific (CP) forged the trail Canadian continues to follow to Asia. PWA brought a strong western heritage and confidence.

Additional regional strength was added to the mix by Eastern Provincial Airways, founded in Halifax in 1949 and purchased by CP in 1984, and Nordair, an airline created in Quebec in 1957 and sold to CP in 1985. The last to join the Canadian team was Wardair Canada, in 1989. One of the world's most successful charter airlines, the Alberta-founded carrier was created in 1953 from the energy and beliefs of one man, bush pilot Max Ward.

Although Canadian's network spans the globe, Calgarians in particular like to claim the airline as their native child. Because Calgary is second only to Toronto as a head-office location in Canada, it is crucial that Calgary maintain access to global business and leisure travel markets. Canadian Airlines serves this need.

"We are Calgary's airline," says Steve Markey, Vice

CANADIAN AIRLINES INTERNATIONAL IS THE HIGH-SPIRITED DESCENDANT OF A RUGGED PAST (LEFT).

CANADIAN IS THE OFFSPRING OF FIVE PREDECESSOR AIRLINES: CANADIAN PACIFIC AIR LINES, EASTERN PROVINCIAL AIRWAYS, NORDAIR, PACIFIC WESTERN AIR LINES, AND WARDAIR CANADA (RIGHT).

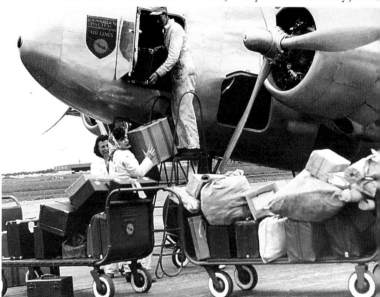

resident Corporate and Government Affairs. "That's the public perception and in many ways that's also the reality."

Canadian dominates the Calgary air transportation market, offering connections to more than 150 destinations from the international airport. The city is home to about 1,800 of Canadian's 16,000 employees, a base for its reservation system, and the crucial Control Centre that co-ordinates all flight activity. It is also headquarters for subsidiary airline Canadian Regional.

Canadian's gateside Business Work Centres and Empress Lounge at the Calgary airport attest to the company's goal of meeting the needs of the business traveller. In addition, Canadian's shuttle service links Calgary, Edmonton, and Vancouver—Western Canada's largest business centres—with departures as often as every half-hour.

## REACHING OUT TO THE WORLD

Key to providing global access for Calgary customers are alliances with other airlines and hospitality providers. These alliances permit each carrier to offer a blanket of unified, coordinated service across their respective networks, including expanded opportunities to accumulate and redeem frequent flyer points. The anchor airlines on Canadian's team are American Airlines and British Airways, the dominant carriers in the United States and the United Kingdom. Other key members of the team are Qantas in the South Pacific and Japan Airlines in Asia.

As it looks to the future, Canadian is more focused than ever on international travel and new opportunities made possible by deregulation and the broadening of its commercial alliances. Passenger capacity into the United States and Asia has been stepped up. The operations of Canadian's Asian hub in Vancouver have been strengthened in anticipation of dramatic growth in travel between North America and Asia.

The vision of a colourful pilot by the name of Grant McConachie has become prophetic for Canadian Airlines. In 1949, McConachie, who would eventually become head of Canadian Pacific, sensed the long-term economic promise in Asia, so he secured flying rights to Hong Kong and Tokyo. McConachie would use a world globe and a piece of string to demonstrate that the Great Circle Route through Vancouver was a shorter and faster corridor to Asia compared to most cities in North America.

Today, all indicators point to the Pacific Rim to lead world economic activity in the future. Canadian flies to eight of the most important business centres in Asia and is well positioned to add more destinations, capturing a larger share of this burgeoning market. Dozens of flights every week carry passengers over the Pacific in comfort and style in wide-body Boeing 747-400s, Boeing 767-300s, and McDonnell Douglas DC-10s. Yesterday's dream has become today's most promising opportunity.

"We're building a high-speed sky highway between two continents," says Kevin Benson, Canadian Airlines President and Chief Executive Officer. "As we consider new routes in the future, we will remember the leaders of the past who set Canadian and its predecessor airlines on this course. From our base in Western Canada, we've positioned ourselves to capitalize on the growth of these markets well into the next century," Benson concludes.

AS ONE OF CANADIAN AIRLINES' PREDECESSOR AIRLINES, CANADIAN PACIFIC CONTRIBUTED ITS UNIQUE PERSONALITY BY FORGING THE TRAIL CANADIAN CONTINUES TO FOLLOW ACROSS THE PACIFIC TO ASIA (LEFT).

TODAY, CANADIAN AIRLINES IS A FULL-SERVICE INTERNATIONAL AIRLINE OFFERING SEAMLESS PASSENGER AND CARGO SERVICE. TOGETHER WITH ITS GLOBAL ALLIANCE PARTNERS, CANADIAN SERVES MORE THAN 300 NORTH AMERICAN DESTINATIONS AND MORE THAN 500 DESTINATIONS WORLDWIDE (RIGHT).

# CARMA DEVELOPERS LTD.

ERHAPS MORE THAN ANY OTHER BUSINESS, LAND DEVELOPERS MUST HAVE vision—an understanding of what the public wants—before the public ever knows it wants it. Carma Developers Ltd. has been anticipating the needs and wants of Calgary residents since 1958. The company is currently the

largest publicly traded real estate development company in Western Canada.

Originally established as a builders' cooperative, formed to ensure a source of sufficient lots for home construction by member builders, Carma's primary focus has always been land development. Carma experienced rapid growth during the 1960s, went public in 1972, and had expanded by the late 1970s into five provinces and seven states. During the economic slowdown of the 1980s,

Carma retrenched, restructured, and refocused ultimately on land development. The company today has about $250 million in assets and revenues in excess of $100 million per year, and is a consistently profitable organization.

Creating lasting value for consumers is Carma's focus, says President and CEO Alan Norris. "We know how to develop communities. The quality of our communities in Calgary is second to none in North America."

Carma has developed 43 neighbourhoods in Calgary alone. In fact, one in five Calgarians—more than 150,000 people—lives in a Carma community. Communities currently under development include Edgemont, McKenzie Lake, Riverbend, Tuscany, and McKenzie Towne.

## MASTER-PLANNED COMMUNITIES

Because of the company's significant land holdings, Carma has the opportunity to create master plans for its communities that look forward into the future. A master plan ensures continuity from one phase of development to the next—for aspects such as architectural standards, community layout, amenities, and the location of parks, schools, open space, and local services. Master planning also ensures that a broad range of housing types and levels is available and integrated into the community in a cohesive manner.

CLOCKWISE FROM TOP: IN ADDITION TO ITS SPECTACULAR MOUNTAIN AND CITY VIEWS AND EASY ACCESS TO ALL PARTS OF THE CITY, TUSCANY OFFERS PRIVATE OUTDOOR RECREATIONAL FACILITIES FOR RESIDENTS.

CARMA HAS DEVELOPED 43 NEIGHBOURHOODS IN CALGARY ALONE. IN FACT, ONE IN FIVE CALGARIANS—MORE THAN 150,000 PEOPLE—LIVES IN A CARMA COMMUNITY.

MCKENZIE TOWNE OFFERS A FRIENDLIER, PEDESTRIAN-ORIENTED ENVIRONMENT.

Indeed, most Carma communities offer a variety of amenities, even in their initial stages of development. The company also gets residents involved, helping to form private residents' associations that ensure that the community's facilities are well maintained and managed. "We like to create opportunities for residents to be in control of their own destinies once we have completed our work as developers," says Norris.

## THE MCKENZIE TOWNE ALTERNATIVE

A recent example of Carma's vision is the McKenzie Towne project, in the southern end of Calgary near the junction of Deerfoot Trail and Highway 22X.

"We try to be conscious of trends and anticipate what the consumer wants years in advance," explains Norris. "We knew that a certain percentage of Calgary consumers were looking for an alternative to conventional suburban communities, with their prominent front-attached garages, winding street patterns, and cul-de-sac layouts."

McKenzie Towne is such an alternative. "With garages moved to the rear and homes positioned closer to the street, it offers a friendlier, pedestrian-oriented environment," says Norris. "It's a place where people can live, play, and work." What differentiates McKenzie Towne from other communities is its focus on "neotraditional town planning"—a blend of the best of the past, with the amenities people expect in the 1990s and beyond.

Tuscany is another example of Carma's vision. This development in northwest Calgary is based on a radial plan with open space links and a central hub. In addition to its spectacular mountain and city views and easy access to all parts of the city, Tuscany offers private outdoor recreational facilities for residents, including a clubhouse; pleasure skating rink with fire pit that becomes a water play area in the summer; regulation-size hockey rink that becomes basketball courts and a roller-blading surface in the summer; and picnic and play areas, walking/jogging paths, and horseshoe pits.

"You can't guarantee a vibrant community," Norris comments. "But you can create the elements that allow communities to flourish and become vibrant."

## AWARD-WINNING COMMUNITIES

The company's strategy has led to significant recognition through the years. McKenzie Towne was named the best new subdivision by the Calgary Home Builders Association. And both Tuscany and McKenzie Towne have received the association's SAM award for Best Pageantry. Carma received the SAM Developer of the Year award in the first year the award was given and placed second in the North American version of the SAM awards for McKenzie Towne's information centre.

In addition to land development, Carma operates two home-building businesses in Calgary. Heartland Homes was established in 1990 to build single-family houses. In four of the past five years, Heartland Homes has won the coveted Customer Choice Award, which is based on a customer satisfaction poll conducted by the Alberta New Home Warranty Program. Hawthorne Homes was established in 1995 to build multifamily and "life-style" homes, and received a National Sales & Marketing Excellence award in its first year of operation. Both home-building companies are intended to further enhance the company's land development activities, as well as complement the activities of other builders.

For the future, Carma will continue its strategy of identifying factors and trends affecting how people live, and further develop its large land holdings. Carma's ultimate goal is to create best value—not just best price. With innovative, master-planned communities like McKenzie Towne and Tuscany, the company is proving it has a vision—and the ability to turn that vision into reality.

MOST CARMA COMMUNITIES OFFER A VARIETY OF AMENITIES, INCLUDING CHILDREN'S PLAYGROUNDS, EVEN IN THEIR INITIAL STAGES OF DEVELOPMENT (TOP).

IN FOUR OF THE PAST FIVE YEARS, HEARTLAND HOMES HAS WON THE COVETED CUSTOMER CHOICE AWARD, WHICH IS BASED ON A CUSTOMER SATISFACTION POLL CONDUCTED BY THE ALBERTA NEW HOME WARRANTY PROGRAM (BOTTOM).

AFTER SEVERAL DIFFICULT YEARS OF BELT TIGHTENING, DOWNSIZING and rethinking its business, Silcorp Limited, owner of Mac's, Mike' Mart, Becker's, and Daisy Mart convenience stores, has emerged with on of the best balance sheets in the North American convenience stor

industry. By combining a sophisticated marketing philosophy born in the 1990s with a sense of the traditional neighbourhood store rooted in its past, Silcorp has developed a plan to tailor each of its stores to its particular community—a plan designed to take the company into the next century.

The original Mac's was founded in 1961 by retailer Kenny McGowan in Richmond Hill. A Scotsman by birth, McGowan adopted the name Mac's and came up with a cat in a tartan kilt as the symbol for his enterprise. By 1972, 375 Mac's convenience stores were operating throughout Ontario, and McGowan sold his chain to Silverwood Dairies, the largest dairy organization in Canada at that time.

Silverwood soon came to the conclusion that the convenience store business offered greater opportunities for future growth than the dairy industry. From 1975 to 1983, the company proceeded to divest itself of its dairy operations and focused on building its convenience store business in Canada. When its last dairy interest was sold in 1983, the company changed its name to Silcorp Limited.

While it was gradually pulling out of the dairy business, Silcorp continued to expand and evolve the nature of the Mac's chain, putting increasing emphasis on convenience items such as beverages, groceries, and non-food merchandise.

During the early 1970s, the company added stores in Manitoba, British Columbia, and Alberta, and in 1978, moved into the Saskatchewan market. A regional office was established in Calgary to oversee operation from the Ontario border to Vancouver Island. According to Kim Trowbridge, Vice-President, Western Canada, there were 31 Mac's stores in the region during the boom in the mid-1980s.

## "CHAIN OF ONE" CONCEPT

However, that same boom led to the over-saturation of convenience stores in North America, increased competition from wholesale clubs and drugstores, and financial difficulties for the industry in general. Downsizing reduced the number of Mac's stores in Western Canada to its current 237.

Silcorp also responded to changing times by developing its Store 2000 concept. This strategy involves considering each individual Mac's outlet as a "chain of one." The company plans for each Mac's store throughout the country to be

enovated and remerchandized ith a marketing approach tai-pred to meeting the particular eeds of the community where it perates. "The Tailored Market-ng Plan is really a return to our pots," says Trowbridge. "It akes us back to the traditional alues of the neighbourhood onvenience store, but not in a aditional store environment."

The Western Canada pro-ram is substantially different om what will be implement-d in Eastern Canada, notes rowbridge. "By design, the rogram is intended to reflect gional differences and con-mer preferences. In the West, e will be focusing on our offer-gs to customers, providing a esh, high-quality approach, s well as a sophisticated decor pgrade. There are also signifi-ant differences within the West-rn Canadian market, as well. lthough Western Canadians re eclectic and well informed, ven about U.S. trends, success-l programs in Calgary do not ecessarily translate well to ancouver."

One aspect of Silcorp's Store coo program involves the min-turization theory. The company searching the continent for accessful marketing concepts apply on a smaller scale. For

example, Silcorp is teaming with Seattle's Best Coffee—a Star-bucks competitor—to provide mini-cafés at selected Mac's stores. These self-serve mini-cafés provide a limited range of prod-ucts, but offer the excitement and "feel" of their larger coun-terparts while using only 50 square feet of space. The first mini-café, which opened in Victoria in 1996, has been a huge success.

Another aspect of the Store 2000 program involves a return to the neighbourhood store—with a twist. Silcorp is seeking out high-quality local suppliers to provide branded goods such as sandwiches and pastries. A nearby bakery, for example, would be able to gain another market for its products. "It's synergistic," says Trowbridge, "a win-win situation for every-one."

Trowbridge is enthusiastic about Silcorp's future. He notes that the six stores in the Victoria region, which were renovated in 1996, are already experienc-ing double-digit growth. There are 15 to 20 renovations planned for Alberta in 1997, with more than half of those targeted for Calgary.

"Calgary is a key market for us," he adds. "The economy

is vibrant and prosperous here." The company's regional office in Calgary employs about 30 people, and each of the 120 stores in Alberta averages five employees. Satellite offices, with about a half-dozen employees each, are located in every west-ern province.

"There's plenty of life in us yet," concludes Trowbridge. "This may not be traditional convenience marketing, but we want customers to recognize us as their local store and come to depend on us as such. We have been serving Calgarians for over 20 years and we plan to continu-ally reinvent ourselves to con-tinue to serve well beyond 20 more."

CLOCKWISE FROM LEFT:
IN AND AROUND CALGARY, SILCORP
IS FOCUSING ON PROVIDING A FRESH,
HIGH-QUALITY APPROACH, AS WELL
AS A SOPHISTICATED DECOR UPGRADE.

SILCORP IS TEAMING WITH SEATTLE'S
BEST COFFEE TO PROVIDE MINI-CAFÉS
AT SELECTED MAC'S STORES.

THESE SELF-SERVE MINI-CAFÉS PRO-
VIDE A LIMITED RANGE OF PRODUCTS,
BUT OFFER THE EXCITEMENT AND
"FEEL" OF THEIR LARGER COUNTER-
PARTS WHILE USING ONLY 50 SQUARE
FEET OF SPACE.

**I**N BUSINESS FOR MORE THAN 50 YEARS, TRIMAC CORPORATION'S ROOT date back to the 1930s, when Scottish immigrant and farmer Jack McCai first established a trucking company to haul milk. In 1945, McCaig an a partner launched Maccam Transport in Moose Jaw, Saskatchewa

marking the official beginning of what is today Trimac Corporation. With its purchase of Calgary-based H.M. Trimble & Sons in 1961, Trimac expanded into Alberta, tapping McCaig's son Bud to serve as president and moving its headquarters to Calgary. "My goal has always been to build a significant Canadian company based in Western Canada," says Bud McCaig. "By the mid-1960s, we saw ourselves as being more broadly in the transportation business. There were no national bulk carriers at that time, and we could see great opportunity for growth."

Today, Trimac Corporation is a bulk trucking and truck leasing business composed of Trimac Transportation Services Inc. and Rentway Ltd.; Bud McCaig remains chairman of the board, and his son Jeff serves as president and CEO.

### QUALITY, SERVICE, SAFETY

With more than 90 branches in North America, Trimac Transportation has grown from a one-truck operation to North America's premier bulk highway carrier. Trimac's fleet carries a wide variety of bulk products,

including cement, chemicals, metal ores, wood chips, food products, and grain.

Trimac Transportation prides itself on its reputation for innovation. The company was one of the first bulk haulers in North America to do two-way hauling with containers that could accommodate both liquids and dry bulk, and among the first in Canada to use lighter-weight aluminum trailers.

Rentway Ltd. provides truck fleet management services, including full-service leasing, rentals, and maintenance services across Canada and several proximate U.S. markets. All of Rentway's Canadian locations have achieved ISO 9002 ratings, assuring cus-

tomers that Rentway has met rigorous set of quality and servic criteria. An important presenc across Canada, Rentway operates the most extensive networ of heavy-duty truck shops in the country.

Trimac Transportation and Rentway are committed to both quality service and the continuous improvement of safety standards, and are both actively involved in industry associations to promote safety Trimac's operating personnel are specially trained to maintain a safe working environmer for employees, customers, and the general public, and this concern is reflected in the Trima Corporation's motto, Service with Safety.

### DIVERSIFICATION

Trimac diversified into the oil and gas business in 1977, and a corporate reorganization in early 1997 saw two entirely separate public companies emerge: Trimac Corporation retained the bulk trucking and truck leasing businesses, while Kenting Energy Services kept the contra drilling businesses. Trimac toda is a company focused on the transportation industry throug Trimac Transportation Service and Rentway.

Trimac's commitment to Calgary includes long-time co porate sponsorships that focu on health- and education-relate institutions, including the Unive sity of Calgary and the Partne in Health Program. An innovativ and growth-oriented company Trimac is sure to continue its long history of success well into the 21st century.

RENTWAY LTD. PROVIDES TRUCK FLEET MANAGEMENT SERVICES, INCLUDING FULL-SERVICE LEASING, RENTALS, AND MAINTENANCE SERVICES ACROSS CANADA AND SEVERAL PROXIMATE U.S. MARKETS.

A LIGHTWEIGHT, THREE-COMPARTMENT, STAINLESS STEEL LATEX SEMITRAILER STOPS NEAR THE GOLDEN GATE BRIDGE IN SAN FRANCISCO, CALIFORNIA.

OR MORE THAN THREE DECADES, PRUDENTIAL STEEL LTD. HAS GROWN within Western Canada by adding new products, introducing leading-edge technology, and watching the bottom line. ❁ Founded by four Calgarians in 1966 as a small pipe-making facility to serve the energy industry, the

company has since grown to become one of the largest Canadian manufacturers of steel tubular products for use in the oil and gas, construction, agriculture, fabrication, and mining industries. Over the years, Prudential has continuously expanded, quadrupling production at its 50-acre manufacturing site on the corner of Glenmore and Barlow Trails to more than 440,000 tonnes per year and employing 500 people. A further expansion is currently under way.

"The area was a cow pasture when we bought it," notes President and CEO Don Wilson. "The city has grown up around us."

## SERVICING THE ENERGY INDUSTRY

Prudential offers three main product lines: line pipe, oil country tubular goods (OCTG), and hollow structural sections (HSS). HSS is geared to the construction industry, line pipe is used for oil and gas gathering systems, and OCTG is used for oil and gas well drilling.

"Although we're a tubular steel manufacturer," says Wilson, "we really consider ourselves an oil and gas industry service company. The energy industry accounts for about 80 percent of our revenues."

"We have a close relationship with our customers," Wilson adds. "Drilling occurs 24 hours a day, and often we get calls in the middle of the night for pipe. We have to be on call 24 hours a day, with enough stock available to meet their requirements immediately." The company keeps inventory on hand in 20 locations in Western Canada to ensure quick delivery.

An emphasis on quality and innovation goes hand in hand with customer service. Prudential was the first pipe mill in Canada to achieve ISO 9001 certification, as well as the American Petroleum Institute's Q1 designation. And the company continues to introduce leading-edge technology in its manufacturing processes. A $13 million capital improvement program in 1994-1995 included the installation of the world's largest solid-state welder on a pipe mill. The technology has improved mill speeds, increased capacity, and further improved product quality and consistency.

In support of advancing technology, the company is also a funding partner for the Chair of Intelligent Manufacturing at the University of Calgary, which focuses on research into improving the automation of manufacturing processes.

Based in Calgary, Prudential is actively involved in community activities. Wilson sits on the board of the Calgary Exhibition and Stampede. The company also has close ties with Spruce Meadows, Calgary's world-quality equestrian facility, and sponsors the Prudential Steel Cup every year. Employees are also encouraged to volunteer in the community.

"When those four guys from Calgary started this company in 1966," sums up Wilson, "I'm sure they never envisioned the outcome."

FOUNDED BY FOUR CALGARIANS IN 1966 AS A SMALL PIPE-MAKING FACILITY TO SERVE THE ENERGY INDUSTRY, PRUDENTIAL STEEL LTD. HAS SINCE GROWN TO BECOME ONE OF THE LARGEST CANADIAN MANUFACTURERS OF STEEL TUBULAR PRODUCTS. FOR MORE THAN THREE DECADES, PRUDENTIAL HAS GROWN WITHIN WESTERN CANADA BY ADDING NEW PRODUCTS, INTRODUCING LEADING-EDGE TECHNOLOGY, AND WATCHING THE BOTTOM LINE.

IS PARENTS WERE PIONEERS IN ALBERTA WHEN THE PROVINCE WAS FIRS being developed. And Howard Gimbel, founder of the Gimbel Eye Centr and co-founder of Gimbel Vision International, Inc., is a pioneer in h own right. ✸ The story of Gimbel's career begins in the fall of 196.

CONVENIENT SCHEDULING, FAMILY INVOLVEMENT IN ALL ASPECTS OF CARE, AND EXTENSIVE EDUCATION PROGRAMS KEEP GIMBEL EYE CENTRE PATIENTS WELL INFORMED AND AT EASE (LEFT).

THE CENTRE HAS ADDED SEVERAL SUBSPECIALTIES, INCLUDING REFRACTIVE SURGERY FOR PEOPLE WITH NEARSIGHTEDNESS, FARSIGHTEDNESS, AND ASTIGMATISM (RIGHT).

when he returned to his birthplace of Calgary to set up an ophthalmology practice. During the first 17 years of practicing general ophthalmology, Gimbel took care of the needs of more than 60,000 Calgarians.

He soon became known as "gadget Gimbel," because of the array of diagnostic instruments he acquired for examining eyes. By 1974, his interest in technology motivated him to become the first surgeon in Canada to use an ultrasonic probe to remove cataracts by phacoemulsification. This procedure was one of a growing number of small-incision surgeries that have revolutionized medicine in the past two decades. These surgeries are less invasive than conventional surgeries, promoting quicker healing and reducing associated health risks.

Frustrated with the growing waiting list at the hospital in the early '80s, Gimbel began offering small-incision cataract surgery with intraocular lens implants in an out-of-hospital setting. Gimbel's wife, Judy, with a master's in public health, joined the organization full-time as its chief administrator in 1982. Because of his commitment to competent, compassionate, convenient care, Judy immediately expanded her husband's already comprehensive high-tech diagnostics and developed the first out-of-hospital outpatient surgical centre to accommodate the long list of patients desiring eye exams and surgery. This led to the opening of his privately owned and operated facility, the Gimbel Eye Surgical Centre, in 1984.

Maintaining his interest in new technologies, Gimbel and

his associates began using a spe cial laser to manage secondary cataracts and to perform delicate internal eye procedures— the first place in Canada to use the YAG laser for eye surgery.

## REFRACTIVE SURGERY FUELS GROWTH

The Gimbel Eye Centre has continued to expand in size and scope, and currently encom passes 33,000 square feet in the Market Mall Professional Building. Several subspecialties have been added, including refractive surgery for people with nearsightedness, farsightedness, and astigmatism. In fac one of Gimbel's associates, Dr John van Westenbrugge, performed Canada's first excimer laser surgery to correct nearsightedness in 1990.

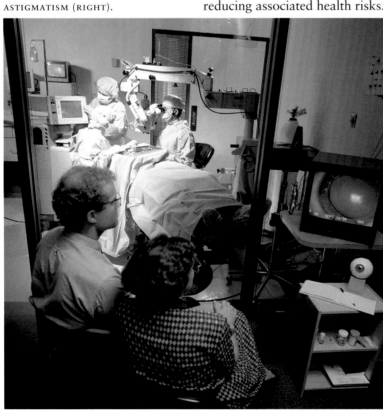

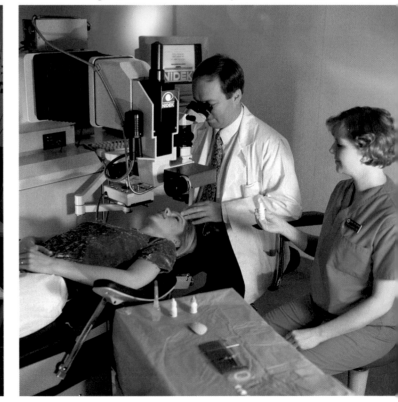

The success of this procedure prompted the establishment of satellite offices. The first one, in Edmonton, opened in 1990, and another opened in Saskatoon in 1994. In 1994, Gimbel Vision International, Inc. (GVI) was founded to pioneer further expansion opportunities, and new centres were established in Toronto and Vancouver, British Columbia, and Las Vegas, Nevada. A public company that owns the refractive surgery portion of Gimbel Eye Centre, GVI provides partners with a wide range of professional support, including staff and physician training, clinical and surgical systems, marketing information systems, and other consultation services. In addition to North America, GVI is focusing its efforts in the Asia-Pacific area and in South America. Fourteen new ophthalmic centres are expected to be opened by the end of 1997, in countries such as China, Thailand, Brazil, and Australia.

## DEDICATION TO PATIENT CARE

Dedication to patient care has been an ongoing commitment at Gimbel Eye Centre. Convenient scheduling, family involvement in all aspects of care, and extensive education programs keep patients well informed and at ease.

Increasingly aware of the links between general health and eye diseases, Gimbel and his associates are active in preventive health education and counseling. For example, high cholesterol can be a factor in some eye diseases that cause blindness. The centre has conducted free cholesterol screenings to increase public awareness of this link, and now offers a registered dietitian and doctor of public health to analyze patients' lifestyles for current risk factors and to counsel them on their overall health.

Gimbel and his associates also contribute to the body of knowledge in the world of ophthalmology through clinical research programs on cataract and refractive surgery, glaucoma, anterior segment surgery, and prevention of eye disease.

Surgeons come from all parts of the world to learn and observe the techniques Gimbel has developed. Gimbel also broadcasts live surgeries by satellite to large groups of doctors attending well-known international meetings in North and South America, Europe, and Japan. He has produced numerous videos and articles for peer-reviewed journals and professional magazines, as well as written chapters for several medical books. In addition, a fellowship program at Gimbel Eye Centre trains one or two doctors a year in clinical, research, and surgical aspects of cataract and refractive ophthalmology.

After 20 years of teaching and the development of numerous new techniques, Gimbel is recognized and often honoured at the frequent meetings he attends. In 1992, he received the Alberta Order of Excellence for his ability to combine technical excellence with the art of caring in an atmosphere of open communication. He was commended for using innovation to raise the standards of medical care in Alberta, and for his global influence as an educator at the forefront of microsurgical developments. And in 1996, he was voted one of the top ophthalmologists in the world by his peers.

Gimbel has been a guest speaker at Harvard, Tufts, and Johns Hopkins universities; the Mayo Clinic; and Cleveland Clinic—to name only a few—and is on the faculty at the University of Calgary, the University of California at San Francisco, and Loma Linda University.

"I'm grateful for having been able to help so many people enhance their vision," Gimbel says. He has a special soft spot for his older patients. "It's especially gratifying to help the people of my parents' generation—the true pioneers of Alberta," he says. Carrying on the pioneering tradition begun by his parents, Gimbel and his associates worldwide will continue to help many more people in the years to come.

GIMBEL EYE CENTRE USES THE LATEST TECHNOLOGY IN EYE CARE (TOP).

JUDY AND HOWARD GIMBEL ARE COMMITTED TO COMPETENT, COMPASSIONATE, CONVENIENT EYE CARE (BOTTOM).

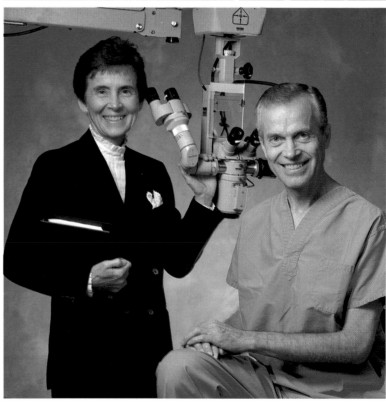

**F**OR TRI-LINE FREIGHT SYSTEMS, GOOD THINGS COME IN THREES. THRE small Western Canadian trucking companies, each with its own mark niche, realized that they could improve their efficiency by merging. S Tri-Line Expressways Ltd. was formed April 16, 1964, with 35 trucks ar

revenues of about $1.3 million per year.

Tri-Line started operations as a private company, went public on the Toronto Stock Exchange in the late 1980s, and is now one of the most profitable private holdings of Eastern Canadian firm Russell Metals Inc. And three is still an important number, as the company now operates in three countries: Canada, the United States, and Mexico. Currently celebrating its 33rd year, the company has grown substantially since the early days. With more than 500 trucks and 800 employees and owner-operators, it is one of the largest trucking companies in the country, with

annual sales in excess of $100 million.

### FIVE DIVISIONS PROVIDE ULTIMATE EFFICIENCY

Tri-Line is structured into five divisions. Two of these—the flatbed and van divisions—account for more than 80 percent of revenues. The flatbed division carries commodities that require crane or forklift loading, such as steel, lumber, and construction equipment. The van division carries dry freight not needing heat or refrigeration, while the reefer division carries goods requiring heat or refrigeration. The fourth division—Tri-Line High-Tech Express—is experi-

encing strong growth. This division hauls expensive, fragile high-tech machinery, such as hospital equipment and compu ers. And finally, the company's logistics division brokers out surplus loads to other trucking companies.

Improving efficiency has always been a focus for Tri-Lin The merger helped ensure tha Tri-Line trucks hauled full loa both ways in the three wester provinces. When it became cle in the early 1970s that truckir couldn't compete with the rail system in transporting goods to Eastern Canada, Tri-Line began to develop a north-sout route. Commodities from British Columbia, Alberta, and Saskatchewan were hauled to Texas and Oklahoma, with oi industry, mining, and farming equipment and supplies makin the return trip to Western Canada. By the late 1980s, Eastern Canada was added as the third point in the triangle, since it made economic sense to haul manufacturing supplie from the southern United State to Ontario and Quebec.

At the same time, Tri-Line added Mexico to its route. Th company's first Mexican job involved transporting 40 truc loads of Christmas trees from southern British Columbia to Mexico City. Tri-Line also transported Mexico's first Ker tucky Fried Chicken store, ori ginally built in Calgary. And the company regularly hauls lumber and prefabricated mater als for the increasing number of Calgarians building homes in Mexico. "Although the de-

luing of the peso has reduced
 me opportunities in Mexico
is past year," notes President
d Chief Operating Officer
om Payne, "the Mexicans are
ll anxious for North American
ods, as well as raw plastic,
emicals, and unassembled
oducts.

"Canadian companies like
i-Line are not permitted to
nsport goods within Mexico,"
yne explains further, "so
e haul loads to the border at
redo, Texas, where our pad-
cked trailers are loaded onto
ower units owned by a Mexi-
n trucking company. The
ansfer itself only takes about
e hour and the goods arrive
e way they were shipped
iginally. Nothing goes miss-
g." Not surprisingly, shipments
Mexico account for a grow-
g portion of the company's
venues.

### FROM DRAGLINES TO DINOSAURS

e largest project ever under-
ken by Tri-Line involved trans-
orting mining equipment from
icago to British Columbia.
is job involved 125 trucks
uling pieces of a huge dragline
be assembled at a coal mine
southern British Columbia.

At the other end of the
ectrum, one of the company's
ost valuable shipments involved
rrying an entire set of ancient,
agile dinosaur bones from
umheller, Alberta, to Calgary,
d then on to Vancouver, where
e bones were loaded on a 747
ound for Japan.

The company is ready to
ckle virtually anything. "We've
ubled in size in the past five
six years," says Payne, "and
'll continue to grow. Other
cking companies suffered
om the recession in the early
90s. Many of them shut down.

We did some downsizing then,
too—but if you downsize too
much, you lose opportunities
for growth. We're continuing
to grow because of our confidence, our commitment, and
our ability to respond quickly."

Customer service for Tri-Line
means having trucks available
for customers when and where
they are needed. The company
has direct terminal facilities in
Vancouver, Edmonton, Calgary,
Regina, Saskatoon, Winnipeg,
Thunder Bay, Toronto, and
Montreal, as well as Houston,
Texas. Agents' offices are located

in Medicine Hat; Halifax;
Dryden, Ontario; and Laredo.

The company also takes
advantage of technology to
enhance customer service. All
trucks can be tracked by satellite, so customers know exactly
when shipments will arrive. "No
one carrries inventory anymore,"
explains Payne. "It's too costly.
Customers expect—and we
provide—just-in-time delivery."

Safety is another aspect
of Tri-Line's customer service
strategy. A full-time environmental manager ensures that
all safety and environmental
regulations are met and that
all employees are well trained
in safety procedures. The company was one of the founders
and participates in the Partners
in Compliance program jointly
sponsored by Provincial Government and the trucking industry.
"We want to set a standard for
the industry we can be proud
of," says Payne.

Threes may be lucky for
Tri-Line, but hard work and
commitment pay off in the end.
As the company's slogan says,
"Your country is Tri-Line
country."

CELEBRATING 33 YEARS OF BUSINESS,
TRI-LINE IS PROUD TO SERVE CANADA,
THE UNITED STATES, AND MEXICO
(TOP).

TRI-LINE'S 1929 FORD IN FRONT OF
THE HISTORIC WAINWRIGHT HOTEL
IN CALGARY'S HERITAGE PARK
(BOTTOM).

TRUE TESTAMENT TO ALBERTA'S PIONEERING SPIRIT, SHAW N Slopes Golf Course is the culmination of one family's vision for t future. Although originally situated on Calgary's outskirts, Shaw Nee now surrounded by new development; many Calgarians assume t

course is as new as the nearby suburban communities, but Shaw Nee was built in 1964 and has been in operation since 1965. Now sporting lush, well-groomed, mature greens and large trees, it is one of Calgary's few semi-private golf courses, open to both members and visitors alike. "We'll make room for anyone from out of town," says Director Eleanor Turnquist. "We want to extend that famous Calgary hospitality."

### CARRYING OUT
### THE VISION

The history of Shaw Nee goes back many decades prior to 1965. In fact, the story starts in 1883, when after a long, arduous journey from Kent, England, Turnquist's great-grandfather, S.W. Shaw, settled in the area called Midnapore with his family and became one of Calgary's earliest pioneers. Since that time, the land—mostly used for farming—stayed in the family, until Turnquist's father, S. William

Shaw II, had a vision.

"My father was a futurist," says Turnquist. "He knew the land would be developed one day and he wanted to preserve a visible piece of our homestead. At that time, there were very few public courses in Calgary— and only a handful of municipal courses. Golf was not a priority sport. He wanted to build a course that would be accessible and affordable for the average Calgarian."

William Shaw built his golf course and was active in its operation until he died in 1990, passing on the business to his three daughters: Turnquist, Mary Bamford, and Lori Rehman. The sisters are proud of their father's vision and their family legacy.

"As a family and as individuals, we have been associated with Calgary all of our lives," says Turnquist. "Dad was an honourary lifetime member in many golf organizations. With his background in agriculture and road construction, he made

significant contributions to golfing in Calgary. He was recognized by other people in the golf business as a resour person you could approach tc answer questions, help solve problems, and get new ideas.

From the start, Shaw involved his entire family in the operation of Shaw Nee Slope His children contributed to th golf course's operations at a young age, driving mowers, repairing equipment, and wor ing in the office. Their mothe was executive chef in the earl years. And even now, under the current management of the three sisters, their father's vision is still being upheld.

### OFFERING ALL
### THE SERVICES

With 300 active members, most of them living in nearby southern Calgary communitie Shaw Nee Slopes still strives to provide affordable golfing opportunities for the average Calgarian. Now considered a

SPORTING LUSH, WELL-GROOMED, MATURE GREENS AND LARGE TREES, SHAW NEE SLOPES GOLF COURSE IS ONE OF CALGARY'S FEW SEMI- PRIVATE GOLF COURSES, OPEN TO BOTH MEMBERS AND VISITORS ALIKE.

...ner-city golf course—located ...nly 20 minutes from down-...own—there are a full 18 holes; ...fully stocked pro shop, man-...ged by an accredited golf pro-...ssional; a complete practice ...cility; electric carts; and a ...ll-service food and beverage ...peration serviced by an accred-...ed chef, and including a ban-...uet facility for 200 people that ...available for year-round use ...y the general public. The sum-...ertime support staff numbers ...bout 80.

In addition to men's and ...dies' programs, Shaw Nee ...ffers a junior program that ...rovides a number of educational ...pportunities, including tourna-...ents, for about 80 youngsters ...learn and practise the sport. ...ennis courts are also part of ...e operation; in the summer, ...tennis pro is available to give ...ssons.

"We don't have oak lockers ...the members' lounges," notes ...urnquist. "Our main emphasis ...to provide an excellent play-...g field—as good as you would ...nd anywhere in Calgary—at ...very competitive price.

"We think our course is user ...iendly," she adds. "Novice ...olfers should be able to have ...n enjoyable time and not be ...oo frustrated, but the course

remains challenging for the refined player."

According to Turnquist, the course is especially appre-ciated by women, whose pres-ence on North American golf courses has skyrocketed in the past five years. Women have full membership rights and privileges at Shaw Nee Slopes and can play at any time. There is a popular nonmember Cham-pagne League for women, as well.

The next generation of the family—William Shaw's grandchildren and S.W. Shaw's great-great-grandchildren—now numbers 10 members, who range from 11 to 31 years old. Al-though only one grandchild works directly in the golfing business—for the Canadian Golf Foundation in Toronto—

their grandfather's vision has had an impact on each of their lives. They all pitch in at Shaw Nee, when required, providing their own special expertise—whether it's an MBA, or mech-anical, accounting, or culinary skills—to help the family busi-ness and preserve the family's heritage.

And, of course, they all play golf—except for Turnquist, whose idea of relaxation is time away from golfing. "Our chil-dren seem to be exploring their individual destinies," notes Turnquist, "but they will always be tied to the land and the family heritage." And William Shaw's dream of preserving a piece of the original homestead will continue to live on in the well-groomed greens of Shaw Nee Slopes Golf Course.

ITH ITS FLAGSHIP PRODUCT, OASyS® (OPEN ARCHITECTURE SYSTEM) Valmet Automation's SAGE Systems Division has captured an unprec-edented 55 percent share of the North American oil and gas pipeline automation market, and is now expanding its position in the electric and water utility industries both at home and abroad.

The organization's roots took hold in Calgary in the early seventies with the founding of SA Engineering, a pipeline auto-mation systems business. The company was subsequently bought in 1986 by Finnish glo-bal industrial conglomerate Valmet. "This represented an increased focus for Valmet in the energy and environment markets," says Dave Jardine, Senior Vice-President and Busi-ness Unit Chief Executive. "Val-met had little previous experience in the pipeline industry, but our success has made us extremely visible to our parent. We are family now."

USING INNOVATIVE TECHNOLOGY AND A NONPROPRIETARY, OPEN ARCHI-TECTURE, OASyS RUNS ON GENERAL PURPOSE COMPUTER PLATFORMS AND IS EASILY INTEGRATED WITH LEADING NETWORKING AND RELATIONAL DATA-BASE PRODUCTS.

## SUCCESS OF THE OASYS SYSTEM

With the Valmet purchase came an infusion of capital, and the development of the OASyS SCADA and Information Man-agement System for remote monitoring and control of crude oil, gas, and refined products pipelines. "Our first major sale was to the Colonial Pipe Line Company in the United States," says Jardine. "This was a very significant contract: The 8,500-kilometre-long Colonial Pipe Line is the world's longest common-carrier refined prod-ucts pipeline. By successfully completing that project, we proved that we could handle just about anything."

OASyS expands the role of the SCADA platform beyond its traditional boundaries to in-clude operations and business management functions such as electronic flow measurement. For electric utilities, OASyS provides distribution and energy management. And for water utilities, OASyS interfaces with laboratory systems that monitor drinking water quality.

Using innovative technol-ogy and a nonproprietary, open architecture, OASyS runs on general purpose computer plat-forms and is easily integrated with leading networking and relational database products. The SAGE Division also manu-factures its own specialized remote terminal units (RTUs). Valmet's systems have built a reputation for saving custom-ers money and reducing environ-mental and public risk through the detection of leaks. In 1995 SAGE Systems won the coveted Alberta Science and Technology ASTECH award for commer-cialization of innovative tech-nology developed in Alberta. "The product continues to prove its value to the market-place," says Jardine.

## THE ELECTRIC AND WATER UTILITY MARKETS

Another milestone in the divi-sion's history was the 1988 purchase of Tejas Controls Inc., a Houston, Texas-based company specializing in electric utility automation systems. "That purchase built up a strong position in the automation of electricity generation, transmis-sion, and distribution," notes Jardine. "Leveraging Tejas' position and adding the OASyS ingredient, we have made sub-stantial headway, as evidenced by high-profile projects such as automation of electrical dis-tribution for Cairo East Distri-bution Company in the city of Cairo, and for the New York City Transit Authority," says Jardine.

"The need for high-quality drinking water is obvious, but people are also realizing that water shouldn't be wasted," says Jardine. "Globally, our technology is becoming important to water utility managers who have selected our systems in Calgary, Lethbridge, and Winnipeg, as well as Helsinki; Houston; and Las Vegas, Nevada, to mention only a few."

The business climate is also changing. "Deregulation brought new appreciation for improved efficiency and competitiveness," says Jardine. He predicts that oil and gas pipeline, electric, and water industries will begin to integrate common aspects of their operations, such as SCADA. Jardine notes, "It's already happening, and we're in an ideal position to take on these projects, since we're the only major player with an established track record in all three industries."

## INTERNATIONAL GROWTH

While North America accounts for approximately 60 percent of the SAGE Division's sales, the international market is growing. The division's association with its well-known parent has also opened some doors. Valmet maintains offices in St. Petersburg and Moscow, Russia, where the division has installed its own Russian-speaking representatives to work with customers like Russian natural gas giant Gazprom.

In addition to a half-dozen systems in China, the division has installations in Argentina, Brazil, Colombia, Mexico, and Peru, and recently scored its first Middle East success with a multimillion-dollar project for Saudi Arabia's Aramco—the largest oil producer in the world. In 1995, Valmet's Calgary team won an Alberta Govern-

ment Economic Development and Tourism award for its international marketing success.

The Calgary office has approximately 230 employees and there are a further 160 people in the Houston office. Both locations have well-equipped centres for training foreign and domestic customers. "We try to hire local graduates in computer science and engineering," says Jardine. Approximately 60 employees are dedicated to research and development, which accounts for about 8 percent of the division's budget.

"While OASyS established a new paradigm when it was introduced," notes Jardine, "it's becoming increasingly difficult to maintain a competitive edge based on technology alone. We are chiefly judged on our ability

to take on large projects and deliver them successfully—to work hand in hand with our customers and partners in a collaborative environment. Our mission is simple: to achieve global leadership in the business by concentrating on making our customers successful. Given the new challenges our customers face due to globalization, new economic and competitive paradigms, and rapid technological advances, we need to be there for them over the long term to give them peace of mind and to assist them in improving their delivery systems." Says Jardine, "We provide this support with the best people, our people, and our foundation product, OASyS, combined to deliver world-class automation solutions."

FOR ELECTRIC UTILITIES, SUCH AS SAN DIEGO GAS & ELECTRIC COMPANY, OASYS PROVIDES DISTRIBUTION AND ENERGY MANAGEMENT.

"'M JUST AN OLD-FASHIONED INNKEEPER," SAYS SAM WONG, GENERAL manager of the International Hotel of Calgary. "Other hotel managers may hide behind a desk, but I'm rarely in my office. I run a small, intimate hotel where I know all the guests and always have time to have a coffee."

Located in the heart of downtown Calgary, the 35-storey, 250-suite International Hotel first opened in June 1970. It has since undergone two complete renovations, and with its emphasis on personalized guest services and extra amenities, the International has no trouble competing with large chain hotels.

The International offers each guest a luxurious, air-conditioned suite at a price normally charged for a single hotel room. The suites range in size from 590 to 800 square feet and include a living room, one or two bedrooms, and either a minibar area or a full kitchen. Complimentary newspapers, remote control cable televisions, and in-room coffee makers are standard for every suite.

In addition, the International provides a full fitness spa with indoor pool, whirlpool, gym, sauna, and in-house massage, as well as a full-service restaurant and three-level lounge. The penthouse on the 35th floor is available for receptions of up to 120 people, and a well-appointed corporate boardroom is available for business meetings.

### CATERING TO SPECIAL NEEDS

The hotel is a favourite for film stars and crews, and Clint Eastwood, Bill Cosby, and Paul Newman have all been guests at the International. It has been the hotel of choice for other celebrities as well, such as Dr. Jane Goodall and the Prince of Monaco. In fact, Wong hosts a by-invitation-only monthly luncheon to allow members of the media to meet and interview some of his famous guests.

Business people also like to stay at the International, which offers a variety of amenities for business travellers, including computer hookups and two telephones in every room. Also, even though the hotel is a convenient walking distance to all downtown locations, a complimentary shuttle service is available on weekday mornings. "This is a nice touch," notes Wong, "especially in the winter months."

While Wong himself is a Calgary institution, he says his hardworking, dedicated staff should be given credit for allowing him the time to devote to public relations activities and to cater to his guests' needs.

"I'm fortunate that most of the staff have been here for a very long time," Wong says. "More than 40 percent of our staff are long-term employees, and that's unusual for a hotel, where the turnover rate is usually quite high." Still, he takes the time to check in with each department every day to ensure the operation is running smoothly.

And run smoothly it does. With Wong at the helm, the International will continue to please guests with its extra amenities, personal service, and luxurious suites for many years to come.

SUITES AT THE INTERNATIONAL RANGE IN SIZE FROM 590 TO 800 SQUARE FEET AND INCLUDE A LIVING ROOM, ONE OR TWO BEDROOMS, AND EITHER A MINIBAR AREA OR A FULL KITCHEN (RIGHT).

THE INTERNATIONAL HOTEL FEATURES A LUXURIOUS CORPORATE BOARDROOM PERFECT FOR SMALL TO MEDIUM-SIZED BUSINESS MEETINGS (LEFT).

OR ALMOST 25 YEARS, CANADIAN HUNTER EXPLORATION LTD. HAS EARNED a reputation in the energy industry as a successful, spirited gas exploration and development company. Founded in 1973, the Canadian Hunter style was set from the beginning under the leadership of John Masters, now re-

red, and current Chairman nd CEO Jim Gray.

Masters and Gray left the algary-based, American oil rm Kerr-McGee to start up eir own exploration comany in Calgary, focusing on Western Canada. Canadian unter was established as a holly owned subsidiary of oronto's Noranda, Inc., a versified natural resources mpany operating in three ctors: mining and minerals, rest products, and oil and s.

Canadian Hunter's first al was to hire exceptionally pable people. "The easiest ay to make money is to surund yourself with excellent ople," said Masters at the me. "You select quality peoe and that solves much of ur problems." With the presce of talented people, decion making could be spread roughout the company, relting in a flat organization ith committed, involved nployees.

## RAPID RISE TO LEADERSHIP

he company's first big breakrough came in 1975 with e discovery of Elmworth, e of the largest gas fields on e continent. That discovery tapulted the company into position of leadership and spect in the industry. Almost years later, about 80 pernt of the company's producon is still focused on gas, with w-cost operating areas in rthern and southwestern berta and in British Columa. The company is one of

Canada's larger gas producers. "We built the company to succeed in Western Canada," says Gray. "That was—and still is—our focus."

Gray is also banking on a bright future for natural gas from the Western Canada Sedimentary Basin. "Canada is an increasingly important part of the North American gas equation," says Gray.

In its efforts to achieve a balanced technical and economic strategy, Canadian Hunter continues to take advantage of technology wherever possible, and to hone its technical skills, as well as its focus on quality. The company has developed a reputation in the industry for conducting business in a responsive rather than an adversarial manner.

"We're not here to tell people we're the biggest," says Gray, "but I do believe we're among the best." The company hopes to maintain its strong economic performance in the top quartile of the industry.

An important factor in Canadian Hunter's success has

been its focus on people and its commitment to achieving a positive balance between performance and caring. A caring attitude and strong interpersonal skills are part of each employee's repertoire, whether he or she is dealing with another employee, business associate, or member of the community. The fact that the company is one of the few with 100 percent of employees contributing to the United Way is one sign of a caring attitude.

"Businesses aren't simply about money," confirms Gray. "They're also about people. Being a caring company results in a competitive advantage."

CLOCKWISE FROM TOP: MEMBERS OF THE CANADIAN HUNTER STRATEGY RETREAT team INCLUDE CHAIRMAN AND CEO JIM GRAY (FIFTH FROM LEFT, STANDING) AND PRESIDENT STEVE SAVIDANT (SEVENTH FROM LEFT, STANDING).

NORANDA BOARD OF DIRECTORS VISIT A CANADIAN HUNTER PLANT.

JOHN MASTERS (RIGHT), NOW RETIRED, AND CURRENT CHAIRMAN AND CEO JIM GRAY SURVEY THE COMPANY'S FIRST BIG BREAKTHROUGH—ELMWORTH, ONE OF THE LARGEST GAS FIELDS ON THE CONTINENT.

PB WIRELINE SERVICES IS THE CANADIAN SUBSIDIARY OF THE PRIVATEL held British oil field service company Wireline Holdings Ltd. Known as th "open hole well specialists," and using its own brand of leading-edge, pro prietary equipment, BPB Wireline Services provides specialized nich

market well logging and evaluation services for energy and mining companies throughout the world.

The company owes its formation to the current Chairman, D.R. "Dick" Reeves, who developed lightweight logging techniques for use in exploring for gypsum for his former employer, the Mining Department of BPB Industries—the leading European plasterboard manufacturer. The techniques were developed principally to delineate subsurface gypsum deposits found within boreholes and to determine the major gypsum, anhydride, and marl content. The solutions provided by the logs were of such quality that BPB Industries suggested that their use could be valuable to the British National Coal Board in determining the thickness and quality of coal seams. This highly successful application, coming at a time of great interest in worldwide coal exploration, proved to be the springboard to overwhelming wireline interest, with the result that in 1969 BPB Industries found its own service department becoming a profit contributor.

In 1970, BPB Industries set up a subsidiary company, BPB Wireline Services, to develop its interest in wireline activity. The mandate of the new company was to actively pursue the commercial opportunities associated with developing "slimline logging" techniques. In no time, the company became a world leader, particularly in coal exploration, with operations in the United Kingdom, Europe, South Africa, Australia, Indonesia, and North America.

A BPB OIL FIELD WELL LOGGING UNIT TRAVELS THROUGH THE ROCKY MOUNTAINS IN ALBERTA.

As worldwide demand for coal exploration services waned, the company moved into the oil and gas sector in the early 1980s, offering conventional oil field open hole services.

"Our first oil field units were introduced in Lloydminster in 1982," says Canadian President Edgar Hulatt. "We survived the National Energy Policy, the oil price crash of 1986, and all of the other ups and downs of the cyclical oil and gas industry. Many people figured we wouldn't make it."

The success of the Canadian operation made an important contribution to a management and staff buy out of BPB Wireline Services from its parent company in 1995. The new private company, U.K.-based Wireline Holdings Ltd., is owned by a majority of its employees.

The Canadian head office is located in Calgary, and operational management, with extensive servicing and technical support, is based in Red Deer. Field units are situated in Grand Prairie, Whitecourt, Lloydminste Medicine Hat, and Red Deer. Each district includes local ma agement, calibration facilities, and quality assurance/maintenance programs.

## R&D—A CRITICAL STRENGTH

In Western Canada, BPB Wire line Services provides resistivit nuclear, acoustic, imaging, an computational services for the evaluation of exploration and development wells. Equipmen manufacture and major researc and development efforts remain at the company's corporate hea office in East Leake, United Kingdom, just south of Nottin ham. Some development is car ried out in Red Deer.

Historically, all profits ha been invested back into researc and development. BPB Wirelin Services brought to market a

lly integrated digital logging
stem in 1982. One year later,
e company introduced the
rst array induction tool.

ne of BPB Wireline Services'
rengths is its internal software
epartment, which, through
s own innovations, brought
market the world's first dip-
eter logs processed real time.
1990, the company also ran
e world's first and shortest
uintuple tool combination
a well in Western Canada.

BPB Wireline Services assists
wide range of clients, ranging
om the major and intermediate
l and gas companies to small
dependents. "We're a small
mpany providing service in
niche market," remarks Hulatt.
s such, we offer a number
strengths. For example, our
les force is very stable. Our
ents deal with the same expe-
enced salespeople year after
ar, building solid, long-term
lationships."

Another strength is the
mpany's flat organizational
ructure. When necessary, cli-
ts can deal directly with the
ople in the United Kingdom
ho design and manufacture
e equipment. Employee own-
ship also ensures that each
aff member has a vested inter-
t in helping the company
cceed.

"In a business dominated
very large, well-capitalized

companies, we've done it our
own way and had success," notes
Hulatt, who, true to his British
roots, takes a fiscally conservative,
long-term approach to helping
the company weather the ups
and downs of the Canadian oil
and gas industry. "Our goal is
to provide high-quality data in
a safe and efficient manner."

## SLIMHOLE APPLICATIONS GROWING

BPB Wireline Services' most
recent venture is the offering
of slimoil logging tools, similar
to the ones originally used by
Reeves to find gypsum and coal
in Britain, but this time in the
oil and gas market. "As the industry moves to smaller diam-
eter holes to reduce drilling costs,
our slimoil logging services are

becoming increasingly valuable,"
says Hulatt.

Slimoil tools can be used
in a variety of situations where
conventionally sized tools will
not fit (for example, slim vertical wells running through the
drill pipe past difficult well conditions, or horizontal wells with
tight build radii sections). Slimoil
tools have diameters between
1.5 to 2.25 inches, contrasting
with 3.5 to 5.5 inches in diam-
eter for conventional tools.

With a reputation for innovative technology and operational efficiency established over
25 years, BPB Wireline Services
is a leader in providing both open
hole and slimhole logging services. It is this tradition of success that the company plans to
continue long into the next
century.

CLOCKWISE FROM TOP LEFT:
AN EXPERIENCED AND DEDICATED
TEAM OF PROFESSIONALS PROVIDES
TECHNICAL AND INTERPRETATIONAL
SUPPORT TO CLIENTS.

A FIELD ENGINEER RETRIEVES A
DIPMETER SONDE FOLLOWING THE
ACQUISITION OF SUBSURFACE DATA.

DATA PROCESSING PERSONNEL RECEIVE
WELL LOG DATA DIRECT FROM A WELL
SITE VIA SATELLITE.

anCANADIAN PETROLEUM LIMITED IS AMONG THE TOP THREE OIL AND GA[S] producers in Canada. One of Canada's most active drillers, with a drilling suc[cess] cess ratio regularly above 80 percent, PanCanadian has experienced unprec[edented] edented growth in recent years. In fact, the company has doubled in size i[n]

the last five years, with plans to double again in the next five.

"Our goal is to be a leading global energy company in the exploration for and production of oil, gas, and natural gas liquids," says President and CEO David Tuer. Unlike other oil companies who have experienced downsizing in recent years, Tuer believes that in order to grow, companies must add resources—not take them away. "Our current slogan is Double Up in Five—although growth also must be accomplished in an economic and efficient manner."

## A LONG HISTORY

PanCanadian's roots go back almost to the beginning of the Canadian Confederation, when important transportation links began to tie the country together. The company grew out of the Canadian Pacific Railway (CPR), which received cash payments and land grants in return for building the TransCanada Railway. The CPR sold some of this land to settlers, but retained the mineral rights. By the time the railway was completed, the company owned the petroleum or petroleum and natural gas rights for a total of 9.6 million acres of land.

By 1958, the CPR decided to create the Canadian Pacific Oil and Gas Company (CPOG) to hold these mineral rights and to undertake an aggressive oil exploration and production program. Amalgamation of CPOG and Central-Del Rio Oils took effect on December 31, 1971, and the merged compan[y] was called PanCanadian Petroleum Limited.

## DOMESTIC AND INTERNATIONAL OPERATIONS

After rationalizing its vast lan[d] holdings, PanCanadian now holds more than 10 million net acres of highly prospective, undeveloped land. Its holdings are primarily in Alberta, Saskatchewan, and Manitoba, but extend into northeastern British Columbia and offshore of Canada's East Coast. Tradi[tional] tional oil and gas field operation[s] are located in Brooks, Drumheller, Elk Point, Hardisty, Ponoka/Grande Prairie, Provost, Weyburn, and offshore Nova Scotia. In the mid-1990s, drilling activities were initiate[d] in western Newfoundland.

At the same time, the com[pany's] pany's profile on the internationa[l] scene is changing significantly. Through acquisition, and by forming alliances with other companies, PanCanadian has established a presence in the North Sea, South Africa, Aus[tralia,] tralia, and Venezuela, and is currently researching other opportunities in South Americ[a.] A significant part of the company's future growth is expecte[d] to be derived from international activities, which will complemen[t] production from the Western Canadian Sedimentary Basin.

## TECHNOLOGY DEVELOPMENT

One of PanCanadian's key strengths, according to Tuer, is its expertise in heavy oil. It

DOUBLING THE COMPANY'S PRODUC-
TION BETWEEN 1997 AND 2002 IS
THE KEY FOCUS OF PANCANADIAN'S
1,600 EMPLOYEES AND ITS HUNDREDS
OF CONTRACTORS.

a leader in developing new
heavy oil technology such as
downhole oil/water separators,
and rodless screw pumps. The
company is also the world's
largest user of slant drilling,
which has helped reduce capital
costs by up to 25 percent and
trimmed operating costs.

In support of the continuing
development of new technology,
PanCanadian was one of the
first companies in Canada
to appoint a chief technology
officer. "I believe we commit
our funds wisely for research,"
says Tuer, "and our people are
recognized worldwide for their
expertise."

In recent years, PanCanadian
has also diversified into the
production and marketing of
electric energy. For example,
the company has acquired a
25 percent interest in a 100-
megawatt, cogeneration project
near Kingston, Ontario. For the
life of the project, the company
will supply 22 million cubic feet
of gas per day. A U.S. subsidiary
provides natural gas and electricity services to producers,
industrials, utilities, and retail
markets throughout the United
States, and markets all of Pan-
Canadian's gas sold directly in
the United States, as well as
third-party producer volumes.

## GIVING BACK TO
## THE COMMUNITY

A major source of pride for Tuer
is PanCanadian's commitment
to the communities where it operates. The company is regularly
recognized for its community
service activities and recently
received an award for outstanding community support from
Mayor Al Duerr of Calgary.

The company's numerous
local activities, many of them
in support of youth, education,
and the arts, include the sponsorship of the first Students'
Choice Awards for Teachers

in the Calgary public school
system, as well as sponsorship
of cultural events such as Alberta
Theatre Project's playRites.
PanCanadian also supports local
crime prevention and administers
the Police and Community Telephone (PACT) program, which
alerts community residents to
crimes in their neighbourhoods.

In addition, PanCanadian
works to develop positive relations with the people living in
the communities where it operates. "We want to develop a
mutually beneficial environment," says Tuer, "because we
know we'll be there for the
long term."

PanCanadian's community
involvement also demonstrates
a commitment to the environment. For example, in 1996,
the company reduced its green-
house gas emissions by 436,500
tonnes of carbon dioxide equivalent—four times the reduction
reported in 1995.

In only a short 25 years,
PanCanadian has leveraged

an enviable land base—and the
talent of its 1,600 employees—
to become one of the country's
largest producers and market-
ers of fossil fuels. To meet its
ambitious growth plans, the
company will strive to unleash
the energy of its employees
and its community business
partners—confident that prosperity follows commitment
and purpose.

TECHNOLOGICAL EXCELLENCE, WHICH
INCLUDES THE DEVELOPMENT OF
LEADING-EDGE TECHNOLOGIES, IS
A KEY ELEMENT OF PANCANADIAN'S
GROWTH STRATEGY.

WITH BUSINESS INTERESTS IN AFRICA,
AUSTRALIA, EUROPE, AND SOUTH
AMERICA, PANCANADIAN IS SUCCESS-
FULLY BUILDING AN INTERNATIONAL
PRESENCE.

A LBERTA ENERGY COMPANY LTD. (AEC) HAS MET THE CHALLENGE of Alberta's volatile energy industry through a long-term, solidly based vision. Growth in shareholder value comes through AEC's success in domestic and international exploration, production, transportation,

storage, gas processing, and natural gas hub services.

The company was initially formed to give Albertans and other Canadians the opportunity to participate directly in the development of the province's vast natural resources: AEC would act as a private sector company, and the government's role would be limited to ownership, not management.

The company's first public offering in 1975 was oversubscribed, with more than 60,000 Albertans purchasing the $75 million offering. It was one of the largest single share offerings in Canadian history.

AEC acquired the oil and gas rights on the Suffield military base and the Primrose Air Weapons Range, and has since developed a unique expertise in the safe and environmentally sound exploration and development of oil and gas properties within active military ranges.

"Over the years, AEC's oil and gas operations grew substantially, and the company also diversified into a number of other resource businesses, which have

since been sold," says Gwyn Morgan, President and Chief Executive Officer, and one of the company's earliest employees. "The handsome profits realized from these sales were reinvested to expand the company's core business of upstream oil and gas exploration and production, and its unique midstream activities of pipeline transportation, natural gas storage, and processing."

The government continued to reduce its investment in AEC, and by the end of 1993, all of its remaining shares were profitably divested. While the Alberta government reaped a handsome profit, AEC was now positioned

on a level investment field with other oil and gas producers.

### MERGING MEANS SUCCESS

The strategic initiatives to dispose of non-core assets financially positioned AEC for major growth through acquisition. A $1.1 billion merger substantially increased the size of the company and transformed it into a decentralized, business-unit-based organization. All business units are autonomous, entrepreneurial entities that have clear sets of objectives and growth targets within a formula for success. Each is supported by the financial strength of a major company with a small head office focused on adding value not bureaucracy.

"Every successful company establishes a formula for success that is constantly reviewed and improved," says Morgan. "Ours is based on the business unit concept featuring entrepreneurial teams of high-performance entrepreneurs with a passion for their work and the ability to add shareholder value."

The AEC formula sets growth targets at 10 percent on a sustainable basis, with a stretch target of 15 percent. A dominant presence in very large focus areas is fundamental to the company's competitive advantage, as is the ability to control operating and processing infrastructures and implement efficiencies to economic advantage. The value of upstream assets is complemented by unique, entrepreneurial, non-regulated midstream activities, such as pipelines/processing and gas storage, which provide a stable and solid source of cash flow.

AEC West is the dominant presence along the west edge of the Western Canadian Sedimentary Basin, from northeast British Columbia through western Alberta, and south to the Blackfeet Reservation in Montana. Alberta's West Peace River Arch is the most industry-intensive region of the Basin, and AEC West has maintained a dominant position in exploration, land, reserves, gas gathering, and processing. AEC West's growth strategy includes expanding its liquids-rich sour gas prospects in several regions on large, concentrated landholdings; targeting deep, multizone gas prospects along the foothills of the Rocky Mountains; and developing up to 10 additional high-impact

exploration plays each year.

While AEC East has been anchored by cost-efficient, shallow natural gas properties, it has increasingly become a major heavy oil exploration and production centre. AEC East is pursuing production and reserves growth targets through relatively low-risk exploitation of 3,000 square miles in large, contiguous land blocks at Primrose and Suffield, two of Canada's military training ranges. AEC East is aggressively acquiring other large land blocks outside the military ranges, including exploration and development agreements on Indian reservations in North Dakota. AEC East is also applying recently developed thermal and drilling extraction technologies to the aggressive pursuit of attractive heavy oil opportunities in the Plains area of Alberta.

Another business unit, AEC Syncrude, includes the company's position as the second-largest owner of Syncrude, the world's largest producer of synthetic oil. Annual production from Syncrude is the equivalent of more than 10 percent of Canada's current oil needs.

AEC International invests approximately 10 percent of the company's exploration and development capital on projects in four countries outside of

North America. The unit's first investment was in Argentina, and additional prospects are now being explored.

AEC's Transportation, Storage, and Processing business units manage the company's "midstream investment." AEC Pipelines Ltd. is the largest transporter of oil within Alberta. Pipeline assets include the Syncrude and Cold Lake pipelines, as well as others that serve oil producers in northeast Alberta. AEC has a 50 percent interest in the Express/Platte system, which delivers crude oil to major markets in the U.S. Rocky Mountain and midwestern states. Also, AEC holds interests in two natural gas liquids extraction plants at Empress, Alberta.

The Storage and Hub Services business unit includes storage facilities in Canada and California. The AECO C HUB™ and Market Centre, located at Suffield, is the largest independent natural gas storage facility in North America and serves as the main Canadian reference point for spot gas prices.

"AEC is in an enviable position to fund growth," notes Morgan. "The foundation for meeting future challenges is our exceptionally solid base of exploration land, long-life reserves, quality midstream assets, and talented people."

# TRIZECHAHN
# CORPORATION

**T**rizecHahn Corporation is one of North America's largest real estate companies. It combines tremendous real estate expertise with financial strength and a commitment to innovation and growth. ❋ TrizecHahn owns an outstanding portfolio of dominant retail centers and landmark

office properties in major metropolitan markets. It has a strong presence in Calgary, Montreal, New York, Houston, Denver, Dallas, and Los Angeles. From strong foundations in North America, TrizecHahn is expanding into key global markets.

TrizecHahn was created in 1996 from the merger of Horsham, a major Canadian company with substantial financial resources, and Trizec, a leading real estate company with more than 35 years of development and operating experience.

In Calgary, TrizecHahn is the leading landlord of premier office space. It owns and manages a high-quality portfolio of office properties in the heart of downtown. With more than 25 years of experience in Calgary, the company has built a strong roster of blue-chip tenants including the Royal Bank, CIBC, Talisman Energy, Canadian Pacific Limited, and Bennett Jones Verchere. Its team of highly skilled management and leasing professionals are focused on ensuring the company main-

tains its leadership as Calgary continues to prosper and grow.

"Calgary is one of the most dynamic cities in North America," says Gregory C. Wilkins, President. "We are committed to being the landlord of choice for Calgary's growing companies by providing high-quality office space and superior service in the best locations."

TrizecHahn's Calgary portfolio consists of six distinctive downtown properties, including the landmark Bankers Hall, a prestigious 50-storey tower built in 1989. In addition to its office space, Bankers Hall has an outstanding three-level retail atrium offering a collection of international fashion retailers including Mondi, Aquascutum, Henry Singer, and Laura Ashley.

TrizecHahn has maintained a strong presence in Calgary since the early 1970s, when it developed the Royal Bank Building and Calgary Place. It also owns and operates Fifth & Fifth, Western Canadian Place, and Scotia Centre, a mixed-use office complex with a vibrant two-level retail center.

"We own and manage some of Calgary's premier office properties," says Evan Welbourn, Regional Vice President, Western Canada. "But our competitive advantage comes from our ability to develop and successfully implement innovative services for our tenants."

Innovations like centrally controlled technical services ensure that TrizecHahn provides prompt customer service, while the company's state-of-the-art building operations improve

TrizecHahn's Calgary portfolio consists of six distinctive downtown properties, including the landmark Bankers Hall (right) and Calgary Place (below).

268

CALGARY

verall efficiency and reduce
enants' costs.

TrizecHahn was the first
ompany in Western Canada
o introduce a comprehensive
ervice Advantage program
or its tenants. Under this part-
ership program, the company
rovides its tenants with pre-
erred service and value pricing
rom major business suppliers.
y harnessing the buying power
f more than 1,000 tenants
cross Canada, TrizecHahn
elps tenants reduce costs.

One element of TrizecHahn's
ervice Advantage program is
he Concierge Service—a unique
rogram that entitles employ-
es of TrizecHahn's tenants to
njoy discounts and special
ervices on a variety of leisure
ctivities and accommodations.
or example, just by working
n a TrizecHahn building, em-
loyees have access to preferred
ates on hotel rooms, theatre
ickets, and special events.

TrizecHahn is the only
Canadian company to win the
nternational Building of the
ear award for its property
nanagement of a large office
uilding. Indeed, the company
as won twice—for Bankers
Iall in Calgary and Canada
lace in Edmonton.

TrizecHahn's marketing
nd promotional programs have
lso gained recognition for their
reativity and effectiveness.
he company has won local,
ational, and international
wards for marketing campaigns
t Bankers Hall and Scotia
Centre. The accomplishments
f the company's engineering
nd operating team have also
ained industry recognition,
inning awards for improving
perating efficiency, energy
onservation, and barrier-free
ccess.

The company's commitment
o Calgary is reflected in a num-
er of ways. In addition to sup-

porting its tenants' charities,
TrizecHahn actively contributes
to a number of valuable community programs aimed at enhancing the quality of life in the city.
These include giving to Grace
Women's Health Centre, AIDS
Calgary Awareness Associations,
and the United Way. Trizec-
Hahn is also a contributor to
the sports program at the University of Calgary and is sponsoring
the Festival Bowl, the annual
football game between the University of Calgary and the
University of Alberta.

In Calgary, TrizecHahn is
particularly committed to the
Special Olympics. TrizecHahn
employees take great pride in
their role as founding sponsors
and organizers of the Sports
Celebrities Festival Breakfast
and Silent Auction, a major
annual event that raises funds
and awareness for the local

and provincial chapters of the
Special Olympics. Attended
by more than 700 people, this
event enjoys growing success.

"We believe Calgary is
quickly becoming a great international city," says Wilkins.
"As the leading real estate company in Calgary, TrizecHahn
has been and will continue to
be a part of the city's tremendous growth and prosperity."

# 1975-1996

| 1975 | GALVANIC COMPANIES |
|------|--------------------|
| 1975 | NORTEL |
| 1975 | QUANTEL VECO ENGINEERING LTD. |
| 1976 | CANADIAN FRACMASTER |
| 1976 | COLT ENGINEERING |
| 1976 | ROBYN'S TRUCKING SERVICES LTD. |
| 1978 | PROGAS LIMITED |
| 1980 | CALGARY FLAMES |
| 1982 | THE RIDER TRAVEL GROUP |
| 1983 | NOVATEL |
| 1984 | CANFER ROLLING MILLS LTD. |
| 1984 | HONGKONG BANK OF CANADA |
| 1987 | MAXX PETROLEUM LTD. |
| 1988 | WESTFAIR FOODS, LTD. |
| 1990 | ASM INDUSTRIES |
| 1991 | RYAN ENERGY TECHNOLOGIES INC. |
| 1993 | SAP CANADA INC. |
| 1994 | SPM/CALGARY INC. |
| 1995 | SHAW |
| 1996 | STONE & WEBSTER CANADA LIMITED |

# GALVANIC
# ANALYTICAL
# SYSTEMS LTD.

THE STORY OF GALVANIC ANALYTICAL SYSTEMS LTD. BEGAN MORE than 20 years ago with its founding by entrepreneur Doug Fraser—the 1995 winner of the Calgary Chamber of Commerce's Small Business Owner of the Year Award. ❈ "In 1975, I was the Canadian manager for a Houston-based operation," says Fraser. "When they decided to close it, I bought the inventory with a $20,000 loan from the Federal Business Development Bank and set up shop with three employees."

By the time Galvanic began distributing in the fall of 1996, not only did Calgary-based Galvanic distribute and service its state-of-the-art instrumentation equipment, but the company had also created a publicly owned manufacturing department.

## COMPETING WORLDWIDE

Alberta is the world's leading exporter of elemental sulphur, a by-product of the processing of sour natural gas. This spin-off industry has led the need for Galvanic's state-of-the-art sulphur measurement equipment.

Initially, the company only distributed and serviced sulphur analyzers from a number of U.S. manufacturers to the growing Western Canadian energy industry. In 1982, with a service outlet already in Camrose, Alberta, Galvanic opened an office in Vancouver, British Columbia, to serve the pulp and paper industry.

In 1990, Galvanic began its own manufacturing operations. This division eventually became the publicly owned subsidiary Galvanic Applied Sciences Inc. (GASI), which manufactures and sells sulphur measurement products and SCADA remote terminal units to petrochemical, refinery, and pipeline businesses worldwide. GASI went public in 1996 with a listing on the Alberta Stock Exchange. Also in 1996, GASI opened a Houston office.

In addition to these ventures, Galvanic Analytical Systems owns a 50 percent interest in ESG Filtration Inc., a private company that markets industrial filtration products.

## A BETTER MOUSETRAP

A major portion of Galvanic Analytical Systems' sales are derived from traditional lead acetate tape analyzers, but GASI now manufactures state-of-the-art equipment and has improved

GALVANIC'S OXYGEN STACK ANALYZ-ERS ARE USED TO OPTIMIZE COM-BUSTION EFFICIENCY AT STEAM INJECTION PLANTS (LEFT).

PETER CARMELL, INTERNATIONAL TECHNICAL SERVICE REPRESENTATIVE FOR GALVANIC APPLIED SCIENCES INC. (RIGHT)

n the technology. "We've added high-tech microprocessor," says Fraser, "and convenience options such as lower maintenance requirements, so the units can be left unattended for longer periods of time—for as long as six weeks. In addition, response time has been improved from three minutes to one minute."

With more than 300 installations of its 900 Series lead tape analyzer and more to come, Galvanic has virtually monopolized the Canadian market. Every Canadian gas transmission company now uses Galvanic's lead tape analyzers for pipeline monitoring. NOVA Corporation alone has 40 units installed. International sales and marketing efforts began in 1994, with a strong focus on the Gulf Coast, the U.S. eastern seaboard, Europe, and the Middle East.

"Canadians have much to offer—especially in the gas, petrochemical, and petroleum industries. We take pride in being Canadian and in bringing Canadian technology to world markets," says Fraser.

Galvanic has also developed a replacement market by building retrofit kits for old-style analyzers manufactured by a U.S. company. The retrofit kit updates the analyzer's electronics, as well as offering a number of enhancements.

## NEXT-GENERATION TECHNOLOGY

The company's biggest source of pride is its new Sulfalyzer, a chemiluminescent chromatograph that can analyze any sulphur species individually, as a group, or as total sulphur. Fewer than a handful of companies are developing this new technology, which boasts a much higher degree of sensitivity than traditional lead tape analyzers. "The Sulfalyzer can measure all of the components in sulphur, in-

cluding mercaptanes, carbonyl sulphides, and hydrogen sulphides," notes Fraser. "It will also measure the sulphur in diesel fuel and gasoline."

The equipment was first introduced to the global market at the annual Instrumentation Society of America show in late 1995, and efforts have begun to market it internationally, including the establishment of a worldwide distribution network and the implementation of the ISO 9000 certification process.

The Sulfalyzer is the result of three years' R&D efforts, with the support of the National Research Council of Canada. Some $400,000 was devoted exclusively to R&D in 1996 alone. Galvanic also has developed an analyzer for the laboratory market. Five GASI employees—technologists and an electronic designer—focus solely on in-house applied research and development. Continued emphasis is being placed on developing improved chemiluminescent and lead tape analyzers.

Not only is its technology superior, but Galvanic provides a first-rate technical support and service program for its customers. Five factory-trained service employees are dedicated to providing customer support. "No

CLOCKWISE FROM TOP LEFT: GALVANIC MANUFACTURES STATE-OF-THE-ART SULPHUR MEASUREMENT EQUIPMENT, INCLUDING SULPHUR-SPECIFIC PROCESS GAS CHROMATOGRAPHS, THE 801 CONTINUOUS H2S/TOTAL SULPHUR ANALYZER, AND THE 901 H2S/TOTAL SULPHUR ANALYZER.

one makes that type of commitment in our industry," notes Fraser.

While the Canadian energy industry provides an ideal incubator for the development of sulphur-related technologies, environmental agencies around the world are continually tightening the screws on regulation, requiring sulphur compounds to be monitored with increasing accuracy and at lower levels than ever. "You can't determine environmental impacts unless you can measure and quantify what's there," says Fraser. "We're part of the process to solve environmental problems—part of the solution."

ORTEL—FORMERLY NORTHERN TELECOM—HAS BEEN REGARDED AS CAN ada's high-tech treasure for decades. Founded in 1895 as Northern Elec tric and Manufacturing Co., a manufacturer of telephones, Nortel ha reinvented itself a number of times in its evolution into a multina

tional corporation with some 68,000 employees around the world. A world leader in network technology, Nortel spends more on research and development than any other private sector company in Canada to ensure it retains its competitive edge.

Headquartered in Toronto, Nortel established operations in Calgary in 1975 during a cross-Canada expansion. In the early years, the company operated a small manufacturing plant with about 38 employees to produce cable and wiring harnesses for a single customer— the local phone company, AGT (now known as Telus).

During the early 1980s, the Calgary operations began to grow, focusing on manufacturing for digital switches and small-business communications systems. Nortel Calgary's many achievements have earned both local lines of business the distinction of being global centres

of excellence for the company. These successes enabled expansion, over the years, to include three manufacturing facilities, a development centre, and several office towers.

Nortel is currently organized into four lines of business that are comprised of a number of business units, each delivering a specific solution to customers. One line of business is Public Carrier Networks, which provides products for phone companies around the world. Another is Broadband Networks, with cable TV companies and new long-distance carriers being the major customers. The two remaining lines of business— with global manufacturing operations in Calgary—are Enterprise Networks, which provides internal communications systems for organizations; and Wireless Networks, which creates products for the cellular phone and personal communications systems (PCS) industries.

The business units in Calgary are part of some of the fastest-growing areas within Nortel.

### ENTERPRISE AND WIRELESS NETWORKS

The Calgary element of the Enterprise Networks group currently focuses on producing the Millennium public pay phon systems, consumer products such as residential and small-business phones, and Norstar integrated communications systems that provide a portfolio of communications solutions for small businesses. In addition to manufacturing, this division is responsible for the R and D, product development, and mar keting for these products, and Calgary is the global business centre for these business units.

The Enterprise Networks facility alone consumes five ton of plastic per day, and inbound supply shipments and outbound product shipments from the

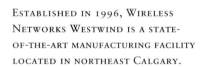

ESTABLISHED IN 1996, WIRELESS NETWORKS WESTWIND IS A STATE-OF-THE-ART MANUFACTURING FACILITY LOCATED IN NORTHEAST CALGARY.

ant fill seven aircraft and 14 ucks daily. Approximately 65 ercent of the business commu- cations systems and residential nones produced by Enterprise etworks are sold internationally.

The growth in the Wireless ne of business has been explo- ve over the past few years. his was made possible by the announcement in 1990 that algary had been chosen by ortel to manufacture two ew parts of the digital cellular roduct line. The announcement nade Calgary the corporation's anufacturing centre for cellu- r infrastructure equipment. his was tremendously exciting, the digital cellular project as one of the most important ew directions for Nortel at ne time. Currently in Calgary, Vireless Networks is a global nanufacturer for three of the ading wireless phone technolo- es, including analogue and digi- l standards for cellular and CS network service providers. his group has continued to xperience rapid growth as a esult of the increasing demand or cellular services. A major ilestone marking this growth nd Nortel's investment in Cal- ary was the rapid construction f a new 285,000-square-foot, ate-of-the-art Wireless Networks lant in 1996.

## CALGARY PRESENCE

lortel's Enterprise Networks nd Wireless Networks both have strong presence in Calgary, vith a total of three manufactur- g plants, five office/distribution acilities, and more than 2,300 vorkers, making the company major employer in the city.

Nortel's economic impact n the city is also substantial. Vith a total investment in the Calgary operations of more nan US$200 million, Nortel pends more than US$300 aillion in Alberta each year

on salaries, supplies, and equip- ment. The Calgary operations export more than US$1.3 billion in products each year to more than 80 countries around the world.

Calgary also benefits from Nortel's community involvement. It is Nortel's belief that assisting the communities in which it does business strengthens the company's commitment to both its employees and its customers. As examples, the company has sponsored the Chair for Intelli- gent Manufacturing at the Uni- versity of Calgary, and is one of the founding members of the Calgary Corporate Challenge. These examples illustrate Nortel's commitment to support the education of youth in science and technology, and to advocate community and employee spirit. These elements are important to Nortel's success in the local community and in the global marketplace.

## COMMITTED TO QUALITY

A key competitive edge for Nor- tel is the strength of its people and their can-do approach to meeting the needs of businesses. Employees have an ongoing involvement in the development of the organization, which has a culture grounded in team-based management and a total quality commitment.

Another key factor in Nor- tel's international success is its "customer first" philosophy. Nortel is constantly working to learn more about its customers' challenges and needs, with cus- tomers directly involved in the development of new products and services.

"Our vision of a 'world of networks' recognizes that cus- tomers want more than equip- ment," says Bill Hews, Assistant Vice-President Global Operation Enterprise Networks. "They want network solutions that give them a competitive advantage. Nortel is unique in being able to provide customers with an extensive global presence, broad product portfolio, and digital net- work leadership." And it is these qualities that will keep Nortel in the forefront of the high-tech telecommunications industry for many decades to come.

CLOCKWISE FROM TOP LEFT: ENTERPRISE NETWORKS EMPLOYEES CELEBRATE A MAJOR MILESTONE— THE PRODUCTION OF THE 1 MIL- LIONTH VISTA 350.

NORTEL EMPLOYEES HAVE AN ONGOING INVOLVEMENT IN THE DEVELOPMENT OF THE ORGANIZATION, WHICH HAS A CULTURE GROUNDED IN TEAM- BASED MANAGEMENT AND A TOTAL QUALITY COMMITMENT.

THE ENTERPRISE NETWORKS MANU- FACTURING FACILITY IS THE GLOBAL CENTRE FOR NORSTAR.

O UR PEOPLE TRAVEL TO THE FOUR CORNERS OF THE WORLD," SAYS DOU⟨
Rogers, Vice-President, Business Development, of Calgary-based Quant⟨
VECO Engineering Ltd. "As Calgarians, we have world-scale technolog⟨
ical know-how. We also wave the maple leaf flag a lot, since othe⟨
countries like working with Canadians."

The private engineering company, which specializes in the design, engineering, and construction of oil and gas production and pipeline facilities, began operations in 1975 as a small consulting firm named Quantel Engineering Ltd. Its first big break came in 1981, when the company was contracted by Peace Pipe Lines to handle engineering and construction for a major pipeline expansion into the Western Canadian Sedimentary Basin.

QUANTEL VECO ENGINEERING LTD. SPECIALIZES IN THE DESIGN, ENGINEERING, AND CONSTRUCTION OF OIL AND GAS PRODUCTION AND PIPELINE FACILITIES. AT RIGHT IS THE BURNT TIMBER GAS PLANT IN ALBERTA, CONSTRUCTED FOR SHELL CANADA LIMITED.

QUANTEL BEGAN IN 1975 AS A SMALL CONSULTING FIRM, BUT BY 1981 HAD CONTRACTED TO HANDLE ENGINEERING AND CONSTRUCTION FOR A MAJOR PIPELINE EXPANSION INTO THE WESTERN CANADIAN SEDIMENTARY BASIN. OTHER PROJECTS INCLUDE THIS PIPELINE INSTALLATION IN ALBERTA.

### MARKETING TO THE WORLD

By the early 1980s, Quantel was gaining recognition for its high quality of work in Western Canada from major producers such as Shell, Esso, and BP. In the meantime, Quantel President Said Arrata began a long-term, visionary campaign to market the company around the world. His unique marketing approach was to offer training to locals in remote locations such as Libya, Egypt, Indonesia, and Saudi Arabia.

In 1990, Quantel embarked on a major strategic alliance with Gulf Canada Resources, and through that relationship, obtained its first international project. Valued at $100 million, the KomiArcticOil Project in the Komi Republic of Russia, inside the Arctic Circle, provided the opportunity for Quantel to carry out feasibility studies, preliminary engineering, and detailed design of production facilities, pipeline gathering systems, field satellites, and

related infrastructure. "The severe climate and remote location made this a very challenging project," notes Rogers.

Then followed another big opportunity, this time in the Middle East, for a $30 million acid gas recovery project in Abu Dhabi. By 1994, Quantel was focusing on developing its corporate vision and devising a game plan to locate a strategic investor who could help the company secure larger international contracts.

In 1996, after a year of negotiation, Quantel got its finan-

cial boost by merging operation⟨ with Veco Engineering, a company based in the United States and the formation of a new corporation called Quantel VECO Engineering Ltd. Worldwide, Veco Engineering has a total of 1,100 employees, operating out of branch offices on a global chain of projects stretching from Australia to Kazakhstan.

The headquarters for Veco'⟨ international operations, Quante⟨ VECO itself has a staff of 425 employees in offices in Calgary; Vancouver, British Columbia; and the United Arab Emirates. The company has quadrupled in size since 1990 and manage⟨ more than $2 billion in capital projects each year, 40 percent of which are overseas. "We're anticipating doubling in size again by the year 2002," notes Rogers.

In addition to providing services for heavy and conventional oil facilities, sour gas processing, pipelines, gathering systems, compressor and pump stations, enhanced oil recovery projects, offshore topside facili ties, process control systems,

nd pipeline leak detection sys-
ms, Quantel VECO has also
ained expertise in environmen-
l clean-up technologies. The
mpany has an exclusive Cana-
ian licence for the Superclaus
ulphur recovery system, which
nproves efficiency and recov-
y levels for sulphur recovery
nits. Quantel VECO has so
r installed seven Superclaus
stems in Western Canada,
cluding the world's largest
Alberta Energy's Sexsmith
lant.

## A SEAMLESS
## ORGANIZATION

uantel VECO is proud to offer
s clients a seamless organiza-
on. "We often send work
o our office in Abu Dhabi by
ternet," says Rogers, "and
e project comes back com-
leted the following day. We
ave local Calgarians in our
ternational offices to ensure
at the standards and quality
ur customers expect are main-
ined. We also have a lot of
hnic diversity in our Calgary
ffice to help us understand the
nguage and the culture of the
untries where we do business."

Quantel VECO's standards
e the highest possible. In 1994,
uantel VECO became only
e second engineering, procure-
ent, and construction contrac-
or in Canada to be certified
o ISO 9001, the international
uality standards that are be-
oming increasingly essential
o conducting business overseas.

In addition, the company
rives to live up to its motto—
he Team That Delivers—by
eating each client as unique
nd spending time up front to
etermine the project's special
arameters, whether it's a tight
eadline or a challenging engi-
eering problem.

The company also expresses
ride in its staff. "We bring in
ood people who are keen and

motivated," notes Rogers. "And
we provide a flexible organization and framework for them.
There are few rules and regulations. Our turnover is very low,
perhaps a few percent per year."

This commitment to people
also extends outside of the company. Quantel VECO is actively
promoting the development of
a project management program
at the master's level at the University of Calgary, and offers
four scholarships each year to
local students in undergraduate
engineering.

Quantel VECO has been
recognized by the local business
community for its work. It was
named one of the city's top
100 private companies in 1994

and 1995. In addition, Arrata
was a finalist in the 1995 Entrepreneur of the Year Award sponsored by the Calgary Chamber
of Commerce.

The future looks bright
for Quantel VECO. Rogers
predicts that Calgary will continue to boom. "I believe there
may be as much as $2 billion
in project work in the next few
years, if you go by what has
been proposed recently," Rogers
sums up. "I think Quantel
VECO is in a strong position
to secure its share of that work."

It's clear that Quantel VECO
expects to live up to its vision
as a "family of professionals,
united in spirit, with the burning desire to succeed."

BY THE EARLY 1980S, QUANTEL
WAS GAINING RECOGNITION FOR ITS
HIGH QUALITY OF WORK IN WESTERN
CANADA FROM MAJOR PRODUCERS
SUCH AS SHELL, ESSO, AND BP. ONE
EXAMPLE IS SHELL CANADA LIMITED'S
SCOTFORD REFINERY IN BRITISH
COLUMBIA.

FORTY PERCENT OF QUANTEL'S
PROJECTS ARE OVERSEAS, SUCH AS
THIS ACID GAS PIPELINE FOR ABU
DHABI GAS CORPORATION (GASCO)
IN THE UNITED ARAB EMIRATES
(LEFT).

QUANTEL HAS GAINED EXPERTISE IN
ENVIRONMENTAL CLEAN-UP TECHNOLO-
GIES, AND HAS AN EXCLUSIVE CANADIAN
LICENCE FOR THE SUPERCLAUS SULPHUR
RECOVERY SYSTEM. THE COMPANY
HAS INSTALLED SEVEN SUPERCLAUS
SYSTEMS IN WESTERN CANADA, INCLUD-
ING THIS ONE FOR SUNCOR INC., IN
ALBERTA (RIGHT).

## CANADIAN

## FRACMASTER

STABLISHED IN 1976, CANADIAN FRACMASTER IS AN INTERNATIONAL OI and gas well service and oil production company headquartered in Calgary Since its founding, the company's focus on technology and innovation ha earned it a position as one of Canada's largest suppliers of cementing

acidizing, fracturing, and coiled tubing products, services, and technologies, including industrial and pipeline services. Through its engineering, laboratory, and fabrication facilities in Calgary, Fracmaster researches, develops, and manufactures products, services, and specialized equipment for use throughout the world.

"We're committed to developing environmentally compatible treatments and procedures that incorporate safety and pro-

CANADIAN FRACMASTER IS HEAD-
QUARTERED IN DOWNTOWN CALGARY.

vide value for our customers," says President Les Margetak.

### AN INTERNATIONAL PRESENCE

Fracmaster's operations are currently structured in two divisions: North American Well Services and Joint Enterprise Services. North American Well Services provides well stimulation, cementing, and coiled tubing services to the North American petroleum industry. Joint Enterprise Services includes the company's Russian joint venture operations, as well as activities related to the provision of materials, services, equipment, and technology primarily to the Russian ventures.

Canadian Fracmaster is the only major Canadian oil field services company designing and building its own equipment for the international marketplace. A large part of its success is due to the company's substantial, long-term Russian operations. Fracmaster's activity in the Soviet Union began in 1986, and increased after the Soviet Union dissolved in the late 1980s, enabling Fracmaster to be one of the first foreign companies to pursue opportunities in the country's new economic environment. Fracmaster was a participant in the first foreign joint venture in the energy business to become operational in Russia.

In addition to Russia's geographical and political challenges, there were a number of other difficulties facing Fracmaster. "A big issue was how we would get paid," notes Margetak. "There was no hard currency

available, and roubles were non-convertible at that time, so we pioneered a new concept, equity-for-service—being paid with incremental oil production."

As a result of the early initiatives and an innovative approach to problem solving, Fracmaster is currently one of the largest foreign oil producer in Russia, and now operates fou joint ventures there. And as th country's economy stabilizes, Fracmaster is moving from equity-for-service payment to the more traditional fee-for-service payment, and expects to do all its business in this manner from 1997 onward.

The company has also been active in China since 1994, when a series of nine technologically challenging fractures were undertaken to demonstrate the company's expertise to the Chinese oil and gas industry. This program led to the successful negotiation of a production-sharing agreement with the China National Oil and Gas Exploration and Development Corporation involving the rehabilitation of 720 oil wells.

A business development uni was established in 1996 to identify and evaluate growth opportunities for the company in the Middle East, North Africa, and Latin America, as well as addi tional opportunities in China. American Fracmaster, a joint venture in which Canadian Fracmaster holds 50 percent, also was established to oversee U.S. operations in Texas and New Mexico.

The company's main strat egy for moving into the international marketplace is the

evelopment of mutually benefi-
al alliances with indigenous
ell service companies. Through
ese technical alliances, Frac-
aster provides technical assis-
nce and custom training
rograms, the licensing of the
mpany's technology and trade-
arks, the sale of Fracmaster
quipment and supplies, and
cess to Fracmaster research
d development.

## A FOCUS ON
## TECHNOLOGY

Technology will continue to be
e Fracmaster advantage," says
argetak, "and we will continue
be the leader in this area."

For example, Fracmaster
constantly developing new
plication-specific cement
ends for its cementing services
at are used during the drilling,
mpletion, and recompletion
ases of a well. For acidizing
rvices, which stimulate a well
increase production, Frac-
aster has developed special
id treatment packages for use
carbonate reservoirs, an iron
ntrol agent that provides a
ore cost-effective package,
d an acid gellant that is com-
tible with corrosion inhibitors.

Fracmaster has the largest
arket share in Canada for
acturing services, a well stim-
ation process that improves
oduction. In this area, too,
search and development are

ongoing. Fracmaster has applied
for patents for a special $CO_2/$
$N_2$ fracturing process that pre-
vents formation damage, allows
rapid clean-up, and is more cost-
effective in shallow formations.
The company has also developed
specialized gels and gellants with
increased proppant-carrying
ability.

Fracmaster is an industry
leader in both conventional
coiled tubing services and coiled
tubing drilling in Canada. Conventional coiled tubing—joint-
less, high-pressure, flexible steel
pipe—is used for well clean outs,
acid treatments, stimulations,
solvents, and cement squeezes,
as well as the delivery and
operation of downhole tools.

Coiled tubing is also well
suited for drilling vertical and
horizontal extensions to existing wells, as well as for use in
underbalanced drilling, where

the reservoir pressure is higher
than the hydrostatic pressure
of the drilling fluids, and formation damage is thus greatly
reduced. In 1995, Fracmaster
designed and built the industry's
first hybrid conventional/coiled
tubing drilling unit. Two such
units are now in operation.

"All of our products are
developed in response to market demand for cost efficiency
and will support the sale of
our technology to foreign
service companies," says
Margetak.

Being a Canadian company
is also an asset, according to
Margetak: "We cut our teeth
on the challenges of the Canadian energy industry, and our
strong Canadian operations,
as well as our devoted employees, give us the ability to move
successfully into the international marketplace."

CLOCKWISE FROM TOP LEFT:
FRACMASTER HAS DRILLED 65 UNDER-
BALANCED HORIZONTAL WELLS AND
MORE THAN 400 VERTICAL EXTENSIONS
USING COILED TUBING.

ACTIVITIES AT FRACMASTER'S RESEARCH
AND DEVELOPMENT FACILITIES IN CAL-
GARY INCLUDE DEVELOPMENT OF NEW
PRODUCTS, AS WELL AS DAY-TO-DAY
SERVICE WORK ON STIMULATION FLU-
IDS, ACIDIZING SYSTEMS, AND QUAL-
ITY CONTROL.

IN 1996, FRACMASTER PERFORMED 254
OF 537 FRACTURE TREATMENTS ON A
FEE-FOR-SERVICE BASIS, COMPARED
TO 12 OF 401 IN 1995, AND ANTICI-
PATES A COMPLETE SWITCH TO THIS
WAY OF DOING BUSINESS IN 1997.

IN 1996, FRACMASTER SUCCESSFULLY
NEGOTIATED A PRODUCTION-SHARING
AGREEMENT WITH CHINA NATIONAL
OIL AND GAS EXPLORATION AND
DEVELOPMENT CORPORATION.

FEW YEARS AGO, WHEN ONE OF CANADA'S LEADING BUSINESS NEWSPAPER wanted to recognize Colt Engineering as one of the 50 best-run firms i the country, Colt said, "Thanks, but we're just not comfortable with tha kind of exposure right now." ❋ Any other firm would have jumped at th

opportunity. Free publicity and unsolicited praise are usually enough to turn the head of any corporation. But not Colt. The company pays little attention to advertising or promotion. Its interests are directed at refining the services that have helped Colt become the major facilities engineering contractor in Alberta's oil and gas, refinery, and petrochemical industries.

This pre-eminent position is the result of a process that began 25 years ago, in 1973. That is when Colt's founders opened the company's doors for business in Edmonton. Operating from an office above a welding shop, the first partners fused their entrepreneurial skills to the disciplines of consulting engineering. This combination attracted customers and the company prospered.

In 1976, the company moved its head office to Calgary, where most Canadian oil companies are headquartered.

Given Colt's focus on designing and building oil and gas facilities, this was a good move. And so was retaining their refinery, petrochemical, and industrial roots in Edmonton. This broad-based, two-city strategy enabled Colt to perform services throughout Alberta.

### CREATIVE PEOPLE WITH INNOVATIVE SOLUTIONS

As the company matured, it continued to attract people who thrive in an environment that encourages the blending of business acumen with engineering expertise and innovative problem solving. Colt's capabilities quickly expanded to cover the full spectrum of project services, from project management, engineering, and procurement to construction. In 1978, Cord Projects Ltd. was established as Colt's construction division to handle

both EPC lump-sum turnkey and direct-hire construction projects.

Endeavoring to develop repeat business and build long-term relationships with customers, Colt adopted a very simple strategy of earning the next job by delivering good work. In this way, the company captured a number of evergreen contracts and established an ongoing rapport with a large number of firms of all sizes.

This variety of project wor combined with the company's longer-term relationships, helpe Colt develop the basic principle and operating guidelines for what became its edge in competing for engineering business in the 1990s: the strategic alliance.

Colt currently enjoys a number of these long-term alliance relationships with many of Canada's prominent oil and gas, refinery, petrochemical, and oil sands companies. Generating a diverse breadth of projects of all sizes and types, alliance work includes upgrading, revamping, maintaining, and expanding existing facilities, as well as developing new grassroots facilities. Projects range up to several hundred million dollars in size.

These alliance relationships—several of which have been in place for more than seven years—have had a very positive effect on Colt's long-term stability. Whereas engineering companies tend to be subject to the ups and downs of a resource-based economy, alliances have given Colt a ver

THESE THREE COLTS PERFECTLY SYMBOLIZE THE SPIRITED, STRONG, AND RESPONSIVE CHARACTER OF COLT ENGINEERING.

able platform for growth and development. It's an exceptional foundation for future operations and gives Colt a unique strength in the marketplace.

With offices in Calgary, Edmonton, Sarnia, and Toronto, Colt has more than 1,500 experienced people with proven abilities in gas processing, liquids extraction, heavy oil facilities, oil sands, major pipelines, Arctic projects, refinery and petrochemicals, cogeneration, environmental, and a variety of new technologies. Operations have expanded into the United States and international activities are increasing.

Over the past few years, Colt has participated in $1.5 billion worth of projects annually. These impressive volumes have been achieved by a strong and flexible management team that's adept at meeting constant changes in the marketplace, while keeping the company focused on being the engineering contractor of choice for clients and staff.

## QUALITY, SERVICE, VALUE

Colt's reputation for listening to customer needs is a product of its own corporate culture.

For 25 years, the company has worked hard to deliver quality, service, and increased value to its customers. And it has learned that the most effective way of delivering these benefits is by encouraging its own people to be creative and innovative in the delivery of Colt's services.

Colt's ownership philosophy also appeals to clients. The company strongly believes in hands-on, active ownership at all levels. With more than 100 senior staff shareholders working in all areas of the company, owners participate directly in the performance of Colt. Their financial stake ensures a strong and personal commitment to continually enhance Colt's operations and future development.

Many customers also appreciate the fact that Colt is considerate of the needs of its own employees. The company's stability—its large client base, strategic alliances, and wide variety of exciting projects to work on—creates exciting opportunities for advancement. But productive people need more than just career options and interesting challenges. They need a work atmosphere that is good for the soul, too.

The word on the street is that Colt is a good place to work. Visitors to any Colt office can see this for themselves. From the receptionist on up, there is a sense of positive energy in action. It is a work ethic that can only come from self-motivated people with a strong entrepreneurial spirit.

If that energy could be harnessed, the result would be the essence of an Alberta success story that's being written, right now, by a company called Colt Engineering Corporation.

CLOCKWISE FROM TOP: THROUGH ITS ALLIANCES, COLT IS RESPONSIBLE FOR THE ENGINEERING NEEDS OF SEVERAL MAJOR REFINERY AND OIL SANDS FACILITIES.

COLT IS RESPONSIBLE FOR SEVERAL MAJOR PIPELINE PROJECTS.

COLT'S GAS PROCESSING AND LIQUIDS EXTRACTION EXPERTISE IS A KEY FACTOR IN THE COMPANY'S SUCCESS.

**R**OBYN JACKSON IS LIVING PROOF THAT OPPORTUNITY CAN LEAD TO great things. ❄ In 1972, Jackson was running a service station in Edmonton, Alberta, when his brother, who was in the business of moving temperature sensitive products, was struggling to find a reliable refrigerated

carrier. Jackson had experience in oil field hauling, and saw this as an opportunity to start his own small business. After borrowing enough money to buy one tractor and one "reefer" (refrigerated) trailer, Robyn's Trucking Services Ltd. was born.

Jackson drove the trucks himself for the first three or four years, gradually building his customer base by providing refrigerated service to the food industry of Alberta. In 1976, he opened a branch of his business in Calgary, and in the early 1980s was able to establish terminals in Lethbridge and Vancouver, making his head office

in Calgary. By the end of the decade, and assisted by the purchase of a small, temperature-controlled transportation company in Richmond, terminals had also been established in Victoria and Nanaimo, British Columbia.

Currently, Robyn's Trucking operates six terminals in Western Canada, and maintains a fleet of some 60 tractors and 180 reefer trailers carrying "clean freight"—usually meat and food products—across Canada and the United States. "We haul everything from hanging beef to boxes of crackers," says Jackson. Ninety percent of this business involves what is called LTL, or "less than load," freight.

Recently the company expanded into the United States with irregular routes, bringing world-famous Alberta beef to the American Midwest. Jackson now has a staff of approximately 200, enabling Robyn's Trucking Services Ltd. to haul more than 40 million pounds of trailer load and LTL freight, making some 18,000 deliveries each month.

### SERVICE AND SAFETY

Jackson says the company's focus always remains on customer service, as that is basically what the transportation business is offering. The demand from cus-

ROBYN JACKSON, FOUNDER OF ROBYN'S TRUCKING, IS LIVING PROOF THAT OPPORTUNITY CAN LEAD TO GREAT THINGS.

mers is greater than ever, especially with the increasing need
or just-in-time deliveries. In
striving to provide the best
possible customer service, the
company's computer system is
being upgraded to provide EDI
(electronic data interchange)
capability. "We need to be able
to get the information to our cus-
omers as quickly as possible,"
says Jackson. "They want to
know where their product is
and when it was delivered, and
we need to provide accurate
and reliable weekly and monthly
reports." Robyn's Trucking has
also established a toll-free customer service number to provide
easier access for customers across
North America.

Until recently, Jackson had
been handling most of the marketing and sales calls himself.
His personal credibility has been
the main reason for the company's growing number of new
accounts. "I like to personally
meet with my customers, even
if I need to hop on a plane,"
says Jackson. "After our discussions, I let them know of
any problems I anticipate. They
appreciate my frankness and the
fact that when a mistake is made
or a problem arises, we can and
will admit to it."

Jackson realizes that developing management and administration is an absolute necessity.
He has implemented new policies
and procedures over the years,
and as he takes his company
through the nineties, Jackson
will revise and restructure to
suit the need. The driver manual
has been updated and refined,
and a company uniform was
introduced to ensure that employees are easily recognized
by the public. An employee
assistance program has been
established to ensure employees
receive any help they may need
to resolve problems affecting
either their personal lives or
their job performance.

Safety is another important
focus for Jackson. The company
provides a Professional Driver's
Improvement Course, where
topics include how to improve
driving skills, how to avoid
accidents and collisions, and
hints on improving image and
attitude. Robyn's Trucking has
a corporate awards program
that recognizes different levels of
accident-free driving. Directly
relating to the focus on safety,
one of the company's drivers was
recently the recipient of one
of the most prestigious awards
that a driver can receive, Driver
of the Year. Jim White was
honored with the 1996 Driver
of the Year award by the Alberta
Trucking Association (ATA),
in conjunction with the Alberta
Trucking Industry Safety Association, an organization established jointly by the ATA and
the Workers Compensation
Board. White has been driving
for nearly half a century, and
has more than 5 million miles
of safe driving under his belt—
having not caused a single
accident.

## LOOKING TO THE FUTURE

"The arrival of the North American Free Trade Agreement has
opened up tremendous opportunities between Canada, the
United States, and Mexico,"
says Jackson. "I just have to

establish a partner there, just
as other carriers already have."
Jackson expects to do that within
three years. Not that the company
is hard pressed for business at
the moment: Over the past 10
years, the company's revenue has
tripled and is expected to double
again in the next five years.

Jackson reports that Robyn's
Trucking generates about 90
percent of its business hauling in
Western Canada, with about 10
percent coming from the United
States. He looks forward to
expanding further into the United
States and possibly Mexico, but
the company will continue to be
Calgary based.

"It's been fun, no doubt
about it," says Jackson, who
is still moving boxes for his
original customer—his brother
in Edmonton. Jackson isn't
driving the trucks anymore, but
he certainly is driving the success of his company, and is
looking forward to what the
future holds.

JACKSON NOW HAS A STAFF OF
APPROXIMATELY 200, ENABLING
ROBYN'S TRUCKING SERVICES LTD.
TO HAUL MORE THAN 40 MILLION
POUNDS OF TRAILER LOAD AND
LTL FREIGHT, MAKING SOME 18,000
DELIVERIES EACH MONTH.

OUNDED IN 1978 BY 12 OF THE MOST SUCCESSFUL NATURAL GAS EXPLOration and development companies in Canada, ProGas Limited is the country's first producer-owned natural gas marketing company. ProGas meetthe needs of Western Canadian producers to sell natural gas, as well as th

ProGas offices are in the Canterra Tower, located in the heart of downtown Calgary (top).

ProGas transports gas through the pipelines of many companies, including NOVA Corporation of Alberta (bottom).

NOVA CORPORATION

needs of long-term buyers in Canada and the United States to purchase natural gas.

"In essence, we serve two groups of customers: the producers on whose behalf we sell the gas, and the buyers themselves," notes Jan van Egteren, Vice-President of Marketing. "The producers are looking for stable, long-term markets to ensure their investments are recovered, while buyers are seeking reliable supplies of natural gas at market-responsive prices."

## SUCCESS AND GROWTH

"Our continuing objective," says van Egteren, "is to sell gas from our pool to incremental markets throughout North America on a long-term contract basis."

ProGas has demonstrated ongoing success in meeting this objective. Growth has been steady, despite deregulation in 1984 and 1985 that introduced competition into the industry for the first time. The company's supply capability has increased to more than 1 billion cubic feet of natural gas per day, with netback prices that have been generally the highest in Western Canada.

With 20 years of experience, this niche player in the energy industry attributes its success to a number of factors. First, the company has a broad-based supply pool, with more than 4 trillion cubic feet of supply contracted with more than 170 Western Canadian gas producers. Secondly, ProGas holds a diversified sales portfolio, with about half the gas flowing to the United States under long-term contracts; the remainder is sold domestically. In the domestic market, about 20 to 25 percent is sold on a day-to-day basis, with the remainder sold on a term basis, usually for one year.

The third factor is the contracts ProGas holds for firm transportation to much of the midwestern United States, northeastern United States, and California, ensuring access to major North American markets. Finally, through regular discussions with producers, customers, and transporters, ProGas staff maintain an in-depth understanding of industry trends, technological advances, transportation issues, and regulatory matters, so the company can respond quickly to its customers.

"I believe we're very ethical in our business dealings," van Egteren adds. "We tell our customers what we can do—and then we do it. There are no surprises. We always try to be honest and up front."

ProGas also carries out activities under two wholly owned subsidiaries: ProGas Enterprises and ProGas U.S.A. Inc. ProGas Enterprises provides fee-based marketing and transportation services within Canada, enhancing flexibility for producers. ProGas U.S.A. manages transportation and gas transactions in the United States, as well as facilitates the import of gas from Canada to the United States.

For the future, ProGas plans to continue its steady growth, while adapting to changing environments and providing more services than ever before. With its history of continuing success in the energy industry, ProGas is well positioned to attain its goal.

THE RIDER TRAVEL GROUP WAS FORMED IN 1982 BY MARK RIDER, a former petrochemical engineer. As a frequent business traveller, Rider knew that business travel demands services and attention that leisure travel does not. As such, The Rider Travel Group began as a

travel management company dedicated exclusively to meeting the needs of business travellers.

From the beginning, The Rider Travel Group set out to be different: Never before in Canada had any company attempted to focus its business offering on only one sector of travellers. Within a newly deregulated environment that enabled companies to realize savings, however, Rider found its niche market as the travel management company of choice for business travellers across the nation.

### UNPRECEDENTED GROWTH

Rider expanded its presence in the Canadian corporate community through the 1980s and into the next decade. As time progressed, Rider gradually expanded nationwide to serve local needs, since the needs of one region of the country are often different from another. Apart from meeting the need for increased service and additional locations, these new offices emphasized local responsibility: each location employed local residents, and profits remained within the community.

Recognizing the need for local presence, Rider established an office in Calgary in 1989, which was to become the regional centre of operations for Western Canada. In addition to core agency services such as counselling, ticketing, and travel management, the Calgary location included training resources, as well as consultative expertise in international destinations and

consolidator and charter fares.

Rider's growth in Calgary has been strong and steady—in 1996 alone, the office grew an unprecedented 90 percent, and the trend is continuing. According to Vice-President, Western Region David Kruschell, Rider's growth mirrors Calgary's economic boom: "It's a vibrant time for the city, and business travel is a sure indicator of corporate growth."

While Rider's growth in Calgary does, in part, reflect Rider's increased market share, the Western Region (as is the case with the rest of the company) maintains a relatively small, yet select client base. As a result, the majority of Rider's success has come one client at a time, as well as through the growth and consolidation of existing clients' needs.

Rider's success is also related to a changing ideology about the feasibility of outsourcing. Companies like The Rider Travel Group, which provide an alternative to the internal development and management of resources, are gaining more recognition as a viable option. "Western companies, more and more, are embracing the need for outsourced travel management," says Kruschell. "The enhanced services Rider offers, combined with proprietary technology and a partnership approach to travel management, provide companies with benefits that self-managed travel cannot provide." Besides removing the burden of managing a specialized department, such as travel, an outsourced travel program can realize sav-

ings that, ordinarily, most businesses could not negotiate by themselves.

Today, with 18 offices and 800 employees nationwide, The Rider Travel Group continues to grow and expand its service offerings; however, the company's primary focus remains the same: to be the supplier of choice for Canadian corporate business travellers and provide them with the services and technology necessary to streamline the travel process.

TOP: According to Vice-President, Western Region David Kruschell, Rider's growth mirrors Calgary's economic boom: "It's a vibrant time for the city, and business travel is a sure indicator of corporate growth."

BOTTOM: Director of Operations Connie Holtan (standing, far right) and Rider's team of business travel counsellors are proud to provide the services and technology necessary to streamline the travel process.

BILL MOSES

BILL MOSES

O N MAY 21, 1980, HOCKEY'S ATLANTA FLAMES BECAME THE CALGARY Flames, moving their franchise to the Corral on Calgary's Stampede grounds. Adopting a fiery new emblem, the Flames have become one of the premier franchises in the National Hockey League (NHL). ❄ The Atlanta Flames

began when a group of Georgia businessmen was granted an NHL franchise in 1972. A contest was held in Atlanta to determine the team's name, and the Flames moniker was selected to commemorate the burning of the city during the U.S. Civil War by General William Tecumseh Sherman.

But by 1980, the team was up for sale. Vancouver businessman Nelson Skalbania purchased the Atlanta franchise, and immediately sold a 50 percent interest to local Calgary businessmen. Sixteen months later, Skalbania sold the remainder of his interest, and ownership of the Flames rested entirely with six prominent Calgarians. The current owners are Dr. Grant Bartlett, Murray Edwards, Harley Hotchkiss, Ronald Joyce, Alvin Libin, Allan Markin, J.R. McCaig, Byron Seaman, and Daryl "Doc" Seaman.

The most memorable year the team has so far experienced in Calgary was 1988-1989, when it won the coveted Stanley Cup, defeating the Montreal Canadiens in a best-of-seven series by winning four games to two. Other individual trophies and awards earned that year included the Lady Byng, Emery Edge, and Molson Cup, with three team members named to the NHL all-star team: Joe Mullen, Al MacInnis, and Michael Vernon. MacInnis also won the Conn Smythe Trophy for most valuable player in the playoffs that year. In addition to the Stanley Cup, the Flames have won two President's Trophies, two Clarence Campbell Conference titles, five regular season divisional titles, and

two Smythe Division playoff championships.

### CANADIAN AIRLINES SADDLEDOME

Since 1983, the Flames have been playing in the Canadian Airlines Saddledome, which is now under Flames management. The Saddledome was built in anticipation of the arrival of the Flames, and Calgary's successful bid to host the 1988 Winter Olympic Games. During the Games, the Saddledome

was a star attraction, successfully hosting the figure-skating and hockey competitions.

"The Saddledome, which seats more than 19,000 for hockey, is one of the best entertainment facilities in North America," notes Ron Bremner, President and Chief Executive Officer of the Flames.

The Saddledome's unique saddle design is representative of Calgary's strong western heritage. Inside the building, everyone has a great view of the action. This is because the

e no pillars, and the longest
ght line from any seat in the
ouse is only 200 feet.

A major, $37 million reno-
tion of the Saddledome took
ace in 1995. The newly reno-
ted facility includes premier
ning and meeting facilities;
Chrysler Club suites, which
e 14 rows from the ice, plus
other 26 suites on row 40;
d a club seating section with
clusive restaurants and lounges.
ountry music superstar Reba
cEntire opened the new
ddledome with an electrify-
g, sold-out performance.
ficial reopening ceremonies
re celebrated at the Flames'
95-1996 season home opener.

Annually, the facility plays
st to more than 150 events,
ended by more than 1.35 mil-
n guests. "The Saddledome
s something for everyone,"
tes Bremner. "It has hosted
-ticket concerts, NBA basket-
ll, rodeos, circuses, ice shows,
d conventions, in addition
hockey games."

For promoters, the Canadian
rlines Saddledome offers
rvices to ensure that events
off without a hitch. The
ddledome provides top-quality
curity, an event management
rice, backstage lounges,
d dressing rooms, as well
a medical room. The state-
-the-art Sony Jumbotron
d its four matrix panels can
programmed to accommodate
e unique requirements of each
ent, including messages, graph-
, and on-screen videos. And
ile the on-site merchandising
tlet, called the Flames Fan
tic, offers a full line of Calgary
ames products, arrangements
n also be made to accommo-
te the sale of promotional
ms for other events.

**ART OF THE COMMUNITY**

hen they're not working hard
the ice, the Flames players

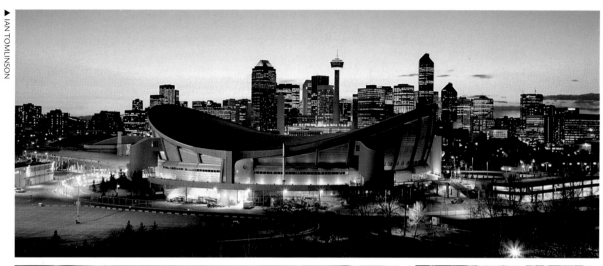

▲ IAN TOMLINSON

▲ BILODEAU

and management are working
hard for a number of charitable
causes, according to Bremner.
"It's a responsibility, and an
opportunity to reciprocate the
support and loyalty of the community," he adds.

Activities are numerous, and
include a wide variety of youth
education, sports, and community programs. The objective of
the Calgary Flames Community
Relations program, while utiliz-
ing the club's unique resources,
is to have a positive impact on
the quality of life for a cross
section of Calgarians. Each
member of the Flames has a
firm and demonstrated commitment to the community, as
well as to the children who view
the players as role models. In
addition, a number of fund-
raising activities are undertaken
by the team, the Flames Wives,
and the Calgary Flames Alumni
Association on behalf of the
Calgary Flames Foundation.

The Saddledome Foundation
was also created to support the
Calgary community and national amateur sports programs.
Through the year 2015, the
Calgary Flames will be responsible for generating over $12
million that will be used to
develop amateur sports for three
groups: the Parks Foundation
Calgary, Canadian Hockey
Association, and Calgary Olympic Development Association.
Each group has a separate purpose and mandate in using
these funds.

While the Flames and Canadian Airlines Saddledome have
combined to put Calgary on
both the national and international hockey maps, the organization has not lost touch with
the local community. Through
the team's strong level of commitment and dedication, the Flames
have helped contribute to a great
sense of regional pride for Calgarians and all Albertans.

"THE SADDLEDOME, WHICH SEATS
MORE THAN 19,000 FOR HOCKEY, IS
ONE OF THE BEST ENTERTAINMENT
FACILITIES IN NORTH AMERICA,"
NOTES RON BREMNER, PRESIDENT
AND CHIEF EXECUTIVE OFFICER
OF THE FLAMES (TOP).

A MAJOR, $37 MILLION RENOVATION
OF THE SADDLEDOME TOOK PLACE
IN 1995. IT NOW INCLUDES PREMIER
DINING AND MEETING FACILITIES; 46
CHRYSLER CLUB SUITES, WHICH ARE
14 ROWS FROM THE ICE; AND A CLUB
SEATING SECTION WITH EXCLUSIVE
RESTAURANTS AND LOUNGES (BOTTOM
LEFT AND RIGHT).

ALGARY IS INCREASINGLY EARNING A REPUTATION AS A HIGH technology centre, thanks to such companies as NovAtel Inc. NovAt specializes in high-end applications for Global Positioning System (GP markets, in which it is an influential member. GPS markets are expecte

to reach approximately US$3 billion by the year 2000, representing a projected compound annual growth rate of more than 30 percent.

NovAtel designs, markets, and supports a broad range of products that determine precise geographic locations using GPS. The system is comprised of 24 earth-orbiting satellites that transmit radio signals 24 hours a day worldwide. GPS receivers calculate the distance from the satellites to the receiver using

a triangulation technique that determines exact geographical locations. GPS is used for a variety of purposes, including navigating, tracking, mapping, and conducting geographical surveys.

NovAtel focuses on high-end GPS applications such as surveying, geographic information systems (GIS), agriculture, aviation, marine, and mining and machine control. These applications require the high levels of accuracy, real-time positioning, and reliability that can be achieved through the use of NovAtel's technically innovative products.

## FROM AVIATION TO ANCIENT RUINS

NovAtel is an important part of the most significant development in aircraft navigation since the introduction of radio-based navigation. GPS technology is being used to increase the safety and efficiency of air travel, and NovAtel products are at the forefront of this navigation revolution.

NovAtel GPS receivers are being used by the U.S. Federal Aviation Administration (FAA) in the Wide Area Augmentation System (WAAS) functional verification system. NovAtel receivers also are used in the Geostationary Uplink Subsystem (GUS) with the INMARSAT III AOR East satellite.

GPS has applications for en route navigation, precision approach, and landing of aircraft. And the worldwide availability of GPS satellite signals presents an opportunity for establishing a single, integrated

Global Navigation Satellite System (GNSS).

An agricultural technique known as site-specific farming also benefits from NovAtel's products. This is a technique that involves subdividing larg areas of land to determine pre cise requirements, such as for fertilizers, thereby increasing crop yields and reducing costs NovAtel's GPS receivers increa the speed and accuracy with which fields can be mapped and also are used to guide machine operators in the field

In marine applications, NovAtel's products provide high levels of accuracy and contribute to the safety and productivity of those who live and work on the water. Seism surveying, pipeline and under sea cable deployment, harbor channel dredging, and oil-rig positioning all benefit from th precise positioning provided t NovAtel's GPS receivers.

Archaeologists also benefi from NovAtel's technology. NovAtel's GPS units are used to map the ancient ruins of th Angkor empire in the Indochir Peninsula. In addition, mining companies use GPS units to improve the accuracy of their drilling operations and shovel control. And security compani are incorporating NovAtel's products into robotic vehicles that patrol exterior warehouse fence perimeters, and open-pi hazardous waste storage sites.

"Our technology offers high accuracy, integrity, and reliability," notes President an CEO Pascal Spothelfer. "We' one of the few highly specialize GPS companies that can provic accuracy from one meter to th

bcentimeter level." In addition being compact and powerful, ovAtel's GPS products can perate under adverse conditions.

NovAtel has developed riginal equipment manufac- rer (OEM) products that excel a variety of applications and orking environments. OEMs e the backbone of NovAtel's usiness and have been an im- ortant source of growth. As ell, NovAtel's entry into the d-user markets with the launch survey and mapping products dded a new growth dimension the business.

The company has attracted rge corporations like Hughes formation Technology Systems, arl Zeiss GmbH, and Nikon c. as strategic partners. "Our rategic alliances add technologi- l depth and breadth," says othelfer. "They also increase ur marketing efficiency and rovide the resources for pro- ams that would otherwise be yond our scope." New oppor- nities for strategic alliances e pursued to ensure the com- any's continuing growth well to the next millennium.

The company also recognizes at flexible and responsive stomer service is an integral

component of overall customer satisfaction. Customers are provided quick turnaround time in addressing concerns, and qualified engineers and techni- cians provide advice and support.

NovAtel has undergone a change in business focus. The company was established to develop, manufacture, and market cellular systems and cellular telephones. The Alberta government owned all or part of the company until 1992, when a major restructuring took place and the company was privatized. In the same year, the company made its first GPS sale. By 1996, all non-GPS activities were sold, and by 1997, a public offering was completed, resulting in the company's becoming listed on the Nasdaq stock market under the stock symbol NGPSF.

---

### CONTINUING RESEARCH

"Our customers demand con- stant innovation," notes Spothelfer. "Our strength in research and development, com- bined with our superior cus- tomer service, are geared to allow us to grow by anticipat- ing the continually changing needs of the marketplace."

NovAtel's research focuses on its core technology. This approach positions the com- pany as a technological leader in the high-end GPS industry. By searching for true innova- tion in RF and digital design, signal processing, and embed- ded software and firmware, NovAtel continues to strengthen its technology portfolio. This research effort provides the ba- sis for products with higher performance and more function- ality at lower cost, and supports a competitive position in the marketplace.

The company completed construction of a new corpo- rate head office in Calgary in May 1997, which has been custom designed to facilitate the challenges unique to GPS development.

"There are lots of telecom- munications and electronics businesses in Calgary," notes Spothelfer. "The university has an excellent geomatics program, and the expertise we require is usually available. Plus, this city provides an excellent quality of life, so it's easy to bring people from elsewhere if needed. Cal- gary is an ideal location for the company."

NOVATEL EMPLOYS GPS SPECIALISTS WHO ARE CONTINUALLY PUSHING THE BOUNDARIES OF TECHNOLOGY, MAINTAINING THE COMPANY'S POSI- TION AT THE FOREFRONT OF THIS INDUSTRY.

**C**ANFER ROLLING MILLS LTD. IS A MANUFACTURER OF LIGHTWEIGH prefabricated building components, which are utilized in constructic by the pre-engineered metal building industry. Today's pre-engineere steel buildings have one foot in the 21st century; Canfer is assisting

getting the other one there.

Gone are the drab box shapes and faded military colours of older prefabricated structures, which were mostly used for warehouses and workshops. The vast array of designer colours now available (made possible by space age polymers), along with imaginative new structural designs, has created a metal building in the market that is extremely attractive, functional, cost effective, and easy to install.

Today, in the Calgary market and throughout the province of Alberta, Canfer is introducing new ideas to the pre-engineered metal building industry that utilize these new architectural shapes and colours. Canfer's new approach allows it to produce the right product at the right price; its timing has catapulted the company's growth to such an extent that *Profit* magazine has recognized it as one of Canada's 50 fastest-growing companies.

In 1984, Carlo Simonelli, P. Eng., who trained as a machinist in his youth and had been extensively involved in the conventional steel building industry in Alberta, founded Canfer armed with the seed of an idea—to introduce lightweight, cold-formed channels to the conventional steel building industry. Drawing from his past practical experience, Simonelli cashed his retirement savings and set about designing and constructing his first roll forming mill. Simonelli's wife, Erika, and son, Marco, lent support during those formative years by working long hours alongside him to produce those initial products.

Canfer began with one 1,600-square-foot facility, which was so inadequate that, in order for the roll forming mill to process material, the shop doors had to be kept open to accommodate the space required for the finished product. Subsequent refinement of its existing mills, and the design and construction of additional roll forming mills, allowed Canfer to expand its product line, which resulted in the cautious, phased expansion of the facility to the 33,000-square-foot plant that the company is housed in today. Plans and preparations are under

way to build a state-of-the-art 110,000-square-foot facility tha will house the next stage of th operation's expansion.

## THE RIGHT PRODUCT AT THE RIGHT PRICE

Canfer's strength lies in the fac that it has strategically locate its manufacturing facilities— for lightweight cold-formed structural sections, which mal up the "bones" of pre-engineere metal buildings, and for assoc ated products such as claddin, panels, which form the "skin" of the buildings—right in the centre of its market area. "Th ability to provide the right product at the right price with the quickest possible delivery times gives Canfer its competitive advantage," says Marco Simonelli, company Vice-President.

The production equipmer which is designed and built in-house, is constantly being modified and improved, offerin an ever increasing product lin to Canfer's customers. The con

FOUNDER CARLO SIMONELLI (MIDDLE), WITH HIS SON, MARCO, AND DAUGHTER, MONICA, WHO HAVE JOINED HIM IN MAKING CANFER ROLLING MILLS LTD. A SUCCESS.

A GROWING SEGMENT OF CANFER'S BUSINESS TODAY IS THE DEVELOPMENT AND CONSTRUCTION OF TURNKEY PROJECTS. THE COMPANY IS ABLE TO WORK CLOSELY WITH ITS CLIENTS AND ASSIST THROUGHOUT THE ENTIRE BUILDING PROCESS, FROM ARCHITECTURAL CONCEPTION TO CONSTRUCTION COMPLETION.

ny continuously seeks out inno-
tive approaches to maximize
ficiency, and works closely
ith its clients to identify their
eds and requirements. Can-
r also makes available to its
ients the ways and means to
hieve cost savings. For example,
nventional steel building com-
nents can sometimes be sub-
tuted with cold-formed sections
oduced by Canfer, resulting
substantial savings. Cold-
rmed sections are a fraction
the weight of conventional
eel, and weight is a main fac-
r in the cost of steel products.
he company's components are
refully engineered to cut costs
ithout compromising the qual-
 of the product or the integ-
ty of the structure.

Canfer's growth is the direct
sult of the company's ability
respond to the market's
mands and needs. A growing
gment of Canfer's business
day is the development and
nstruction of turnkey projects.
he company is able to work
osely with its clients and assist
roughout the entire building
ocess, from architectural con-
ption to construction comple-
on. The Canfer product has
en readily accepted in the
arketplace, and can now be
und in manufacturing plants,
arehouses, sawmills, office/
stribution terminals, and agri-

cultural and residential applications across Western Canada.

Today's marketplace is increasingly demanding in regard
to the quality and flexibility of
product that it is willing to accept.
"Canfer's ability to provide a
product that satisfies those needs
and, at the same time, exhibits
built-in qualities that allow flexibility in design and construction
is becoming one of its most valuable assets," says Carlo Simonelli.

Canfer's efforts have been
rewarded with steadily increasing sales and growth. The company and its affiliates now have
a work force of nearly 100 employees; with increasing interest
in its products from such places
as Atlantic Canada, Spain, the
Philippines, and Jamaica, that
figure is expected to double
in the near future.

The Province of Alberta,
and the City of Calgary in particular, is expanding its image
beyond cattle, wheat, and oil.
Alberta's vision to diversify its
business sector, realized with
the help of the Western Diversification Program, has contributed to Canfer's success. Canfer
is continually evolving to facilitate the expansion of its market;
technical and managerial consult-
ants are being retained so that
all of the subtle nuances of
the industry may be gleaned
and harnessed to maximize
efficiency.

Canfer Rolling Mills Ltd.
reflects Calgary's exhilarating
pioneer spirit and entrepreneurial confidence, and shares its
pride in the city's flourishing
economy and sense of
community.

LIGHTWEIGHT, PREFABRICATED BUILD-
ING COMPONENTS ARE MANUFACTURED
IN CANFER'S ROLL FORMING MILLS.

THE BIG ROCK BREWERY AND THE
BULK TEC INTERNATIONAL BUILDING
ARE EXAMPLES OF THE INNOVATIONS
MADE IN ARCHITECTURAL DESIGN AND
COLOUR AVAILABILITY IN THE PRE-
ENGINEERED BUILDING INDUSTRY.

ONGKONG BANK OF CANADA WAS ESTABLISHED IN VANCOUVER I
1981 after changes in Canadian legislation opened the market to oversea
owned banks. A wholly owned subsidiary of HSBC Holdings plc, head
quartered in London, Hongkong Bank of Canada is part of on

of the world's leading international banking and financial services organizations, with major consumer, commercial, investment banking, and insurance businesses operating under long-established names in the Asia-Pacific region, Europe, the Americas, and the Middle East.

The bank's Canadian subsidiary has been strengthened by a series of acquisitions, including the Bank of British Columbia in 1986; Midland Bank Canada in 1988; Lloyds Bank Canada in 1990; Metropolitan Trust Company of Canada and institutional research broker BBN James Capel Inc., both in 1995; and Barclays Bank of Canada and the investment management firm of M.K. Wong & Associates in 1996.

Hongkong Bank of Canada has 117 branches within Canad and two branches in the western United States, and is now the seventh-largest bank in Canada.

Hongkong Bank of Canada operates five full-service branche in Calgary, as well as the headquarters for the Western Region that includes Alberta, Saskatchewan, and Manitoba It is the largest international bank in Canada, employs Canadian staff, and has strong Canadian representation on the board of directors.

"We're a full-service bank with a strong retail and commercial base," says Michael Papadatos, Senior Vice-Presiden Western Region. "Because we took over the Bank of British Columbia and Lloyds Bank Canada, we have many loyal employees with more than 20 years of service. Our staff is dynamic, motivated, and customer oriented."

### EMPHASIS ON THE GLOBAL MARKETPLACE

While it's a full-service bank, with services ranging from operating and term loans and deposit services to foreign exchange and discount brokerag services, Hongkong Bank of Canada provides trade finance as a key business segment.

As more and more Calgary based companies begin to do business in the global marketplace, they can take advantage of such services as import and export letters of credit or intro ductions for local commercial customers doing business over seas. "We can provide the glo

al banking network, which
essential in the delivery of
uperior trade finance," says
apadatos.

All the Canadian branches
re connected electronically
o more than 5,500 offices
n 79 countries and territories.
n addition, HSBC James Capel
anada Inc. and Hongkong
ank Discount Trading Inc.
rovide access to every major
ock exchange in the world to
atisfy investor needs through-
ut Canada.

The bank has also taken
dvantage of electronic commu-
ications technology to enhance
he speed, accuracy, and secu-
ty of international banking
rvices. For example, the bank
as the first in Canada to intro-
uce on-line discount trading—
s Net Trader service—on the
ternet.

"Furthermore," adds
apadatos, "we offer competi-
ve pricing on foreign exchange.
Ve operate one of the world's
iggest trading operations,
ased in London, New York,
nd Hong Kong. Here in Calgary,
ustomers can open foreign
urrency accounts in seven
urrencies—the French franc,
he pound sterling, the Deutsche
Iark, the Swiss franc, U.S. funds,
he Japanese yen, and the Hong
ong dollar."

Finally, the bank's interna-
onal mutual funds are managed
y local specialists, who have
much deeper understanding
f the market in the country
volved. "We benefit from the
xpertise of local funds manag-
rs," says Papadatos.

## A FOCUS ON
## RELATIONSHIPS

Faster, smarter, friendlier"
the bank's slogan, and this
rong customer orientation
as been crucial in its success
date. The bank takes a team
pproach to each account: Cli-

ents are called and visited regularly, so all key staff members
have a thorough understanding
of each client's needs. The bank
does not consider itself a trans-
actional bank. "We don't do
a deal and then walk away,"
says Papadatos. "We develop
long-term relationships with
our clients." This focus has
helped the Calgary branches
acquire a loyal local customer
base, as well as some large,
international clients who had
been doing business with the
bank in other countries.

In a recent independent
survey by the Canadian Banking
Association, Hongkong Bank
of Canada ranked as number
one in a majority of categories
of service provided small- and
medium-sized businesses, as well.
Customer satisfaction was an
outstanding 94 percent, which
is 20 percent above the average
for Canadian banks.

The bank also contributes
to the communities where its
branches are located. In Calgary,
the bank provides support for
the arts and the United Way,
for example, by sponsoring
Alberta Ballet productions.

Papadatos himself has been
vice-president of the Hong Kong
Canada Business Association
for a number of years, and the
bank is one of the founders of
the city's annual Dragon Boat
Festival. The bank's Chinatown branch manager is the

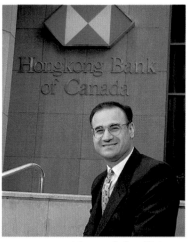

HONGKONG BANK OF CANADA
OPERATES FIVE FULL-SERVICE
BRANCHES IN CALGARY.

"WE'RE A FULL-SERVICE BANK, WITH
A STRONG RETAIL AND COMMERCIAL
BASE," SAYS MICHAEL PAPADATOS,
SENIOR VICE-PRESIDENT, WESTERN
REGION.

current president of the Chinatown Merchants' Association,
one of Calgary's leading Chinese
business organizations.

With its focus on service,
long-term relationships, and
strong international connections,
it's no surprise that Hongkong
Bank of Canada is growing
rapidly. And the Western Region
is the fastest-growing region
in the country, according to
Papadatos. "In 1986, there
were under 10 employees in
Calgary. There are now 131
in Calgary alone," he says. "In
the last four years, we've doubled
our business in Calgary.

"Some people in Calgary
still ask: Who is Hongkong Bank
of Canada?" says Papadatos.
"We have been here for a long
time and are part of the fabric
of this city. We have a loyal
client base, and we want to
continue to be a bank for all
Calgarians."

AXX PETROLEUM LTD. WAS FOUNDED IN 1987 AS A JUNIOR CAPITAL POO on the Alberta Stock Exchange. Since then, the oil and gas company ha shown impressive, steady growth in production and cash flow. In 1992, th oil and gas company was listed on the Toronto Stock Exchange. ❋ Max

was founded by current Chairman, President, and Chief Executive Officer Burl N. Aycock, along with colleague Peter Whiteway, who resigned from the company in 1996. "In our early years, we focused on acquisitions as a means to grow," notes Aycock, "but our objective has always been to grow through exploration, and now we are accomplishing that goal."

### THREE PRIMARY OPERATIONS

Although Maxx has some natural gas holdings, the company has chosen to focus on the development of oil reserves because of the volatility of gas markets. Oil markets have generally demonstrated more strength in the past few years, and generate significantly higher netbacks. Future prospects for oil are forecast to be strong.

Maxx has operations in three primary areas: Saskatchewan, Alberta, and, more recently, Kansas. The company is continuing to expand its oil operations in southeast Saskatchewan. With the use of 3-D seismic, vertical, and horizontal drilling technology, Maxx has been able to access reserves that otherwise would not be economical to develop. "Our Saskatchewan holdings represent more than 50 percent of our annual crude oil production and almost 40 percent of our total oil and gas production," says Aycock, "making it our largest net-producing area.

"Our success in southeast Saskatchewan has encouraged us to look for other areas where horizontal drilling could improve

oil recovery from shallow carbonate reservoirs," he adds.

Early in 1996, the company identified an oil-producing area in west-central Kansas with almost identical characteristics to its oil fields being developed in Saskatchewan. Moreover, the Kansas oil fields were at the same stage of development as the Saskatchewan fields were 12 to 15 years earlier, with limited use of the latest technology.

With attractive land also available at low cost, Maxx acquired more than 18,000 gross acres of oil leases in Kansas with a joint venture partner in the United States. An aggressive development program has been initiated. "The Kansas project is our first major venture outside Canada," Aycock notes. "We believe it will be a relatively low-risk, high-reward undertaking with the potential to develop several million barrels of high-quality oil reserves."

In Alberta, Maxx has established a new core area in the Wildmere field in the east-central

part of the province. Recogniz ing the potential of applying new technologies to producing heavier crude oil, Maxx has committed itself to pursuing significant exploration and devel opment activity in this area.

"We intend to be a major player in the Wildmere area," says Aycock, "and through th use of new technology, such as advanced completion technique and state-of-the-art pumping equipment, we expect to increas efficiency and reduce operating costs."

### EXPLORATION AND DEVELOPMENT

Maxx's major successes in add ing new oil reserves have all incorporated the application of the latest technologies, including 3-D seismic, horizonta drilling, new well completion practices, new production equipment, and new operating techniques. "We will continue to focus on areas where these technologies have proven suc-

BURL N. AYCOCK, CHAIRMAN, PRESIDENT, AND CHIEF EXECUTIVE OFFICER OF MAXX PETROLEUM LTD.

essful," says Aycock, "as well as continue to investigate new technologies and opportunities where technology can give us the upper hand."

Maxx is also working diligently to reduce operating costs and improve efficiency. At Wildmere, central processing and oil-gathering facilities were built, eliminating third-party processing fees and reducing trucking expenses. This infrastructure will improve the economics of the company's expanding exploration and development program in the area. Maxx is also selling interests in minor properties that are either non-core or have high operating costs.

The company is building a team of professionals, both at the management and at the technical levels, to ensure sufficient resources for continued growth. "We're technically strong in all the disciplines—geology, geophysics, land, engineering, and financial," says Aycock. All of Maxx's 50 employees are stockholders, and hence have a vested interest in the success of the company.

Although still a young company, Maxx has not neglected its contribution to the community. In addition to supporting employees' volunteer efforts, the company contributes regularly to charitable causes. One program is especially appreciated by employees: The company makes a financial contribution to the library of every school that is attended by an employee's child.

With its excellent track record and the largest inventory of new exploration drilling prospects in its history, Maxx continues strive to achieve a balance between growth and investment opportunities. The company is committed to growth through full-cycle exploration.

"We are technically very thorough, and when we confirm the viability of new technology, we aggressively pursue opportunities to exploit development of new oil and gas production," says Aycock. "We believe this helps minimize risk and maximize the return on our investment. To date, we have been able to steadily grow our company, with our cash flow per share increasing at an average rate of about 50 percent over the past five years."

JOHN GALESKI (STANDING), VICE-PRESIDENT EXPLORATION, AND TERRY MCLEAN, MANAGER GEOPHYSICS, REVIEW A 3-D SEISMIC PROJECT USING ONE OF MAXX'S GEOPHYSICAL WORK STATIONS.

A DRILLING OPERATION IN SOUTHERN ALBERTA

THANKS TO COMPANIES LIKE WESTFAIR FOODS LTD., CALGARY IS NOW the hub of the wholesale and retail grocery business in Western Canada. Ironically, though, mention the company and most Canadians will give you a blank look. It is the stores that Westfair owns that are familiar: the

real Canadian Superstore, Extra Foods, the real Canadian Wholesale Club, and Western Grocers, Westfair's wholesale arm.

A subsidiary of Loblaw Companies limited, Westfair moved its head office from Winnipeg to Calgary in 1988. "Calgary is a central location for us," says Public Affairs Director David Ryzebol. "Plus, its airport offers easy access to the rest of Western Canada." The company's stores are spread

from Vancouver Island to Western Ontario to as far north as Whitehorse, with new sites always under construction.

Westfair's continuing success over the years has prompted many other western food suppliers and manufacturers to relocate to Calgary. "I believe that 70 percent of retail grocery business decisions for Western Canada are now made in Calgary," notes Ryzebol.

### A WINNING FORMULA

While Westfair's real Canadian Superstores are big in size—some are as large as 140,000 square feet—they don't look like warehouses. They're bright and nicely decorated, with state-of-the-art equipment. The ceilings are high, the aisles are wide, and the shopping carts are extra large.

Superstore has achieved significant success and tremendous growth since 1979, based on a three-part strategy: low prices, one-stop shopping, and large selection. With such slo-

gans as Permanent Discount and Everyday Low Prices, the store attracts families who buy large quantities of groceries, are pressed for time, and are interested in saving money. Surveys conducted by the Consumers Association of Canada and local television station CFCN confirm that Superstore's prices are consistently the lowest.

With a wide selection of goods and services, in addition to groceries, Superstore offers a mind-boggling 50,000 products that cater to the interests and needs of families, well-travelled baby boomers, and Canada's growing ethnic communities. "Our produce department alone is the size of a conventional grocery store," says Ryzebol. "We've introduced produce that was previously unavailable in Canada, and is now available on a daily basis."

In addition, since the late 1970s, the company has featured three lines of award-winning products, each developed to answer customers' demands. First, in response to the lagging economy of the late 1970s, Westfair became the first company in Western Canada to offer generic products under the No-Name brand. "During those years, customers were being squeezed financially," says Ryzebol, "and they wanted extra value."

Then, during the 1980s, baby boomers who travelled extensively were interested in foreign and gourmet cuisine. Westfair began to offer its own line of unique, high-quality products, the President's Choice line, that couldn't be bought anywhere else. Many of these

roducts helped would-be gourmet cooks create exotic dishes
with little effort. Such products
s the company's renowned
Memories of Szechwan peanut
auce have won many awards.
resident's Choice products are
ow available in gourmet food
tores throughout North Amer-
:a. Finally, driven by the envi-
onmental movement of the late
980s, Westfair introduced its
Green Line of environmentally
riendly products.

"This business is so dynam-
:," says Ryzebol, "that you
an't predict next week. New
roducts are always under de-
elopment, and customers vote
vith their dollars."

## SERVING ITS COMMUNITIES

ecause of their size, Superstores
re situated in larger communi-
ies. Extra Foods, Westfair's
ther food stores, are sized like
onventional food stores—ap-
roximately 30,000 to 50,000
quare feet—and are likely to
e located in smaller commu-
ities, such as High River,
Cochrane, and Stettler, Alberta.
s the local neighbourhood
tore, they meet the needs of
he smaller market.

The real Canadian Whole-
ale Club stores, of which there

are two in Calgary, cater to another group. These stores offer
products in large sizes for institutional buyers, such as restaurants and food service suppliers.
The Western Grocers operation
supplies products to the company's retail food stores, as well
as independent grocery stores.

Ryzebol believes that the
growth of Westfair's stores has
been beneficial to the industry,
as well as to consumers. "We've
been in Saskatoon since 1979,
and there are still plenty of
thriving and prosperous small
food stores in operation there,"
he says. "What we provide is
healthy competition among
major grocery retailers, with
the end result being that consumers experience a consider-
able reduction in the cost of their

groceries, wherever they shop."

Furthermore, a big part of
Westfair's Western Canadian
influence and management is
reflected in the company's generous support of charitable
community projects.

The company's Calgary sup-
port includes donations to the
United Way, Interfaith Food
Bank, Mustard Seed Registry,
medical research at the Univer-
sity of Calgary, Alberta Ballet,
Alberta Children's Hospital,
Calgary International Children's
Festival, Calgary Philharmonic
Orchestra, and the Multiple
Sclerosis Society Super Cities
Walk. Ryzebol concludes, "We
want to contribute to the well-
being of the communities where
we operate—to enhance the
quality of life."

CLOCKWISE FROM TOP LEFT:
WITH A WIDE SELECTION OF GOODS
AND SERVICES IN ADDITION TO GRO-
CERIES, SUPERSTORE OFFERS A MIND-
BOGGLING 50,000 PRODUCTS THAT
CATER TO THE INTERESTS AND NEEDS
OF FAMILIES, WELL-TRAVELLED BABY
BOOMERS, AND CANADA'S GROWING
ETHNIC COMMUNITIES.

"OUR PRODUCE DEPARTMENT ALONE
IS THE SIZE OF A CONVENTIONAL GRO-
CERY STORE," SAYS PUBLIC AFFAIRS
DIRECTOR DAVID RYZEBOL.

SUPERSTORE HAS ACHIEVED SIGNIFI-
CANT SUCCESS AND TREMENDOUS
GROWTH SINCE 1988, BASED ON A
THREE-PART STRATEGY: LOW PRICES,
ONE-STOP SHOPPING, AND LARGE
SELECTION.

ONE OF CALGARY'S MOST DELIGHTFUL CHARACTERISTICS IS ITS "CAN-DO" entrepreneurial attitude. ASM Industries demonstrates that attitude in spades. ❋ The private company was founded by President Ray Gertz in 1990, when he purchased the assets of ARTS Sheet Metal. With about

a dozen employees, ASM initially focused on contracting work for commercial and industrial heating and ventilation applications. But within two years, the company was expanding into custom metal manufacturing.

"We still do a lot of heating and ventilation work," notes Gertz. "But custom work is the area we're focusing on for growth. There's an edge there for us."

The company now fabricates custom products from stainless steel and other alloys. Installation of these products occurs on commercial, institutional, and industrial sites. Many of ASM's long-time customers are from the packing oil field and mining industries. About 90 percent of its business is local, and most of its clients are obtained by referral.

As a first step toward its goal of becoming a full-service metalworking shop, ASM expanded its facilities in 1993 from 6,500 to 11,000 square feet, and then to 16,000 square feet

in 1996. The company also began to purchase specialized computer-controlled equipment, including a computer numerical control turret punch and a computer numerical control plasma and torch cutting table. "These types of equipment are great labor-saving tools, however, they do require highly trained personnel to operate," comments Gertz.

### FLYING HIGH FOR PRATT & WHITNEY

The custom projects ASM has tackled over the past few years have been both challenging and diverse. By far the biggest challenge was to build a large exhaust system for testing aircraft engines for Pratt & Whitney in Lethbridge, Alberta. Because the job was so technical, ASM ended up being the only company to bid on this $800,000 contract. Involving lots of custom fabrication work inside the test booths, the project demanded very high levels

of accuracy—tolerances were within one ten-thousandth of an inch.

"We also had a very tight schedule," says Gertz. "We had only two months to do the project, and there were 40 people working day and night to get it done. But we completed the job on time, and our customers were pleased with our work."

ASM has also been involved in fabricating components for the oil and gas industry, such as belt guards, tanks, and pump and oil rig parts. ASM's work for packing houses, restaurants, and restaurant supply businesses includes fabricating conveyors, work tables, shelving exhaust systems, and hoods. Custom cabinets and sinks are also provided.

For example, the company has built all the kitchen equipment for the Joey's Only chain of seafood restaurants since 1994. The Calgary-based chain is undergoing continuing expansion with restaurants opening across Canada and in the United States.

ASM INDUSTRIES WAS FOUNDED BY PRESIDENT RAY GERTZ IN 1990 (LEFT).

ONE OF ASM'S MOST CHALLENGING PROJECTS WAS BUILDING A LARGE EXHAUST SYSTEM FOR TESTING AIRCRAFT ENGINES AT THE PRATT & WHITNEY FACILITY IN LETHBRIDGE (RIGHT).

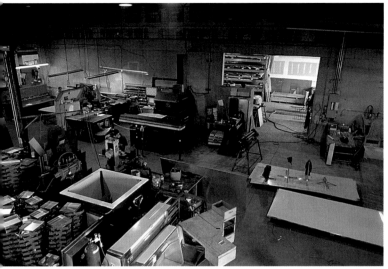

ASM won the ongoing contract by offering competitive pricing, quality workmanship, and uniformity of product.

For this contract, ASM does custom fabrication of sinks, dish tables, counters, and tables and hoods, in addition to standard items for all the chain's sites, such as carts and shields. So far, the company has completed about $100,000 worth of work for Joey's Only.

## SUCCESSFULLY MANAGING PEOPLE AND GROWTH

Some start-up companies have difficulty moving into the next phase of operational growth, but ASM's growth has been managed well. A conservative approach has ensured that the company is financially secure. Today, the company boasts annual revenues of more than $5 million, compared to $800,000 in its first year. Furthermore, ASM now has 50 full-time employees.

Gertz also credits his hands-off philosophy and his skill at dealing with people, noting that staff turnover is negligible. Most of the employees who started with the company are still there.

"I had no personal experience in sheet metal—my background was in construction,"

Gertz notes. "I certainly didn't have the skills to actually do the work, so I learned how to manage. Today, I consider our office staff to be the most dedicated and experienced in the industry. Together with a great group of highly trained and efficient tradesmen, we are able to tackle any metal project efficiently."

In addition, the company has been certified by the Canadian Welding Bureau, which sets quality-assurance-type standards for welding procedures. Safety is also a concern for ASM, since welding and related activities are sometimes quite dangerous. The company joined the Partners in Injury Reduction (PIR) program of Alberta Labor's Occupational

Health and Safety branch in 1995. The program has helped generate a very positive safety record, with no significant injuries having occurred since that time. An added bonus is that the company's cost for workers' compensation has fallen as a result.

But the bottom line for ASM is that Calgary can-do attitude. "There are very few companies who can do the custom work we do—maybe only one or two in the city," says Gertz.

"We're very diverse and we try to be innovative," Gertz concludes. "Our contacts know that if they can't get it done anywhere else, they can come to us. We're not afraid to tackle new projects."

ASM FABRICATES CUSTOM PRODUCTS FROM STAINLESS STEEL AND OTHER ALLOYS FOR ITS CUSTOMERS, WHICH INCLUDE RESTAURANTS, PACKING HOUSES, RESTAURANT SUPPLY BUSINESSES, AND THE OIL AND GAS INDUSTRIES. PICTURED CLOCKWISE FROM TOP LEFT ARE ASM'S SHEET METAL FABRICATION FACILITY, AN EMPLOYEE WELDING STAINLESS STEEL TANKS, AND A COMPUTER-CONTROLLED BENDING OPERATION.

**A**S THE ONLY CANADIAN PUBLIC COMPANY SOLELY DEDICATED TO horizontal and directional drilling, Ryan Energy Technologies Inc. has been riding the wave of the Canadian petroleum industry renaissance. ❊ Ryan Energy was founded in 1991 by Rick Ryan, who now serves as

President and CEO. In the summer of 1996, the company became listed on the Toronto Stock Exchange. Shareholders saw the value of their shares skyrocket from 70 cents in January 1996 to close at $9 at the end of July 1997.

### NICHE MARKETING KEY TO RYAN'S SUCCESS

Ryan is organized into three divisions: Horizontal and Directional Drilling Services; Measurement While Drilling and Logging While Drilling Services; and Research, Development, and Engineering. The company competes with large, multinational companies that provide a variety of services to oil and gas companies.

"Where I think we are very competitive against bigger companies is the skill of our people in applying our technology," says Ryan, who was recognized as an Emerging Entrepreneur by the 1996 Canadian Entrepreneur of the Year Awards. "We are more nimble and responsive than larger firms because we can make decisions quickly. In terms of our horsepower-to-weight ratio, I think we deliver a lot for the size of our company."

Canadian customers have been pleased with the quality and responsiveness of the Ryan team. The company's current client list reads like a who's who in the Canadian oil and gas industry. Clients include Shell Canada, Texaco, Petro-Canada, Northstar Energy, and Talisman, as well as a number of smaller and mid-size oil and gas companies.

Ryan is also making inroads in the U.S. market. In early 1997, the company announced the purchase of Directional Technologies, Inc., a directional

drilling company based in Lafayette, Louisiana. The purchase is expected to significantly increase the company's horizontal and directional drilling capacity in North America, as well as provide the platform for further introduction of Ryan's new technologies into the southern U.S. market. The business is now operating under the name Ryan Directional Technologies Inc.

### STRONG COMMITMENT TO ONGOING RESEARCH

Ryan's ongoing research and development focus has been a major factor in its success. "New technology is improving our customers' ability to locate, drill, and produce new and existing oil and gas reserves," notes Ryan. "It's also contributing to the improvement of economic returns by reducing exploration and drilling risk while increasing recoverability of reserves."

The company's commitment to developing new technology

RYAN ENERGY TECHNOLOGIES INC. IS COMMITTED TO DEVELOPING NEW TECHNOLOGY IN ANTICIPATION OF CUSTOMERS' NEEDS. AT LEFT, WORKERS ARE RETRIEVING A DOWN-HOLE ELECTRONIC PACKAGE THAT RECORDS AND UPDATES ALL DIRECTIONAL DATA PERTAINING TO THE WELL BORE TRAJECTORY, AND, AT RIGHT, RECORDING OPERATIONAL DATA OF ALL DIRECTIONAL DOWN-HOLE TOOLS.

TOM WALKER

n anticipation of customers' needs is evident. Early research resulted in the development of a top-quality Measurement While Drilling (MWD) device to complement Ryan's drilling services. Based on principles similar to those used in missile guidance systems, the proprietary MWD technology transmits critical data from the bottom of the well. This information allows drillers to "see" where the well is going and to make appropriate adjustments, fine-tuning the position of the well bore in the best part of the reservoir.

In addition to the MWD device, the company has developed a Logging While Drilling (LWD) device that measures and transmits to the surface geological data about the formation through which the drill bit is moving. Real-time logging information can be used to adjust the trajectory of the well bore during the drilling process. As a result, the well bore can be positioned in the highest-quality reservoir, enabling maximum production rates and recoverability.

One of Ryan's research projects, the development of its proprietary Geological Steering Instrumentation (GSI) technology, has been successfully completed. This technology facilitates the measuring and real-time transmission to the surface of additional geological and reservoir information. By applying this technology, Ryan's clients can optimize the placement of the well bore for purposes of enhancing their oil and gas production and recoverability.

Furthermore, Ryan is one of only a few companies in the world to have access to commercial electromagnetic technology for drilling oil and gas wells. This proprietary solid-state technology allows the company's MWD/LWD equipment to communicate down-hole information to the surface without drilling fluid. The technology will form the foundation for the company's subsurface communication systems for the next five to 10 years. It will also allow Ryan to develop a commercial market in under-balanced drilling and air drilling applications.

Four of the company's 12 current research projects are expected to be ready for commercialization during 1997. Furthermore, Executive Vice-President and Chief Technical Officer Derek Logan is one of the founders of the Petroleum Technology Alliance of Canada, established in the summer of 1996 as a collaborative think tank for the development of new technology for the oil and gas industry.

In addition to leading-edge technology, superior job performance has been a key component in the company's growth. As the company's technology becomes increasingly sophisticated, additional technical training for staff is needed. A new, formal facility, using the latest educational tools, ensures the company can provide superior personnel to meet expanding operations.

In the coming years, the company plans to expand overseas, bringing Canadian technical know-how to South America and the Middle East. Ryan's next major challenge will be learning how to grow, while remaining nimble and responsive at the same time. With the strides the company has made thus far and the energy with which it strives to attain its goals, Ryan will, no doubt, meet the challenge successfully.

TECHNOLOGY DEVELOPED IN RYAN'S RESEARCH, DEVELOPMENT, AND ENGINEERING FACILITY PROVIDES THE SOLID FOUNDATION FOR CONTINUED GROWTH AND SUCCESS (LEFT).

CONFIGURING THE MWD DEVICE TO MAKE APPROPRIATE ADJUSTMENTS FINE-TUNES THE POSITION OF THE WELL BORE IN THE BEST PART OF THE RESERVOIR (RIGHT).

▼▲ TOM WALKER

PARTNERSHIP, LEADERSHIP, AND INNOVATION ARE THE CORNERSTONES OF SAP Canada's success, according to Carol Burch, District Director for the company's western operations. SAP delivers enterprise-wide software solutions with the primary goal of maximizing the business performance and profitability of its customers. More than 40,000 people in Canada are now using SAP's innovative software systems to do their work more efficiently, and that number is rapidly growing.

SAP—which stands for Systems, Applications, and Products in Data Processing—has become a North American phenomenon in a very short time. In business for 25 years, the company's global headquarters is in Walldorf, Germany, and it now has operations throughout Europe, Africa, North and South America, Asia, Australia, and New Zealand.

"We are currently the market leader in providing enterprise-wide applications in the client/server environment," says Burch. "This is supported by several industry and business studies. We expect our worldwide annual revenues to increase significantly above industry averages each year through the year 2000."

### R/3 SOFTWARE

SAP's major product is the R/3 application software for open client/server systems. Companies can choose to implement any one function, or a complete suite of applications. The power of SAP software on a departmental, divisional, or global scale lies in providing real-time integration, linking a company's business processes and applications, and supporting immediate responses to change throughout the organization.

According to Burch, R/3 is an important strategic tool in the competition for market share and in the pursuit of profitability. With R/3 providing a flexible software base for their business infrastructure, organizations of all sizes—and in all sectors of industry—can profit from the quality and functionality of the applications.

SAP's Canadian operations are headquartered in Toronto, and regional offices have been established in Montreal, Vancouver, and Ottawa. SAP has been active in Calgary since 1991 and opened a small office in 1993. Now located in the Canterra Tower downtown, the Calgary office has grown significantly and oversees all Western Canadian operations. The Western District is expected to be home to approximately 75 employees by the end of 1997. "Calgary is centrally located to handle all of Western Canada," comments Burch. "Plus, it is quickly becoming the city of choice for many head offices."

In Calgary, SAP serves a range of clients from multinational corporations to small

THE AWARD-WINNING CANTERRA TOWER IS HOME TO THE WESTERN CANADA OFFICE, ONE OF SAP'S FASTEST-GROWING DISTRICTS WORLDWIDE.

businesses. A sample of customers includes Petro-Canada,
TELUS, Canadian Pacific Railway, TransAlta Corporation,
Husky, Alberta Energy and
Utilities Board, NOVA, Agrium,
Nowsco, and Precision Drilling.
In addition to the oil and gas
industry, the company is addressing the needs of the public sector, utility, telecommunications,
financial, consumer products,
and transportation fields.

## STRATEGIC PARTNERSHIPS

Complementing SAP's own
consulting services, the company's strategic partners provide
their own expertise and a full
range of products and services
in support of SAP projects,
including business case development, industry and best business practices, as well as support
for system implementation,
hardware, and database options.
Local partners include such
well-established companies
as IBM, Digital Equipment,
Hewlett Packard, OmniLogic,
Deloitte & Touche/ICS, Price
Waterhouse, KPMG, and Ernst
& Young. In direct response
to customer demand, SAP has
also developed a unique partnership with the University of
Calgary to offer courses on the
benefits of R/3 and how to
use the software.

## HIRING THE INDUSTRY'S BEST

SAP's management believes to
provide innovative solutions, you
need innovative, committed
employees. "At SAP, we hire
the best and the brightest," says
Burch. "Calgary has a very good
pool of expertise and we hire
locally whenever possible. We
look for people with a strong
business background—at least
two years' business experience—in

addition to the required technical
background. A business background is important, since employees must be able to walk
into a new client's environment
and understand their processes
and organization, as well as work
with staff and management to
develop the most effective solutions. Quite often, the processes
themselves require reengineering.
So far, our greatest challenge
is finding the right people
quickly enough."

In addition to hiring local
talent, SAP demonstrates its
commitment to the local community through a number of
sponsorships. "We're a major
sponsor of the Calgary Philharmonic Orchestra," says
Burch. The company has also
sponsored a 100-mile run for
Hostelling International, matches
employees' charity contributions
dollar for dollar, and actively
supports clients' fund-raising
events and charities. This trans-
lates into substantial support for
local non-profit groups who are
dependent on personal and corporate donations.

SAP's commitment to
the community is ultimately
demonstrated through its business. "We help companies work
more efficiently," concludes
Burch. "In addition, for every
single employee we hire, five
additional workers are hired
by our partners to help implement a SAP solution. That's
an important contribution to
both the local and Canadian
economies."

A "FOUR-FINGER PHILOSOPHY" HELPED SPM/Calgary, Inc. ACHIEVE $30 million in sales in 1996 and the number one rank in operational perfor mance over all sister SPM plants in the world. ❀ General Manager Tom Jackman explains: "Our management philosophy is very simple. We be

lieve all employees should provide 100 percent effort and be honest, professional, and mature. We select our people very carefully. If they have these four qualities, then there is no need to have a highly controlled environment, and we can be assured of operational excellence through the contribution of our people. We train extensively, empower employees to do their jobs, and improve processes to better service our customer needs."

Most of SPM/Calgary's 250 employees work in the company's 80,000-square-foot plastics factory, producing telephone components for telecommunications companies such as Northern Telecom (Nortel). In fact, the plant began opera-

tions in 1994 on the basis of a contract with Nortel, which produces several new telephone models each year.

Since start-up, however, SPM has acquired ISO 9002 quality certification, expanded its customer base, started providing additional value-added services, and positioned itself as a precision manufacturer of high-tech plastic components. Sales have quadrupled, and the plant now operates 24 hours a day, seven days a week.

## VALUE-ADDED SERVICES THROUGH PARTNERING

While initially operations only involved moulding plastic components, in response to custom-

ers' demands SPM has added front-end services such as tooling design, and prototype development. At the back end, subassembly of parts is now a common feature of the company's operations.

"We're involved in the whole process," says Jackman, "from concept through to production. We're a one-stop shop and we like to partner with our clients. Nortel used to handle the other operations themselves but they've outsourced many of these functions. We are a plastics company; we can do some of those jobs in a more focused way, allowing them to concentrate on their core competencies—like product development and marketing."

SPM/Calgary operations include 27 moulding machines, automated robots and assembly lines, pad printing, ultrasonic welding, a state-of-the-art tool room, a quality lab, and CAD/CAM systems. Many of the processes are fully automated. For example, after moulding the plastic casing, telephone handsets are assembled on a conveyor belt, tested electronically, welded, and packaged—all through the

use of robots. In addition, all machines are linked to a computerized system to ensure that quality standards are maintained and production is entered into the system.

While all of its equipment is state-of-the-art, SPM is especially proud of its compact, portable metalization machine—the only one of its kind in Canada and one of only five in North America. This equipment puts a wafer-thin metal coating on the inside of a cellular telephone, for example, to eliminate radio frequency interference, and does it in an environmentally friendly way.

As well as supplying telephone parts for world-class telecommunications companies, SPM also does work for a local furniture company; an Edmonton company that has developed a new dental suction tube; a local company that has developed a new, portable emergency flasher; and other businesses that require high-performance plastic mouldings.

## JUST-IN-TIME PRODUCTION

One challenging aspect of SPM's operations is the focus on just-in-time production. With more and more companies reducing inventories and improving response time for their customers, suppliers like SPM, in turn, must also be more responsive than in the past. "We often only find out in the morning what we have to ship that afternoon," says Jackman. "We make deliveries every four hours and it's often very hectic. There's no room for error—no margin.

"The plastics industry is really booming," he adds. "It's grown 15 percent each year for the last 20 or 30 years. We're hustling to keep up with demand. This industry used to be family-

based with small factories, but now larger companies and conglomerates are acquiring the smaller plastics operations."

The SPM group is owned by parent company Dynacast, a global manufacturer of small, precision components for products such as cameras, cars, computers, appliances, and electronic equipment. Dynacast, in turn, is a subsidiary of Coats Viyella, headquartered in the United Kingdom and a huge international conglomerate that does about $5 billion in global sales per year.

There are 13 other SPM operations in North America; one in Monterrey, Mexico; and another in Wales. As a result of SPM/Calgary's success, seven of these plants are now also producing components for Nortel. The entire SPM group has about 2,000 employees and achieves about $300 million in sales annually.

While industry growth accounts for some of SPM/Calgary's success, a large portion is also due to its committed and dedicated work force. Employees include business-minded individuals, designers, and operations workers. New employees receive three full

days of training from a full-time trainer in their first three months of work. SPM also has an active safety program. "The plastic is heated to 500 degrees Fahrenheit and moulded under tremendous pressure, up to 20,000 pounds per square inch," Jackman notes, "so if something went wrong, it could result in a serious accident."

In keeping with its four-finger philosophy, SPM/Calgary has an employee recognition program in effect. Employees are nominated by their peers for Employee of the Month, in recognition of their commitment to the company's philosophy. SPM's success is proof that keeping a business approach simple works.

EADQUARTERED IN CALGARY AND CELEBRATING ITS 25TH ANNIVERSARY, Shaw is a diversified Canadian communications company and one of the largest cable television providers in the country. Headed by JR Shaw, Chairman and Chief Executive Officer, and Jim Shaw, President

and Chief Operating Officer, the publicly traded company provides cable television and communication services to approximately 1.5 million customers, representing about 20 percent of the Canadian cable television market. Shaw is more than just a cable television company, however, and over the next few years, as the company rolls out a variety of innovative and leading-edge services and products, it will become more things to many more people.

"Cable has changed television, and we've changed cable," Jim Shaw notes. "What started out as a commitment to give Canadians more choice in television programming has evolved into a technological revolution that is helping shape and define the world of tomorrow."

SHAW PROVIDES SERVICES TO APPROXIMATELY 1.5 MILLION CUSTOMERS, WHICH AMOUNTS TO 20 PERCENT OF THE CANADIAN CABLE TELEVISION MARKET.

HEADQUARTERED IN CALGARY AND CELEBRATING ITS 25TH ANNIVERSARY, SHAW IS A DIVERSIFIED CANADIAN COMMUNICATIONS COMPANY.

## EXPANDING INTO NEW ARENAS

The realization of Shaw's new vision began in 1992, with a series of acquisitions that expanded the company's cable television base from approximately 550,000 customers to 1.5 million in 1997.

As the owner of 11 radio stations across the country, the company sees radio as an important target area. Notes Jim Shaw, "It's cost effective for advertisers and it complements the cable business." Shaw also offers music programming subscriptions for businesses through its satellite-delivered Digital Music Express (DMX). DMX features uninterrupted, talk-free, CD-quality music in such formats as rock, classical, jazz, blues, country, international hits, and many more.

The company has also taken on an increasing role in specialty television programming through its ownership of Country Music Television, YTV network, and TreeHouse (a preschooler's service), and its interests in Teletoon, SEGA Channel, and the Comedy Network.

The Shaw Televisual networks, including Broadcast News, TV Listings, Real Estate, Wheel and Wave, Classified TV, and the Shopper's Teleguide provide commercial customers with cost-effective advertising opportunities, while viewers receive up-to-the-minute news and enjoy the convenience of shop-at-home services.

Shaw is also a participant in the Canada Television and Cable Production Fund, which provides financing to producers and broadcasters across the country on a first come, first served basis, and without subjective evaluation.

## FOCUSING ON CHILDREN

Children's programming is also a key area for the company. Shaw has dedicated $27.5 million through the Shaw Children's Programming Initiative, which helps fund the production of quality children's television programming.

In addition, through the Cable in the Classroom program, all elementary and secondary schools in Shaw's service area have access to news packaged for young people, political coverage, educational programming in French and English, curriculum specific materials, and local programming.

For parents, Shaw offers a booklet of guidelines to help mothers and fathers choose appropriate television programs for their children. The company also is playing a key role in the development of the V-Chip, which will allow parents to block out any violent, profane, or explicit programming content.

## VISION FOR THE FUTURE

One example of the company's vision is its recent expansion into direct-broadcast satellite communications. Pending regulatory approval, Shaw will acquire a majority interest in Star Choice Communications. "Star Choice is already delivering a wide choice of video and audio programming by satellite direct to people's homes across Canada," notes Mark Pezarro, President and Chief Operating Officer of Star Choice.

Through Shaw FiberLink, commercial organizations are served with data, voice, and video transmission over secure networks, while new technology is also being used to enhance existing residential cable services. Shaw is extending its fibre-optic network over the next three years, and has introduced digital video compression technology to allow the company to transmit six or eight channels where subscribers currently only receive one. "This technology gives consumers more choice, higher-quality pictures, and digital-quality sound," according to Peter Bissonnette, Senior Vice-President of Cable Operations.

Other initiatives include WAVE, a high-speed Internet access service that allows customers with PCs to access the Internet at up to 350 times faster than existing alternatives. "Cable has a distinct advantage over other technologies in moving data. We'll be providing a technology platform that will revolutionize how our customers access and use the Internet," says Michael D'Avella, Senior Vice-President of Planning. Shaw also has a 10 percent ownership in Microcell Telecommunications Ltd., which utilizes wireless digital technology to offer a personal communications service that will compete with cellular phones.

Reflecting its origins as a family business, Shaw strives to respect and support the interests and values of the communities it serves. As communications technology continues to change, evolve, and converge, the company's diversification strategy ensures its success in the coming years.

THROUGH SHAW FIBERLINK, COMMERCIAL ORGANIZATIONS ARE SERVED WITH DATA, VOICE, AND VIDEO TRANSMISSION OVER SECURE NETWORKS.

THROUGH THE CABLE IN THE CLASSROOM PROGRAM, ALL ELEMENTARY AND SECONDARY SCHOOLS IN SHAW'S SERVICE AREA HAVE ACCESS TO NEWS, POLITICAL COVERAGE, AND EDUCATIONAL PROGRAMMING.

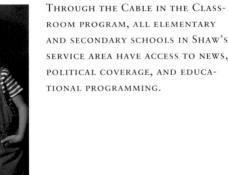

ONE EXAMPLE OF THE COMPANY'S VISION IS ITS RECENT EXPANSION INTO DIRECT-BROADCAST SATELLITE COMMUNICATIONS.

ᴀʟᴛʜᴏᴜɢʜ ʀᴇʟᴀᴛɪᴠᴇʟʏ ɴᴇᴡ ᴛᴏ ᴛʜᴇ Cᴀʟɢᴀʀʏ sᴄᴇɴᴇ, Sᴛᴏɴᴇ & Wᴇʙsᴛᴇʀ Canada Limited can trace its roots back for more than 100 years. The global company reestablished its ties with Calgary in 1996 in response to its growing base of Alberta clients. In association with other Alberta design and

IN 1889, CHARLES A. STONE AND EDWIN S. WEBSTER (TOP) ESTABLISHED A SMALL ELECTRICAL CONSULTING FIRM IN BOSTON. TODAY, STONE & WEBSTER IS A RESPECTED GLOBAL ENGINEERING AND CONSTRUCTION COMPANY.

DESIGN OF THE 70- AND 90-METRE SKI JUMP FACILITY FOR THE 1988 WINTER OLYMPIC GAMES WAS CARRIED OUT BY STONE & WEBSTER (BOTTOM).

construction companies, Stone & Webster provides full engineering, procurement, and construction services to a broad range of clients.

"Stone & Webster is a global leader due primarily to the success of our proprietary technologies in the petrochemical and petroleum processing fields," notes Albert E. Garred, President and Chief Executive Officer. "Having been personally involved in many Alberta projects during the 1970s and 1980s, I'm pleased that the company has reestablished a full design-construction capability in Calgary."

The company dates back to 1889, when Charles A. Stone and Edwin S. Webster, two young Massachusetts Institute of Technology graduates, established a small electrical consulting firm in Boston. From these

modest beginnings, Stone & Webster has become a respected global engineering and construction company.

A member of the worldwide group of Stone & Webster companies, Stone & Webster Canada Limited was federally incorporated in 1950, following many years of engineering and consulting activity in Canada, primarily for electric utility clients. Headquartered in Toronto, the company currently employs more than 400 professional, technical, and support staff.

### PARTNERING WITH OTHERS

The company already has a number of initiatives under way in Alberta. Stone & Webster is playing a major role in providing ethylene technology at NOVA Chemicals' petrochemical and polyethylene complex in Joffre. Stone & Webster is an authorized contractor for SCLAIRTECH™ polyethylene technology and assists NOVA Chemicals in licensing this technology globally. A similar, but more exclusive, arrangement exists for NOVA's crystal and impact polystyrene technology.

In addition, Stone & Webster has established a joint venture with Calgary-based Colt Engineering to provide polymer technology, engineering, and other services capabilities for a grass-roots, first-of-a-kind polyethylene unit at the same site. The polyethylene plant will use NOVA Chemicals' advanced SCLAIRTECH™ technology. In another joint venture with

Cimarron Engineering Ltd., Stone & Webster has formed a strong design-build capability to serve clients in the gas transmission industry. The integration of Stone & Webster's international experience in major gas compression and pipeline projects and Cimarron's track record in Canada provides clients with a unique capability.

In order to serve an even broader process sector client base, Stone & Webster and Optima Engineers and Constructors have formed an alliance to provide full EPC capability. "The combination of our international technology, experience and financial strength with the knowledge and expertise of local companies allows us to offer our Alberta clients a strong team," notes Calgary office General Manager John Hutchinson.

For more than 45 years, Stone & Webster has been undertaking hundreds of assignments for major electric utilities and independent power-producing clients across Canada and overseas. The company's presence in Calgary, with the full support of the Toronto and U.S. power groups, enables it to better serve Western Canadian clients in utility plant rehabilitation and new power generation.

With its strong technology base in the energy field and more than a century of global and domestic experience and leadership, Stone & Webster looks forward to working in partnership with its clients to successfully meet the challenge of capital growth in the near future and beyond.

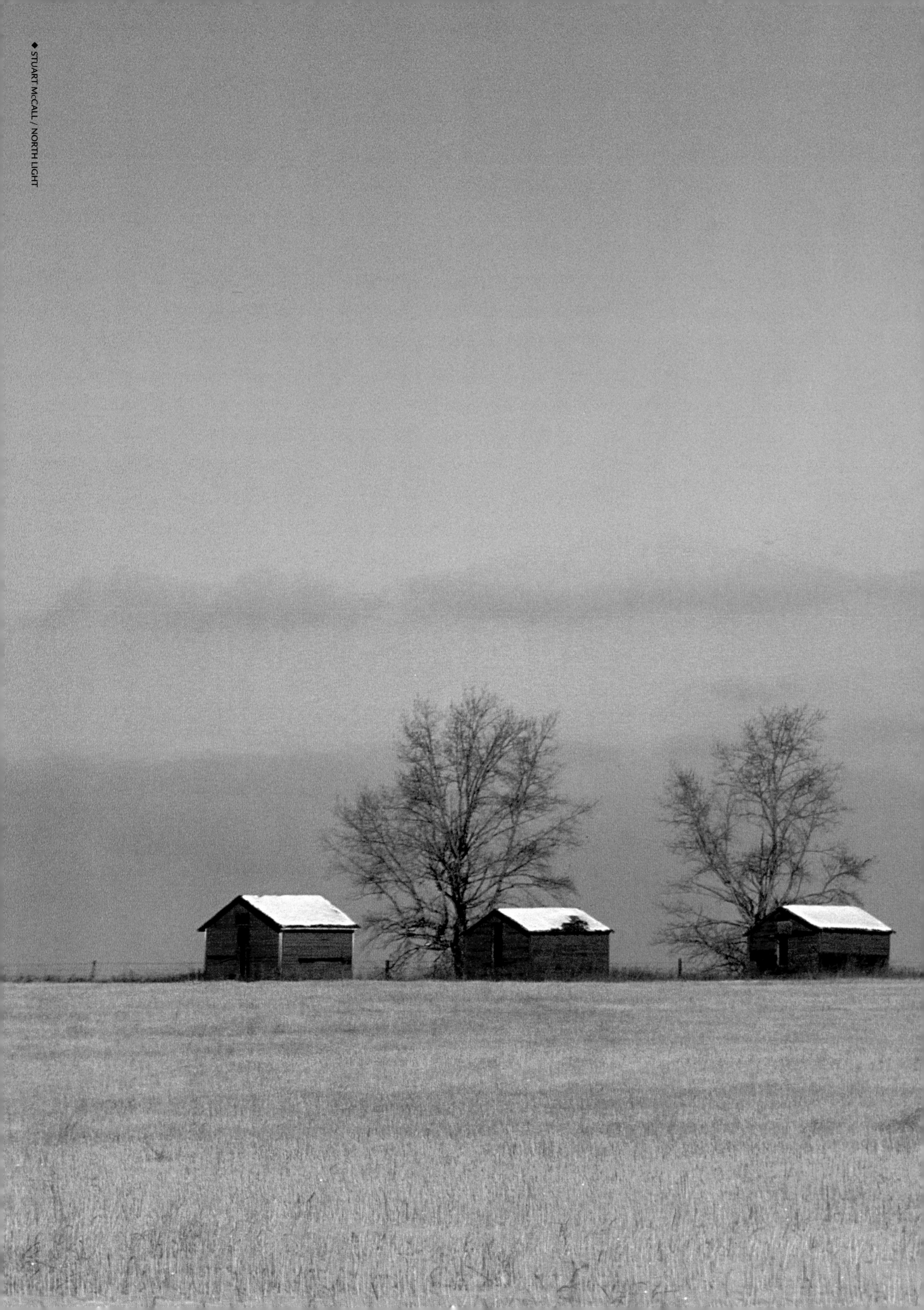

◆ STUART McCALL / NORTH LIGHT

ANGUS OF CALGARY PHOTOGRAPHY LTD. is a studio specializing in commercial, real estate, aerial, and annual report photography, as well as images of oil fields. The outfit is operated by Andy Chetty and Angus McNee, who both served as photographers with the British Royal Navy. In addition, Chetty served with the Royal Marines as a combat photographer and instructor.

DON DENTON is originally from Vancouver, British Columbia, and now makes his home in Calgary with his wife and three children. He has worked as chief photographer and picture editor for a variety of newspapers in Alberta and British Columbia and, for a number of years, pursued his interests in Brussels, where he worked for Reuter News Service. Denton currently works for the *Calgary Herald* and specializes in photojournalism and portraits.

CRAIG DOLICK, originally from Burlington, Ontario, has pursued an interest in the arts since his early teens, when he custom-painted vehicles. When he moved to Calgary in 1980, he took up photography. Beginning as a stock shooter, Dolick grew steadily more interested in photography as a viable career in itself. Today, through his studio, Horizon Photoworks, Dolick concentrates primarily on commercial and architectural photography and believes his work reflects a perfectionist's eye for beauty in the simplest of details.

FIRST LIGHT represents photographers from Canada and abroad. Its files contain a wide range of people, business, industry, scenic, landscape, nature, and wildlife pictures. Maintaining offices in Toronto, Ontario, and Vancouver, First Light prides itself on offering great customer service, intelligent research, and a wide range of innovative photography.

LEE FOSTER is a veteran travel writer and photographer who lives in Berkeley, California. His work has been published in a number of major travel magazines and newspapers, and he maintains a stock photo library that features more than 250 worldwide destinations. Foster's full travel publishing efforts can be viewed on his Web site at http://www.fostertravel.com.

GREG FULMES is a self-employed free-lance photographer from Watrous, Saskatchewan, who spent almost 10 years pounding spikes on the Canadian National Railroad before his photography career took off. Now a resident of Calgary, he has worked for tourism clients; postcard companies; the Calgary Exhibition and Stampede; the *Calgary Herald*; *Datamation* and *Westworld* magazines; public relations and advertising firms; and many corporate clients. Fulmes has also received several awards for his work as a staff newspaper photographer. His favourite subjects are people, especially native Canadians, cowboys, and farmers.

BLAINE HARRINGTON III calls Colorado home when he is not travelling around the globe. For 10 weeks in the fall of 1996, he journeyed 36,000 air miles to 11 countries on photo shoot. In addition, he has worked for a variety of magazines, including *Business Week, Forbes, Time, Newsweek, National Geographic Traveler,* and *Ski.* Harrington has also worked assignments for several National Geographic and Time-Life books, and has taken cover photos for such travel guides as *Fodor's, Frommer's, Insight Guides,* and *Real Guides.*

HILLSTROM STOCK PHOTO, established in 1967, is a full-service, Chicago-based photography agency. Its files include images of architecture, agricultural backgrounds, classic autos, gardens and high-risk adventure/sports.

KEITH LOGAN uses a four-by-five-inch view camera to photograph the natural landscape. When taking pictures, he constantly looks for scenes that capture the spirit of the land. Using black-and-white negatives in conjunction with original transparencies, he produces archival Ilfochrome prints that have a wide tonal range and saturated colour. These prints are featured in various collections of the City of Calgary, TELUS TeleSolutions, Amoco Canada Petroleum Company Ltd., and Edmonton Art Gallery. Currently, Logan resides in the foothills outside of Cochrane, Alberta.

STUART McCALL, a native of Toronto, currently lives in Vancouver, where he works for North Light Images Ltd. and specializes in corporate, editorial, and garden/landscape photography. Among his clients are BC Hydro, Hewlett Packard, Phillip Morris, and Canadian Helicopter. McCall's work has been featured in a variety of publications, including *Time, Forbes, Fortune, CompuServe Magazine,* and *Country Living Magazine.* In addition to being a photographer, McCall is an avid traveller, a lover of good food and wine, a father of two boys, and a 15-year student/instructor of kung fu.

DAVE OLECKO has spent most of his life in Calgary, where he is currently a staff photographer for the *Calgary Herald.* Having studied public relations and photojournalism at Mount Royal College, he specializes in sports, hard news, and feature photography. Olecko has won several major awards, including the Canadian Press Feature Photo of the Year in 1992 and the 1988 Edward Dunlop Award of Excellence for feature photography. His work has been featured in *Maclean's, Financial Times, Flare, Home Life,* and *Calgary: A Year in Focus.*

PHOTOPHILE, established in San Diego, California, in 1967, has more than 1 million colour images on file culled from more than 85 contributing local and international photographers. Subjects range from images of Southern California to adventure sports, wildlife/underwater scenes, business, industry, people, science and research, health and medicine, and travel photography. Included on Photophile's client list are American Express, *Guest Informant*, Franklin Stoorza, and Princess Cruises.

PAT PRICE is a self-employed photographer who makes his home in Cochrane with his wife and two daughters. Price specializes in sports, feature, corporate, and editorial photography, and his clients range from local advertising agencies to worldwide news wire services.

LEIGH REED is an Alberta photo artist who works mainly with western themes, portraitures, and landscapes. Taught basic darkroom techniques at age five by her grandfather, Reed finds that manipulating prints in her private darkroom is what gives her photos their unique, sometimes surreal, quality. Her works are shown in various galleries in Canada, and she holds gallery memberships at the Muttart Public Art Gallery, Station Cultural Centre, Canmore Artisan Guild, and Foothills Camera Club.

MARK REINSTEIN has called Washington, D.C., and Bethesda, Maryland, home, and presently lives in Alexandria, Virginia. As a self-employed photographer, he specializes in taking fireworks, travel, news, and wedding pictures.

WILF SCHURIG spent the early years of his life in Germany, where he became fascinated by the beauty of nature. In search of adventure, he moved to Canada and advanced his career as a pattern maker serving the oil industry. In 1969, Schurig graduated from the North American School of Conservation. Several of his wildlife films have been televised in North America and Europe, and hundreds of his nature photographs have been published in books and magazines, and on calendars.

BRIAN STABLYK, a resident of West Vancouver, originates from Edmonton. Having earned degrees from the University of Alberta and the University of British Columbia, he is a location and stock photographer. He was runner-up in the photojournalism category at the *Western Canada Outdoors* Magazine Awards, and won the Photo of the Year Award in 1991 from *Alaska* magazine. Stablyk has shot five magazine covers, five posters, and more than 100 postcards of Western Canada.

PATRICK MORROW / FIRST LIGHT

TAKE STOCK INC., a stock photography agency established in Calgary in 1987, represents stock photographers and affiliate subagents from around the world. Its library specializes in people, lifestyle, business, and industry images, and is complemented by an excellent collection of images on Canada.

MARK VITARIS, a native of Buffalo, New York, graduated with a communications degree from the University of Ottawa. Currently, he lives in Calgary and operates a small studio for product photography called Mark Vitaris Productions. His images have been featured in such publications as *Calgary: A Year in Focus*, *Share the Flame*, *Husky Oil: A Year in the Life*, and *Photo Digest* magazine. Vitaris specializes in corporate and stock photography.

Other photographers and organizations that have contributed to *Calgary: Harnessing the Future* include Doran Clark, Fotopic, Mark Gallup, Mark E. Gibson, Glasheen Graphics, R. Hartmier, K.A.M., Thomas Kitchin, Jerry Kobalenko, Lyle Korytar, Larry J. MacDougal, Alan Marsh, Ken A. Meisner, Baiba Morrow, Patrick Morrow, Darwin A. Mulligan, Shannon Oatway, Troy and Mary Parlee, G. Petersen, Craig Popoff, Wes Raymond, Dave Reede, Mike Ridewood, Benjamin Rondel, Rick Rudnicki, Kim Stallknecht, Harvey Steeves, Boyce A. Stringer, Eric Swanson, Ian Tomlinson, Ron Watts, and Darwin Wiggett.

# INDEX OF PROFILES

ALBERTA ENERGY COMPANY LTD. ............... 266

A.R. WILLIAMS MATERIALS HANDLING LTD. .... 226

ASM INDUSTRIES ......................... 298

BPB WIRELINE SERVICES .................... 262

BURNCO ROCK PRODUCTS, LTD. ............ 208

CALGARY CHAMBER OF COMMERCE ............ 200

THE CITY OF CALGARY ...................... 184

CITY OF CALGARY ELECTRIC SYSTEM ........... 188

CALGARY COOPERATIVE ASSOCIATION LIMITED .. 242

CALGARY ECONOMIC DEVELOPMENT
    AUTHORITY ........................ 186

CALGARY FLAMES ......................... 286

CALGARY HERALD ......................... 192

CALGARY OLYMPIC DEVELOPMENT
    ASSOCIATION (CODA) ................... 238

CALGARY PHILHARMONIC SOCIETY ............ 240

CALGARY STAMPEDERS ..................... 230

CANADA SAFEWAY LIMITED .................. 218

CANADIAN AIRLINES INTERNATIONAL, LTD. .... 244

CANADIAN FRACMASTER ..................... 278

CANADIAN HUNTER EXPLORATION LTD. ........ 261

CANADIAN NATIONAL RAILWAY ............... 212

CANADIAN PACIFIC ....................... 190

CANADIAN PACIFIC RAILWAY ................ 194

CANFER ROLLING MILLS LTD. ............... 290

CARMA DEVELOPERS LTD. .................. 246

CLAY-ROBINSON LTD. ..................... 220

COCA-COLA BOTTLING LTD. ................. 214

COLT ENGINEERING ....................... 280

ECL GROUP OF COMPANIES, LTD. ........... 232

GALVANIC COMPANIES ..................... 272

GIMBEL EYE CENTRE ...................... 252

HONGKONG BANK OF CANADA ................ 292

IMPERIAL OIL ........................... 210

INTERNATIONAL HOTEL OF CALGARY ......... 260

MAXX PETROLEUM LTD. .................... 294

MOUNT ROYAL COLLEGE ..................... 202

MULLEN TRANSPORTATION INC. ............... 236

NORTEL ................................ 274

NOVA CORPORATION ....................... 201

NOVATEL ............................... 288

PANCANADIAN PETROLEUM LIMITED ........... 264

PETROLEUM INDUSTRY TRAINING SERVICE ...... 241

PROGAS LIMITED ......................... 284

PRUDENTIAL STEEL LTD. ................... 251

QUANTEL VECO ENGINEERING LTD. ........... 276

THE RIDER TRAVEL GROUP .................. 285

RIGEL ENERGY CORPORATION ................ 237

ROBYN'S TRUCKING SERVICES LTD. ........... 282

ROYAL BANK OF CANADA .................... 205

RYAN ENERGY TECHNOLOGIES INC. ........... 300

SAP CANADA INC. ........................ 302

SHAW ................................. 306

SHAW NEE SLOPES GOLF COURSE ............. 256

SHELL CANADA LIMITED .................... 228

SILCORP ............................... 248

SOUTHERN ALBERTA INSTITUTE
    OF TECHNOLOGY ....................... 202

SPM/CALGARY INC. ....................... 304

STONE & WEBSTER CANADA LIMITED ......... 308

TELUS ................................ 196

TRANSALTA CORPORATION .................. 206

TRI-LINE FREIGHT SYSTEMS ................ 254

TRIMAC CORPORATION ..................... 250

TRIZECHAHN CORPORATION ................. 268

UNITED WAY OF CALGARY AND AREA ......... 224

UNIVERSITY OF CALGARY ................... 202

VALMET AUTOMATION ...................... 258

VICTORIAN ORDER OF NURSES ............... 189

WALLACE & CAREY LTD. ................... 216

WESTERN ATLAS INC. ..................... 234

WESTFAIR FOODS, LTD. ................... 296